JANE AUSTEN:
ILLUSION AND REALITY

JANE AUSTEN:
ILLUSION AND REALITY

Christopher Brooke

D. S. BREWER

First published 1999
D. S. Brewer, Cambridge

ISBN 0 85991 557 3

D.S. Brewer is an imprint of Boydell & Brewer Ltd
PO Box 9, Woodbridge, Suffolk IP12 3DF, UK
and of Boydell & Brewer Inc.
PO Box 41026, Rochester, NY 14604–4126, USA
website: http://www.boydell.co.uk

A catalogue record for this book is available
from the British Library

Library of Congress Cataloging-in-Publication Data
Brooke, Christopher Nugent Lawrence.
    Jane Austen : illusion and reality / Christopher Brooke.
        p.   cm.
    Includes bibliographical references (p.   ) and index.
    ISBN 0-85991-557-3 (alk. paper)
    1. Austen, Jane, 1775–1817 – Knowledge – England.   2. Literature and
society – England – History – 19th century.   3. Literature and history –
England – History – 19th century.   4. Women and literature – England –
History – 19th century.   5. England – Social life and customs –
18th century.   6. England – Social life and customs – 19th century.
7. Manners and customs in literature.   I. Title.
PR4038.E46B76   1999
823'.7–dc21   99-33905

This publication is printed on acid-free paper

Printed in Great Britain by
St Edmundsbury Press Ltd, Bury St Edmunds, Suffolk

Contents

For Pauline, Mary and Annie
In memory of Francis

Acknowledgements

My first thanks must be to Jane Austen herself, for the infinite pleasure her novels have given me for nearly sixty years. Next, to Rosalind, my wife, who compelled me to turn my meditations into a book, and has constantly improved it. She has read version after version, 'lopt and cropt', adding constantly and imaginatively from her own deep knowledge to the themes I have explored. Over the years my late brother Nicholas Brooke has shown me how to explore the borders of history and literature: I owe much to his inspiration, but for nothing else in this book can he be blamed. Michael Shaw has encouraged me to publish the book and made it possible. Edna Pilmer has given invaluable help in preparing the book for the printer. David Smith and Jennifer Thorp gave very generous help on eighteenth-century ordinations. In the study of the Church in Jane Austen's time, I owe a special debt to the studies of Stephen Taylor and Irene Collins. The staff of the British Library, and the Librarian and his colleagues in King's College, Cambridge, have given me access to the original ending of *Persuasion* and the original manuscript of *Sanditon*. I owe much to the generous facilities of Gonville and Caius College, and the splendid resources of the Cambridge University Library. I am very grateful to the Publishers – and especially Helen and Richard Barber, Derek Brewer, Pru Harrison and Caroline Palmer – for accepting the book and for much skilled help.

I am heavily in debt to a multitude beyond counting whose comments or studies or research have helped me to such understanding of Jane Austen as I have. I would wish to have acknowledged every debt; but that is not possible – the passage of time and fading memory prevent it. Most of the more important debts are noted in the text or represented in the references, but (I am all too aware) far from all. Anyone who writes on Jane Austen is surrounded by a cloud of witnesses. I have noted major bibliographies under Bibliographical References, and these contain thousands of entries of which few people could claim to have read more than a fraction. I certainly cannot. I have set out to give a view of Jane Austen based on ceaseless, reflective reading of her works. But I owe very much to many others who have done the same.

I first encountered *Pride and Prejudice* in the old film starring Greer Garson and Laurence Olivier, whose relation to the book was at times coincidental. My mother then read me the authentic version when I was in my early teens. In recent years my daughter-in-law Pauline – my 'eldest daughter' – and my granddaughters Mary and Annie have sat me down to the videos of most of the novels. I particularly admire the recent version of *Pride and Prejudice*, which has shown that a modern audience does not need to be palmed off with a travesty; that a reasonably authentic version can command an immense audience; that she appeals to the young as well as to the old. Thus, the dedication reflects a particular debt as well as much else.

1

Prologue

'Can he be a sensible man, sir?'
    'No, my dear; I think not. I have great hopes of finding him quite
the reverse.'[1]

No one who writes a book about Jane Austen in the 1990s can escape Mr
Bennet's censure. The chance of finding something new to say is as slight as a
large prize in the Lottery. But such a person's fate is worse than that; for Jane
Austen's sharp intelligence and crackling wit make rings round us all. It is a
monstrous presumption: nothing less than approaching senility can explain it.
Nothing less than an exceptional devotion to the subject can excuse it.

My life has been spent in studying the foundations of history over a long
span of time. In part this has meant editing medieval texts – thus, for
example, well over 40 volumes passed through my hands as a General
Editor of Nelsons and Oxford Medieval Texts between 1959 and 1987; but
it equally meant exploring the various kinds of historical, legal and literary
texts for the history of marriage (*The Medieval Idea of Marriage*, 1989). In that
enquiry, literary texts – in French, German and English – played a central
role. Most of my life has been spent in the twelfth century, although these
and many other tasks took me forward into the late Middle Ages and the
sixteenth century too. I have been driven into the eighteenth and early
nineteenth centuries by work for *A History of Gonville and Caius College*
(1985) and *A History of Emmanuel College* (1999) – and in Samuel Blackall of
Emmanuel my interest in college history and Jane Austen met (see p. 29).
These studies revealed to me that a radical revision of the stereotyped view
of the eighteenth-century church, from which Jane Austen sprang, was
needed. This led me to the present enterprise: to looking at the materials
for our knowledge of Jane Austen, and especially at her letters and novels,
with a historian's eye – to exploring them with as little presupposition as
possible. This is exceptionally difficult with Jane Austen – as with the
Gospels – owing to the vast accumulation of assumed wisdom which surrounds her. But that only makes the enterprise more worth while, though
it carries many dangers with it. Such an approach is bound to involve

---

[1] *PP* I, c. 13, p. 64.

1

repetition of much which may seem all too familiar to the specialist. That is in the nature of the method, which involves the patient exploration of the evidence on which the dating of the novels and the letters is based, and of the fundamental features of the novels themselves. In my exploration of the plots of the novels the patient reader will find embedded something which I at least have not seen suggested elsewhere, and much which is essential to the exposition which follows – of their role in the history of social structure, marriage, morals and feminism.

It is an essential part of the historical method here pursued that it looks plainly at the novels and makes as few assumptions of knowledge or of 'agreed results' as possible.[2] I hope that this will make it accessible to those who are not specialists. Above all I hope that those who approach Jane Austen primarily from the study of literature will not regard me as an intruder who has rashly braved the barbed-wire entanglements that separate our disciplines, but as a colleague in a common enterprise.

Reading and rereading her novels has been the favourite occupation of my leisure for many years – but I know that there are very many who are in like case. I am a historian, and I am fascinated by the pursuit of someone whom we know well – or think we know well – but chiefly from her own writings. The Austen-Leighs' *Jane Austen, Her Life and Letters: A Family Record* of 1913 represented at that date the furthest extent that family tradition and legend could go in recording the woman who had made the name Austen illustrious. It has recently been brought up to date by Deirdre Le Faye in the *Family Record* of 1989. This is a fine work of scholarship, in which every tiny fragment of family history and family reminiscence, including a number of family diaries, has been sought out from scattered record offices and family collections, sifted and fitted into the intricate pattern of the traditional family biography. Its accuracy is exemplary; it is perhaps ungracious to cavil – or to say that anything different is needed. But the best of the book remains – what it always was – the extracts from Jane Austen's own letters. It is perhaps even more ungracious to admit that I find Deirdre Le Faye's admirable edition of the *Letters* (1995) far more revealing and even more useful than the *Family Record*. With great skill and modesty she goes over again the first-rate edition of R.W. Chapman, and improves it in detail at many points. She thus represents the meeting point of two traditions: of family memory, consummated in the *Life* of 1913, and of precise textual work on novels and letters, of which Chapman was the supreme master. I have checked all the texts from the novels and the letters quoted in this book by the early editions or the original letters – as represented in Jo Modert's facsimile edition – and I have very rarely found Chapman's text of the novels astray, and never Le Faye's of the letters. My

---

[2] This does not mean that I have not read widely in the modern literature on Jane, but it inevitably means that recent debate plays relatively little part in my discussion.

only cavil with Chapman's texts is the cramped print and format in which they – and every edition known to me based upon them – have been published. The Winchester edition of 1911–12, with larger print and more generous margins, is infinitely kinder on the hand and the eye; and it was my constant companion for many years. But there are notorious weaknesses in the text of every modern edition before Chapman; above all it (and its sources) paid no attention to the way Jane Austen punctuated her books. No one who has spent long hours with the editions published in Jane Austen's lifetime – and faithfully represented by Chapman and his successors – can ever be content again with texts which play havoc with her punctuation.

Valuable as the *Family Record* is, the quantity of material in it which comes from genuine reminiscences of those who knew Jane Austen personally is relatively small: precious, because so small, but adding little to the material from her own pen. Such is the charm of her writing, such the stature, that there will always be room for new and readable biographies. But they can add almost nothing to knowledge. One can only learn more about her by burrowing more deeply into her writings, or by portraying the world about her – as Irene Collins has done most attractively in her *Jane Austen and the Clergy* (1993).

Some historians love most of all their own conclusions: they are revisionists, forever presenting to an admiring audience the *results* of their research. I am much more interested in how one gets to results than in what one finds at the journey's end. In every period of history I have studied, the contemporary documents are more interesting than the modern historian's summary of them. How then do I come to write synthetic and analytic history at all? – Should not all my days be spent – as most have been – in editing historical narratives and records? The answer is that modern scholarship – if delicately and efficiently conducted – can add a dimension to our reading of the records of the past. By the same token, Jane Austen's novels are a great deal more worth reading than the volumes of modern criticism on them. Literary critics, like historians, can build a card-house of jargon which gives their thoughts the appearance of much greater authority and originality than they really possess. But I do not at all mean to decry what they do: I have even greater respect for the best criticism I have encountered than for the best historical commentaries on the period. Commentary is worthwhile so long as it does not come between us and the texts we study: and that is peculiarly true of the study of Jane Austen, for she was a woman of quite exceptional subtlety and power of mind, able with a touch of her wand to make fools of us all.

The study of Jane Austen is like a marvellous townscape swarming with visitors and tourists. Many of them genuinely appreciate what they see and have something interesting to say about it; it would be churlish to grudge any of them their pleasure, or their contribution. But the result is a field so crowded it is almost impossible to say anything new. It is exceedingly

3

difficult to read her novels as if they had never been read before, and appraise them as historical, literary and religious literature afresh. So it is a perilous task to write about Jane Austen; but the attempt will always be made. I believe it to be the case that documentary historians and literary critics have not always been in dialogue in their study of her; and in that conviction I have – with much hesitation – gone forward.

For fifty years after her death her family kept silence. There is indeed a Biographical Notice by her good, enthusiastic brother Henry attached to the first edition of *Northanger Abbey* and *Persuasion*. It tells us a little of what she looked like, of the affection in which her family held her, of the image they wished to portray to the public; but very little.

> Though the frailties, foibles, and follies of others could not escape her immediate detection, yet even on their vices did she never trust herself to comment with unkindness. . . . Faultless herself, as nearly as human nature can be, she always sought, in the faults of others, something to excuse, to forgive or forget.[3]

These worthy sentiments cannot survive the briefest perusal of her letters: no reader of them doubts that she was often candid, catty and uncharitable – though they also show she could indeed be often the reverse. When Henry goes on to say 'she was thoroughly religious and devout' we may believe him a little more readily, since some of her prayers are extant – and they reveal a much more than conventional piety.[4] But we believe Henry only when Jane's own word supports him.

The last of Jane Austen's brothers, Frank – Admiral Sir Francis Austen – died in 1865, aged 91, and the family began to think that her memory might be more openly recorded, especially as her surviving nephews and nieces were themselves growing old. Her nephew James Edward was prevailed on to publish the *Memoir*, a fragrant panegyric – yet revealing how little he remembered in detail. The portrait of Jane at work and play, of the delightful aunt, was composed by his half-sister Caroline; and her brief memoir is the best the family produced: a delightful piece of writing, with many clearly authentic touches in it. But it is exceedingly short – only 17 pages in modern print – and very unequal in value.[5] Thus she gives a vivid description of Aunt Jane's charm and beauty, and of a day in Chawton Cottage in her later years – which yet throws no light on how her aunt came to write three great novels in five years.

Her charm to children was great sweetness of manner – she seemed to

---

[3] *Biographical Notice*, p. 6.
[4] *Biographical Notice*, p. 8; *MW*, pp. 453–7.
[5] C. Austen 1952. On Jane Austen's relation to children, see pp. 38–9 below.

love you, and you loved her naturally in return . . . But soon came the delight of her playful talk – *Every*-thing she could make amusing to a child – Then, as I got older, and when cousins came to share the entertainment, she would tell us the most delightful stories chiefly of Fairyland, and her Fairies had all characters of their own . . . As to my Aunt's personal appearance, her's was the first face I can remember thinking pretty . . . Her face was rather round than long – she had a bright, but not a pink colour – a clear brown complexion and very good hazel eyes – She was not, I believe, an absolute beauty, but before she left Steventon she was established as a very pretty girl, in the opinion of most of her neighbours – as I learned afterwards from some of those who remained – Her hair, a darkish brown, curled naturally – it was in short curls round her face . . . She always wore a cap . . . at least of a morning but I never saw her without one, to the best of my remembrance, either morning or evening . . .

Aunt Jane began her day with music – for which I conclude she had a natural taste; as she thus kept it up – tho' she had no one to teach; was never induced (as I have heard) to play in company; and none of her family cared much for it. I suppose, that she might not trouble them, she chose her practising time before breakfast . . . She practised regularly every morning – She played very pretty tunes, *I* thought – and I liked to stand by her and listen to them . . . [As a very little girl, she says elsewhere, I was always creeping up to her, and following her whenever I could.] At 9 o'clock she made breakfast – *that* was *her* part of the household work – The tea and sugar stores were under *her* charge – *and* the wine – Aunt Cassandra did all the rest . . . I don't believe Aunt Jane observed any particular method in parcelling out her day but I think she generally sat in the drawing room till luncheon: when visitors were there, chiefly at [needle]work – She was fond of work – and she was a great adept at overcast and satin stitch . . . She could throw the spilikens for us, better than anyone else, and she was wonderfully successful at cup and ball. After luncheon, my Aunts generally walked out – sometimes they went to Alton for shopping – Often, one or other of them, to the Great House [her brother Edward's country house in Chawton] – when a brother was inhabiting it, to make a visit – or . . . to stroll about the grounds . . . They had no carriage, and their visitings did not extend far . . . My Aunt must have spent much time in writing – her desk lived in the drawing room. I often saw her writing letters on it, and I believe she wrote much of her Novels the same way – sitting with her family, when they were quite alone; but *I never saw any manuscript of that sort, in progress.*[6]

---

[6] C. Austen 1952, pp. 5–9. The italics in the last sentence are mine.

Helpful as this is for the light it throws on Jane Austen's manner of life, it fails entirely to answer the question we most want answered – when and where and how did she write her novels? The notion that she wrote them in the intervals of visits with her sister and mother – and often other members of the family – about her – was credulously repeated, with embellishments, in the *Memoir* and the *Life*, and has won wide currency.[7] But it seems incredible – it passes belief that the systematic writing of her later years, when she produced novel after novel at a steady pace, could have been the fruit of such haphazard opportunities. The evidence of her letters confirms that she was an early riser, and performed her own private tasks before breakfast: several of her letters, especially from Henry's house in London, reveal that they were wholly or partly the work of the space between 7.30 or 8.00 a.m. and breakfast.[8] But one very striking feature of the letters is that they tell us every detail of her day, and occasionally describe a novel on the way – but never refer to time spent in the composition of a novel. After the publication of *Sense and Sensibility* – and especially after *Pride and Prejudice* appeared – she spoke freely in her letters to her family about their publication, about their reception, about how they were read aloud, sometimes to an unsuspecting visitor who was not let into the secret that they were hers.[9] It is theoretically possible that Cassandra suppressed letters which told of Jane's writing; but all the indications are that Cassandra's suppressions were themselves fairly haphazard.[10] It is much more likely that she had early formed a habit of keeping her writing even from her sister – a habit only partially broken in later years when the *results* of her composition were freely discussed in the family. If this is so, we must suppose that she normally wrote her novels at times of day – early in the morning or late at night – when she had privacy. Common sense points the same way. She may have thought out her plots and her dialogues in her walks, in times of reflection, in her sleep. But the composition of some of the most profound and subtle and concentrated works of imagination in any of the world's literature must presuppose periods of peace and quiet. Not perhaps very much: a rough calculation of her most productive years might suggest that in the period 1811–17 she had to write 300 words a day or – if one allows that she wrote little or nothing when away from home or when little nieces interrupted her free hours – 500 words a day. For so assured a writer this is not an excessive harvest: it could have been the fruit of say two hours' uninterrupted writing. Her last novel, *Sanditon*, is the best

---

[7] *Memoir*, c. 6 (1870), pp. 128–30; (1871), pp. 96–7; *Life*, p. 241.
[8] For letters written early in the morning – all in London – see *Letters*, L no. 87, pp. 217–19, C no. 82, pp. 318, 322; L no. 91, p. 235, C no. 86, p. 346; cf. L nos. 96, 98, C nos. 91, 93.
[9] On references to the novels in *Letters*, see esp. Chapman's Index VI in C. For the unsuspecting Miss Benn, C no. 76, p. 297; L no. 79, p. 201.
[10] See pp. 36–8.

recorded, for we have Jane's own notes of the dates of composition in the margin of the original manuscript: these show that roughly 8000 words were written between 1 and 18 March 1817; that is, about 330 words a day. But she was near her death, and she may well have slowed down.[11]

Her letters to Cassandra sometimes seem to imply that Jane was an earlier riser than her sister; and that may well be why she made the breakfast. We do not need to seek far to find the explanation of why Cassandra did most of the housework: by the time Caroline knew them well enough to remember, Jane was a major novelist not in the best of health. The breakfast suggests that the early morning was Jane's; and we may reasonably suppose that the later novels were written before breakfast.

But if this is true, neither Caroline nor her brother – nor any other member of the family – has told us so; we have had to deduce it in the main from the negative evidence of the letters and the positive evidence of the novels themselves. It will be the argument of this book that almost all that is really worth knowing about Jane Austen comes from her own writings; and that her deepest thoughts are only revealed in her novels. But there they have to be perceived as in a mirror: she never presents them face to face.

For this enterprise we need to use the tools both of the historian and the literary critic.[12] Some basic principles need to be established: what is the world Jane Austen describes – how is it related to the world in which she lived? – a question both literary and historical. Did she set out to teach, as some good critics have supposed? – That is, can we deduce the lessons she taught from the face of the novels? Then the historian needs to know the materials of his enquiry – her letters, notebooks, unfinished novels, as well as the novels themselves. The historian is fundamentally interested in chronology; the critic only marginally less so – for the order of the novels and their relation one to another are fundamental to the enquiry.

We should then be ready to explore the major novels themselves. I have deliberately interpolated a reading of each of them at that point: readers intimate with the text of all her novels may find these chapters too familiar. But I have tried to explain how I read the novels as well as what is in them, so they have a vital place in the argument of the book.

Finally, I have taken a sheaf of themes – church and clergy, rank and status, marriage – to see how they are handled in their social and historical setting; and at the end we enquire about Jane Austen's deepest convictions – in what measure can they be validly deduced from the text of her novels? What do we really know?

It is sometimes asserted that a historian learns more from the typical,

---

[11] King's College, Cambridge, Library, MS. of *Sanditon*; *Fragment*, Preface, unpaginated; *MW* pp. 407–27.

[12] I do not enter into the question whether they can, at the deepest level, be validly distinguished: I leave that to the reader to determine.

humdrum literature of a period than from its greatest artists. I believe the opposite to be true. There is indeed much to be learned of taste and outlook and ordinary things even from *Lovers' Vows* both in Germany where it was written and in England where it was all the rage. But if we wish to have our minds stretched, to be shown the limits of human imagination and enquiry, we shall do well to go to the greatest and best.

2

Illusion and Reality

There is no word more dangerous to the literary critic or the art historian than realism: time and again it has deceived them, and a sensible student gives it a wide berth. For it commonly refers to a special skill in illusion: the capacity to deceive the viewers or the readers into thinking that something especially real has been put before them.[1] Even the camera deceives: yet there really is such a thing as a photographic image, whether in painting or literature. But that is clearly not what Jane Austen attempted; and historians who regard her novels as transcripts of life deceive themselves.

Yet at the centre of her art lies the portrayal of ordinary people. *Northanger Abbey*, as we have it, is a relatively early essay by Jane in the contrast between the fantasies of the Gothic Novel and the plain facts of human experience; or, at least, it seems evidently designed to create that impression, even if it is a little obscured for the modern reader by the heavy irony with which the heroine's qualities are compared with the more conventional heroic properties in the novels of the age. Catherine Morland as a child

> had a thin awkward figure, a sallow skin without colour, dark lank hair, and strong features [which did not prevent her becoming remarkably pretty in her later teens]; – so much for her person; – and not less unpropitious for heroism seemed her mind. She was fond of all boys' plays, and greatly preferred cricket not merely to dolls, but to the more heroic enjoyments of infancy, nursing a dormouse, feeding a canary-bird, or watering a rose-bush. Indeed she had no taste for a garden; and if she gathered flowers at all, it was chiefly for the pleasure of mischief – at least so it was conjectured from her always preferring those which she was forbidden to take. – Such were her propensities – her abilities were quite as extraordinary. She never could learn or understand any thing before she was taught; and sometimes not even then, for she was often inattentive, and occasionally stupid. Her mother was three months in teaching her only to repeat the 'Beggar's Petition'; and, after all, her next sister, Sally, could say it better than

---

[1] Cf. Gombrich 1960.

she did. Not that Catherine was always stupid, – by no means; she learnt the fable of 'The Hare and many Friends', as quickly as any girl in England.[2] Her mother wished her to learn music; and Catherine was sure she should like it, for she was very fond of tinkling the keys of the old forlorn spinnet; so, at eight years old she began. She learnt a year, and could not bear it; – and Mrs Morland, who did not insist on her daughters being accomplished in spite of incapacity or distaste, allowed her to leave off. The day which dismissed the music-master was one of the happiest of Catherine's life. Her taste for drawing was not superior; though whenever she could obtain the outside of a letter from her mother, or seize upon any other odd piece of paper, she did what she could in that way, by drawing houses and trees, hens and chickens, all very much like one another. – Writing and accounts she was taught by her father; French by her mother; her proficiency in either was not remarkable, and she shirked her lessons in both whenever she could. What a strange, unaccountable character! – for with all these symptoms of profligacy at ten years old, she had neither a bad heart nor a bad temper; was seldom stubborn, scarcely ever quarrelsome, and very kind to the little ones, with few interruptions of tyranny.

The spinster Jane Austen was always, in novels and letters alike, quite exceptionally perceptive of children's behaviour in an entirely unsentimental fashion. Catherine

> was moreover noisy and wild, hated confinement and cleanliness, and loved nothing so well in the world as rolling down the green slope at the back of the house.
>
> Such was Catherine Morland at ten. At fifteen, appearances were mending; she began to curl her hair and long for balls; her complexion improved, her features were softened by plumpness and colour, her eyes gained more animation, and her figure more consequence. Her love of dirt gave way to an inclination for finery, and she grew clean as she grew smart; she had now the pleasure of sometimes hearing her father and mother remark on her personal improvement . . . [and she even read books] provided that nothing like useful knowledge could be gained from them, provided they were all story and no reflection . . . But from fifteen to seventeen she was in training for a heroine; she read all such works as heroines must read . . .[3]

Many of Catherine's adventures in *Northanger Abbey* are absurd – based on her imaginative life, which is lively, not the everyday humdrum of the

---

[2] Chapman (*NA* p. 289) cites Gay's Fables as the source for this.
[3] NA I, c. 1, pp. 13–15.

parsonage in which she was brought up. But Catherine herself – as she is presented to us – has many or most of the qualities of an ordinary young woman, with more life, vigour and charm than many perhaps; but for the novel to work, she must convince, must at a certain level fulfil the reader's expectations of what an ordinary young woman might be.

A modern 'realistic' novel will commonly tell us much of its heroines' and heroes' sexual experiences. Of such, Jane will tell us nothing: if she had, her readers would have thrown the books out of the window. She is candid about illegitimacy: it is intriguing to compare the single brisk sentence which introduces Harriet Smith – she 'was the natural daughter of some-body' (1816) – with the hundreds of pages of mysterious fuss with which Dickens surrounds the birth of Esther Summerson in *Bleak House* (1853). Jane was, indeed, exceptionally discreet about her heroines' family lives after marriage. When she has peremptorily dismissed Dr Grant to apoplexy and death at the end of *Mansfield Park*, the living of Mansfield becomes vacant, 'just after they [Fanny and Edmund] had been married long enough to begin to want an increase of income, and feel their distance from the paternal abode an inconvenience'.[4] This is even more discreet than Trollope's very similar hint at the end of *Framley Parsonage*. He calls the final chapter indeed 'How they were all married, had two children, and lived happily ever after'; – the conventional ending – though of the four couples he unites in wedlock one at least (Dr Thorne and Miss Dunstable) clearly had no children, and – unlike Dickens with Esther – none is known to have had two. But the principal couple, Lord Lufton and Lucy Robarts, were evidently not childless.

> It is well known to everyone at Framley that old Lady Lufton still reigns paramount in the parish. 'Yes, my dear; the big room looking into the little garden to the south was always the nursery; and if you ask my advice, it will remain so. But of course, any room you please –'
> And the big room looking into the little garden to the south is still the nursery at Framley Court

– which is as near as Trollope chooses to go to saying that the nursery was needed.

The modern novelist is not in any truer sense giving a transcript of reality than Jane – commonly less so, for Jane wrote (in a large measure) about human experience as she encountered it; and there are few things of which we know less than our neighbours' sexual experiences. Both are circum-scribed by the fashions and conventions of their age: not to introduce sex makes a modern novelist – or social historian – coy, prudish, and unrealis-tic. Yet in truth the modern historian of sex has to plough through heaps of

---

[4] *MP* III, c. 17, p. 473; for what follows, see A. Trollope, *Framley Parsonage* (1861), c. 46.

worthless evidence. Jane's portrayal of human life and human emotions can be more readily checked against experience – and she knew it; she was able to create the illusion of realism by exceedingly subtle use of relatively commonplace human experience.

The conversation of Miss Bates in *Emma* – 'a great talker upon little matters'[5] – is perhaps the best known illustration of this truth. When I first read *Emma* in boasting youth, I confess I thought Miss Bates so realistic as to be as boring in the novel as in life. In my own narrative old age, I hang on her every word.

One of Emma's deficiencies is a tendency to avoid Miss Bates and her mother – the widow of a former vicar of Highbury – to escape the ceaseless chatter of the good spinster, and the latest letter from her niece, Jane Fairfax. Miss Fairfax is the chief local rival to Emma in elegance and accomplishment – one whom Emma has neglected on Jane's visits to her aunt and grandmother, and whom Emma accordingly dislikes. So she visits Miss Bates at a time when she is confident no letter will have come from Jane – to be greeted with the news of an unexpected letter from the niece.

> 'Have you heard from Miss Fairfax so lately? I am extremely happy. I hope she is well?'
>
> 'Thank you. You are so kind!' replied the happily deceived aunt, while eagerly hunting for the letter. 'Oh, here it is. I was sure it could not be far off; but I had put my huswife upon it, you see, without being aware, and so it was quite hid, but I had it in my hand so very lately that I was almost sure it must be on the table. I was reading it to Mrs Cole, and since she went away, I was reading it again to my mother, for it is such a pleasure to her – a letter from Jane – that she can never hear it often enough; so I knew it could not be far off, and here it is, only just under my huswife – and since you are so kind as to wish to hear what she says; – but, first of all, I really must, in justice to Jane, apologise for her writing so short a letter – only two pages, you see – hardly two – and in general she fills the whole paper and crosses half . . .'

– and so she goes on, page after page, herself – until Emma manages to slip away,

> happy in this, that though much had been forced on her against her will . . . she had been able to escape the letter itself.[6]

This first major deployment of Miss Bates – though long and rambling – is relatively straightforward; as time passes we are shown her fitting more complex threads together. We are even shown Emma mimicking her. A

5 *E* I, c. 3, p. 21.
6 *E* II, c. 1, esp. pp. 157, 162.

suggestion is made that Mr Knightley may want to marry Jane Fairfax, and Emma pours scorn on it.

> 'How would he bear to have Miss Bates belonging to him? – To have her haunting the Abbey, and thanking him all day long for his great kindness in marrying Jane? – "So very kind and obliging! – But he always had been such a very kind neighbour!" And then fly off, through half a sentence, to her mother's old petticoat. "Not that it was such a very old petticoat either – for still it would last a great while – and, indeed, she must thankfully say that their petticoats were all very strong." '[7]

Miss Bates's final curtain is a very happy one: Jane's engagement to the rich and charming Frank Churchill has been revealed – as a secret, the kind which everyone knows and a few try to keep. Emma goes to congratulate Jane and finds other company there – and when Miss Bates comes in,

> Emma could not help being diverted by the perplexity of her first answer to herself, resulting, she supposed, from doubt of what might be said, and impatience to say everything.
>
> 'Thank you, dear Miss Woodhouse, you are all kindness. – It is impossible to say – Yes, indeed, I quite understand – dearest Jane's prospects – that is, I do not mean. – But she is charmingly recovered. – How is Mr Woodhouse? – I am so glad. – Quite out of my power. – Such a happy little circle as you find us here. – Yes, indeed. – Charming young man! – that is – so very friendly; I mean good Mr Perry! [the apothecary, who has visited Jane when she was ill] – Such attention to Jane!'[8]

This is at once real conversation – the unfinished sentences and confusion of rapid speech – and high art. Some have claimed to know the original of Miss Bates: assuredly they are mistaken – much as the good lady owes to folk Miss Austen had met, her origin lies wholly in Jane's imagination.[9] We might meet Miss Bates anywhere in Jane Austen's England – we shall never meet her save in the pages of *Emma*.

My final examples of Jane's treatment of the real world are very different. Nothing has served to bring literature so much into disrepute with social historians as its witness to age of marriage. There has been much argument, for example, whether the marriage of Juliet at 13 mirrored the customs of Shakespeare's world – a discussion which would have caused him much

---

[7] *E* II, c. 8, p. 225.
[8] *E* III, c. 16, p. 455.
[9] Mrs and Miss Milles have been seen as models for Mrs and Miss Bates – cf. *Letters*, C no. 89, pp. 360–1 and Chapman's note, Index VI, under Emma.

amusement.[10] No serious historian would use Jane Austen's witness as a contribution to demographic statistics. But it is instructive to compare the ages of her leading characters when they entered marriage with those of her own family – and currently accepted mean ages of marriage among similar folk. The score among heroines is as follows: Catherine 18, Marianne 19; Fanny 19 at least; Elinor about 20; Emma probably 21; Elizabeth about 21; Jane about 22; Anne 27 or 28. Among the heroes: Edward about 23; Mr Bingley about 24; Edmund about 25; Henry Tilney 26; Mr Darcy 28; Mr Knightley and Colonel Brandon both about 38.[11] The mean age on current estimate in the first half of the nineteenth century was 25.3 for men, 23.4 for women.[12] But Jane Austen was not interested in mean ages – though she was profoundly interested in the effect of age on choice and outlook. In Jane's family, Charles's first wife was 17 when he married her; Edward's wife 18; her mother married at 24; James's second wife was 25; his first wife had been 33; Henry's first wife was 36 – and while the age of Francis's first wife seems to be unknown, his second, whom he married when he was 54 and a widower with 11 children, was 63.[13] The ages of first marriage of Jane Austen's women were not out of line with the experience of her own family.

On 29 January 1813, Jane wrote to Cassandra in high excitement to tell her that her first copy of *Pride and Prejudice* had come – 'I have got my own darling child from London' – how it had been tried out on the unsuspecting Miss Benn, who had no idea Jane was the author; how delighted she still is with Elizabeth, 'as delightful a creature as ever appeared in print' – and 'Now I will try to write of something else, and it shall be a complete change of subject – ordination . . .'[14] No doubt she uses the word with deliberate pomp and circumstance, to emphasise, in the style of their sisterly banter, that the new book is more solemn. None the less, within reasonable limits she means what she says. Ordination was indeed a minor theme in *Pride and Prejudice*, for Mr Collins had been ordained 'at Easter' before

---

[10] See Brooke 1989, pp. 173–4.

[11] In addition, Lydia Bennet was 16 when she married, Maria Bertram about 21 (*PP* p. 306; *MP* p. 38 makes Maria 20 some months before her marriage). For these details see *NA* p. 252; *SS* I c. 7, p. 34; c. 8, p. 37; c. 22, p. 131; II c. 1, p. 140; III c. 13, p. 369; c. 14, pp. 378–9 – and below c. 8 n. 2. In *PP* Elizabeth was 'not one-and-twenty' in March, so 21 when married (p. 166; cf. p. 403); as the Bennets had been married 23 years at the outset (p. 5), Jane must have been about 22; Mr Darcy was 28 (p. 369), Bingley 23 or so at the outset (p. 16), so 24 when married. In *MP*, Fanny was at least 19 (see below, c. 15 n. 45), Edmund at the outset was 6 years older than Fanny (16, p. 12), so about 25 when married. Emma was nearly 21 at the outset (p. 1), and marries a year later; Mr Knightley was about 37 or 38 (p. 9) – that is, about 38 when he married. In *P*, Anne was 27 or 28 (cf. pp. 26, 225, 237) – all the other women were much younger. These details show how precise Jane Austen could be in matters of age as of chronology.

[12] Wrigley and Schofield 1989, p. 255.

[13] I have gathered these details from the very helpful Biographical Index to *Letters* L.

[14] *Letters*, L, no. 79, pp. 201–2; C, no. 76, pp. 297–8; M, F-236-7.

taking up the living of Hunsdon – in the year before he made his debut among the Bennets.[15] In *Mansfield Park* it is a major theme. Edmund Bertram, Sir Thomas's younger son, is to be a clergyman; and as the book advances, so he prepares himself to go to Peterborough (in whose see Miss Austen quite correctly places Mansfield) for ordination in Christmas week – to return a fully fledged clergyman.[16]

It has often been observed that – then as now – the Church of England recognised three stages of Holy Orders – of bishops, priests and deacons; that a country parson had to be a priest to celebrate the eucharist, though not to read the office; and that according to tradition, and according to canon law as represented by Bishop Gibson's *Codex*, a year should elapse between ordination as deacon and as priest.[17] By implication in the case of Mr Collins, and without any shadow of doubt for Edmund, Jane Austen rolls the two orders into one: he goes to Peterborough a layman and returns a clergyman complete. There has indeed been some discussion whether this was due to ignorance, to deliberate simplification – or to a knowledge of contemporary, irregular practices. The last is perhaps the most improbable. Jane's father and eldest brother, James, were both evidently ordained to the titles of their fellowships at St John's College, Oxford – George as deacon on 10 March 1754, as priest on 25 May 1755; James as deacon on 19 December 1787, as priest on 7 June 1789.[18] By the kindness of Mrs Jennifer Thorp and Professor David Smith, I have been able to learn the practice in two English dioceses – in Winchester, the see in which Jane's father and brothers were beneficed, and in which the family lived during most of her life, and York, to offer a distant comparison.[19] In the see of York there were cases in the seventeenth century of ordination as deacon and priest on the same day, but none in the eighteenth century. In the see of Winchester the pattern was more varied. In the vast majority of cases a full year or so elapsed; in just over 60 of the 2,000 and more ordinations between 1750 and 1817 whose records survive the gap was less, usually of a few months – four months in the case of Jane's brother Henry, but he was ordained in 1816–17 after *Mansfield Park* had been published.[20] Of the 60, 43 had

[15] *P* I c.13, p. 62.
[16] See p. 147.
[17] Gibson 1713, pp. 173–4; cf. Branton 1955.
[18] Tucker 1983 (1998), pp. 26–7, 102–3, 220 n. 14: I have not been able to check the sources for these dates.
[19] From Winchester, Hampshire Record Office, Winchester Diocesan Records F/1/B3–16, analysed for me by Jennifer Thorp; indexed in Willis 1964–65. The York details are as analysed for me by David Smith from the York ordination records in the Borthwick Institute, University of York.
[20] Henry was ordained deacon in Dec. 1816 and priest in March 1817 (loc. cit. F/1/B16/2601, 2615). Cf. Caroline Austen 1986, p. 49; *Letters*, L no. 144, p. 318; C no. 132, p. 461 and note; M, F-409; *FR* p. 212.

intervals between one and eleven months; 8 of within two weeks; five of within a week; five on consecutive days; 9 on the same day. Of these 9, 6 took place in 1751–52, two in the later 1750s – that is to say, in the later years of the great Latitudinarian, Bishop Benjamin Hoadly, who died in 1761. Most of the nine took place in the private chapel of his palace in Chelsea; and two at least were of clergy from the Channel Isles – one of them, perhaps more, a Huguenot minister who was being re-ordained for the Anglican ministry – who may always have had rather separate treatment. None the less, this evidence makes clear that in Hoadly's later years, ordination as deacon and priest on the same day was not an uncommon practice – though still only for a small minority. Only one instance is known under his successor, Bishop John Thomas (1761–81), none under Brownlow North (1781–1820), who was bishop for the greater part of Jane Austen's lifetime. Under Bishop North, there are five cases of ordination on adjacent days – and a few other irregularities. But throughout Jane's life – and the ministry of her father and brothers – the normal practice was to ordain to the two orders at dates far apart, most commonly at least a year apart.[21]

A careful reader of Jane Austen's novels might be led to think that ordinations normally took place at Easter and Christmas. The official rule was to hold ordinations on the Sunday following Ember-Days.[22] The Easter date seems pure fantasy: neither at York nor at Winchester was it ever the practice to hold ordinations at Easter in this period. But Christmas is another matter. At the turn of the eighteenth and nineteenth centuries at York, ordinations were held in July and October; but Archbishop Vernon Harcourt brought in a new pattern, much less regular – save that it included ordination in the week leading up to Christmas. At Winchester this had long been so: both Bishops Thomas and North held ordinations at all manner of times, but regularly (with a few exceptions) in December. In 1812 when *Mansfield Park* was being conceived, North ordained on 20 December; in 1813, when it was awaiting publication, on 18 December.[23]

The date of Edmund's ordination thus clearly suggests genuine knowledge, which is hardly surprising. Mr Collins simply had to be ordained at a convenient period before he packed his bags to go in search of a wife to share the blessings of Lady Catherine de Bourgh's patronage with him. The failure – or refusal – to distinguish the two stages of ordination is more puzzling. Born in a rectory, daughter of one clergyman, sister of one – and eventually two – Jane can hardly have been ignorant of the basic elements of ordination; even if she had never heard it discussed at home – which passes belief – she can hardly have avoided the ordination services on some

[21] For the dates of the bishops, see Horn 1974, pp. 82–3.
[22] Gibson 1713, p. 161; Cripps 1850, pp. 17–18.
[23] See n. 19.

of the innumerable occasions when she handled the Book of Common Prayer. It is conceivable that she was brought up on stories of how Bishop Hoadly had conducted himself. But if she had, she would have known that double ordination on a single day was an abuse, or at best, an exception. Now there are indeed abuses tolerated even in the relatively zealous ethos of *Mansfield Park*.[24] But Edmund is portrayed as a reasonably conscientious parson – and a wholly admirable young man; it is most unlikely that Jane would have admitted to anything irregular in his ordination – and there is certainly not a hint of it. Nor is there much clerical conversation or jargon either – though she allows Edmund and Dr Grant to talk of tithes, allows Edmund and Miss Crawford to dispute about a clergyman's duties, and Mrs Norris to fume at dilapidations.[25] It seems much more likely that she was deliberately avoiding anything so technical, so clerical-sounding, as 'deacon and priest' – that she has deliberately ironed out distinctions and practices which would ruffle the smooth surface of her narrative.

Thus Edmund's is not a real ordination, in the simple sense of these terms. Yet we have Jane's word for it that it is one of the central events of the book in her mind and purpose. She may have been a supreme artist in creating an impression of reality; but all she created was also illusion. Historians must be very wary of taking her characters and their situations at face value as evidence of what was common and normal – but they must be wary in their use of every kind of evidence. In this respect the novel is no different from other genres of historical evidence – it will cheat us if it can.

The great virtue of Jane Austen's novels as evidence is that she set out to create the illusion of reality with far greater artistic skills than most of her kind. She will deceive us if we are too credulous; but if we keep our wits about us, she will allow us to learn.

Yet we can only avoid deception by constant vigilance. At the end of *Persuasion* she reflected on her heroine's predicament. Anne 'gloried in being a sailor's wife, but she must pay the tax of quick alarm for belonging to that profession which is, if possible, more distinguished in its domestic virtues than in its national importance'.[26] Coming from a pious lady in the Regency era, writing not many years after the death of Horatio Nelson, the comment seems on first reflection either preposterous or very innocent. But can one believe in an innocent Jane Austen? Only if one forgets the deep interest in the Navy which *Mansfield Park* and *Persuasion* so amply illustrate – and that one of her sailor brothers had been close to Nelson, the supreme hero of the navy, but no model of domestic virtue. The literary critics have taught us very justly to read books as books and not to be excessively distracted by their context or by imaginary influences from the life or

---

[24] See p. 148.
[25] *MP*, pp. 226, 91–4, 55.
[26] *P* II c. 12, p. 252; cf. p. 273.

the ego of their author. But just occasionally it may be sensible not to follow this doctrine too ruthlessly. We may be allowed to recall that two of Jane's brothers were distinguished sailors and are not likely to have relished her portrait of the wicked old Admiral Crawford, whose vices lubricate the plot of *Mansfield Park*. If I had been one of them I should certainly have asked her to do better by my profession in future; and in doing so have earned her retort. For everyone knew that the sailor's profession was not, in the public eye, distinguished for its marital fidelity; and to the careful reader she struck two blows in this sentence – for she had unkindly observed that the profession was 'if possible, more distinguished in its domestic virtues than in its national importance'. Trafalgar is cut down to size. Doubtless she would have hastened to say that that was not her meaning – but we cannot escape the *double entendre*.

3

A Didactic Novelist?

I believe I have learned more of Jane Austen's inspiration from Marilyn Butler's *Jane Austen and the War of Ideas* than from any other book about her written in the last thirty years.[1] Above all she has shown very clearly how much Miss Austen owed to the highly moral, didactic, conservative, 'anti-jacobin' novels. So substantial is the evidence for their influence that Dr Butler becomes convinced that Jane Austen must have had a like didactic programme in her major novels, and she proceeds to discover it. But a difficulty arises: for all the subtlety and power of Jane's technique as a novelist, she seems to falter in adapting her teaching and her stories. So consistently does Marilyn Butler make her falter that our suspicions are aroused: no small part of Dr Butler's contribution to our understanding lies in the failure of this part of her scheme. If it is a failure, which is a bold claim, it cannot detract from the value of the book: as Albert of Pisa the Franciscan said about the early Dominicans – we owe much to them, and they have sometimes taught us what not to do.

She sees in *Sense and Sensibility* a plain statement of the virtues of Elinor and sense, against Marianne and sensibility. But that is not how the book reads to me; on the contrary, the dialectic between the heroines, which is developed with enormous gusto, proves in the end relatively superficial – relative that is, to the deeper convictions on which they agree. Nor is it true that Marianne is wholeheartedly condemned. She is very young at the outset and barely 19 when she becomes the lady of Delaford House. She is impulsive and absurd at 16 – yet 'sensible and clever . . . generous, amiable, interesting' as well.[2] Even in the early chapters her better qualities are occasionally deployed, and they come out with great effect towards the close. 'She was every thing but prudent'; but Jane did not write the book to propound the tedious doctrine that it is better to be prudent than interesting. Most of the way indeed, as is emphasised again and again, Elinor herself was as much deceived in her love for Edward Ferrars as was Marianne in Willoughby: for from the beginning until almost the very end Edward was betrothed to Lucy Steele. So much for sense.

[1]   Butler 1987.
[2]   *SS* I, c. 1, p. 6; also for what follows.

As in all her mature novels, the action in *Sense and Sensibility* seems to proceed at two levels: there is the more visible level at which both Marianne and Elinor make disastrous mistakes: Marianne in falling on impulse for the dissolute Willoughby, Elinor by falling in love with Edward Ferrars, who (it transpires) is engaged to another. All is at sixes and sevens till very close to the end, when an almost miraculous intervention rescues Elinor and restores Edward to her. In ironical contrast, Marianne's conversion to be the wife of Colonel Brandon proceeds in more humdrum fashion, but (for the faithful reader) with equal conviction. At the deeper level Elinor and Marianne prove to have feelings and convictions in common of more lasting worth than the differences between them. Some might say that this was the didactic lesson Jane Austen sought to teach us – that the hidden virtues matter more than the superficial vices. If so, she could have made it a great deal plainer than she did, for she does not seem to have put the message across to most of her readers. Surely, indeed, high art and plain instruction can only sit ill together. That is not to deny that Jane Austen was a moralist and a teacher: all of us who read her attentively have come away the better for it. But I for one have not learned any simple moral lessons from her.

In all her major novels the discourse proceeds at two levels; and this is most clear and most perfectly presented in *Emma*, the novel which may reasonably be seen as the culmination of her creative purposes. At the superficial level it is one long tale of errors, mistakes and misunderstandings, the fruit of Emma's wilful vanity; and towards the end she allows herself to be carried away in enjoyment of her flirtation with Frank Churchill to be unforgivably insulting to Miss Bates. Yet there are hints here and there throughout the book of a better Emma – not only clever, but thoughtful, considerate, generous minded. It is most conspicuous, from beginning to end of the book, in her consideration for her father. Mr Woodhouse is one of Jane Austen's immortal creations, my favourite male character in the whole *oeuvre*. But he has also a role to play; and part of that role is to keep us aware of Emma's better nature. In the last chapters of the book she appears to have undergone conversion: she is considerate to Miss Bates, attentive to Jane Fairfax – whom she had earlier neglected – and a worthy partner for Mr Knightley. But it seems nearer the truth to say that her superficial follies have passed, leaving no scars, but helping her to find and bring to the fore her deeper, better self.

If we turn back from contemplating Emma to *Sense and Sensibility*, we can see that it is dominated by a similar procedure, less assured, less masterly in its technique – yet astonishingly mature for her first major novel. At a superficial level there is a dialectic between the most obvious qualities of the two sisters – and yet, ironically, Elinor's mistake comes near to being the more disastrous of the two. It was perhaps in the nature of things that the worldly, profligate Willoughby should abandon Marianne and leave her free to make a better choice; Elinor was unbelievably lucky not to lose her Edward to the scheming Lucy Steele. Yet there is a deeper level still, as in *Emma*, at which the two sisters share far more qualities than those which set them apart.

> Among the merits and the happiness of Elinor and Marianne, let it not be ranked as the least considerable, that though sisters, and living almost within sight of each other, they could live without disagreement between themselves, or producing coolness between their husbands.[3]

'Though sisters': this most characteristic swipe – a public joke of the kind she loved, and a private joke for her only sister – disguises with a touch of irony the serious point that Jane has been making: Elinor and Marianne had far more in common of the good qualities of their family and their kind than just being sisters.

It has often been thought that Miss Austen's didactic vein was least apparent in *Pride and Prejudice*, most apparent in *Mansfield Park*. The contrast is very neatly illustrated by two closely parallel passages.

When Lydia eloped with Mr Wickham, Mr Bennet's first reaction – after they were securely married – was to refuse them entry to his house; but Jane and Elizabeth urged on him 'that she should be noticed on her marriage by her parents', and he relented. Not long after came a letter from his cousin, the Reverend Mr Collins, who rejoiced that

> Lydia's sad business has been so well hushed up, and [I] am only concerned that their living together before the marriage took place, should be so generally known. I must not, however, neglect the duties of my station, or refrain from declaring my amazement, at hearing that you received the young couple into your house as soon as they were married. It was an encouragement to vice . . . You ought certainly to forgive them, as a christian, but never to admit them in your sight, or allow their names to be mentioned in your hearing.

– and Mr Bennet comments – ' "*That* is his notion of Christian forgiveness!" '[4] Any ordinary reader, while observing that Mr Bennet himself had begun by taking a sterner line, must surely reckon that Miss Austen is most unlikely to have put her own views into the mouth or pen of Mr Collins.

Pride and Prejudice was published in 1813, and although a first draft is supposed to have been written as early as 1796–7, the only certain fact is the date of publication. There is, however, clear evidence that she was revising it – and took some time revising it – in 1812–13. On 29 January 1813 she wrote to Cassandra that 'I have got my own darling child from London' –

---

[3] *SS* III, c. 14, p. 380.
[4] *PP* III, c. 8, p. 314; c. 15, pp. 363–4.

her copies of *Pride and Prejudice*; and she is as thrilled as anyone might be who had written such a book; there is certainly no hint that she rejected anything in it. On 4 February she wrote again, a little less satisfied – 'the work is rather too light and bright and sparkling; – it wants shade; – it wants to be stretched out here and there with a long chapter – of sense, if it could be had, if not of solemn specious nonsense . . .' we are rapidly aware that Jane is enjoying herself as much as ever.[5] In the first letter she told Cassandra (as I quoted in the previous chapter) that 'Now I will try to write of something else; it shall be a complete change of subject – ordination' – and in case we should have any doubt that she refers to *Mansfield Park* – which was already well under way, and seems to have been finished 'soon after June 1813'[6] – she asks Cassandra a question about Northamptonshire. There is in fact no doubt that the revision of *Pride and Prejudice* and the early stages of *Mansfield Park* proceeded hand in hand. Yet, notoriously, the judgment scene at the end of *Mansfield Park* is more dour than anything in *Pride and Prejudice*. Critics startled by the contrast between the moral judgments of the two books have even claimed that Jane was converted to Evangelical principles – or influenced by them – between the two; but there was no gap between them.[7] Furthermore, if Sir Thomas's moral code were to make Jane an Evangelical, it would have the same effect on Mr Collins, otherwise a delectable parody of a second-rate eighteenth-century country parson. There is no end – as Jane herself might have said – of the mischief the notion of Miss Austen's conversion unleashes upon us.

Mansfield Park was begun in 1811, finished in 1813 – and published the next year; and this marvellous book is the happy hunting ground of exponents of Jane Austen, the moralist – and rightly so, for it reveals the problems of moral education more completely and more starkly than any other of her novels.

Thus Julia Bertram suffers penance at Sotherton from the necessity of being polite to Mrs Rushworth.

> the politeness which she had been brought up to practise as a duty, made it impossible for her to escape; while the want of that higher species of self-command, that just consideration of others, that knowledge of her own heart, that principle of right which had not formed any essential part of her education, made her miserable under it.[8]

The problem of moral education plays a special part in the melodramatic

---

[5] *Letters*, L no. 79, p. 201; C no. 76, p. 297; M, F-236; and L no. 80, p. 203; C no. 77, pp. 299–300; M, F-238. On the date of *PP*, see pp. 44–5, 51–2.

[6] See p. 45.

[7] For what follows, see pp. 126–32.

[8] *MP* I c. 9, p. 91.

conclusion of the book. For this, however, Jane prepares us in her most ironic vein. Fanny Price, whom she has portrayed to us in the most sympathetic colours, yet unmistakably as a prig, has been brought up to worship everything that is right and good at Mansfield Park, and to accept without hesitation every element in the code of Sir Thomas Bertram. So she is miserable in the home of her own family in Portsmouth and longs to return to Mansfield. When the summons finally arrives, it comes coupled with the shocking news that Maria Bertram, Mrs Rushworth, has eloped with Henry Crawford, the worldling who had been courting Fanny herself – and that Edmund Bertram, Maria's brother and Fanny's cousin, whom Fanny deeply loves, is coming next day to fetch her back to Mansfield. It is a situation brilliantly contrived, for it reveals the full horror of the Bertram scandal – and carries Fanny to the gate of heaven. 'She was, she felt she was, in the greatest danger of being exquisitely happy, while so many were miserable' – and in the light of that contrast or ambivalence all the rest must be read. She returns to enjoy the fondest welcome from Lady Bertram – ' "Dear Fanny! now I shall be comfortable" '[9] and the sourest looks from Aunt Norris, the parson's widow, the author (in her own estimation) of the Rushworth marriage, who is shattered by its failure – yet inclined to minimise the moral aspect. To the parents, 'The case admitted of no comfort. Lady Bertram did not think deeply, but, guided by Sir Thomas, she thought justly on all important points' – that is, she thought as he did –

> and she saw, in all its enormity, what had happened, and neither endeavoured herself, nor required Fanny to advise her, to think little of guilt and infamy . . . Whenever Lady Bertram *was* fixed on the event, she could see it only in one light, as comprehending the loss of a daughter, and a disgrace never to be wiped off.[10]

The outcome is that Maria, who had had a relatively brief affair with a man who was not her husband and become the guilty party in divorce – as these things were then understood – suffered a sentence of virtual life imprisonment with Mrs Norris in a distant 'country' – that is, a county far removed from Mansfield. To the modern reader it is a shockingly harsh sentence; and nothing is done to alleviate the stark judgment on Maria – or the contrast between the frivolity in which she has been allowed to grow up and the stern morality by which she was subsequently judged. Sir Thomas realises, indeed, something of what was wrong in his scheme of education for his daughters – that no attempt was made to build a bridge between his own stern aloofness and the spoiling flattery administered to them by Aunt Norris. But he fails to see that this might entitle Maria to mercy at his hands. Jane turns the knife in the wound – without ever a

---

[9] *MP* III, c. 15, pp. 443, 447.
[10] *MP* III, c. 16, p. 449 (*was* italic in both 1st and 2nd edns.).

murmur that there might be a moral code which allowed forgiveness to Maria after penance – by showing with exquisite irony and charm the prig Fanny entering her heaven. Henry Crawford's sin leads to a final breach between Edmund Bertram and Mary Crawford, Henry's sister – and this leaves the path open to Fanny's dearest dream, her marriage to Edmund. The whole sequence is foreshadowed in Fanny's intense delight in receiving that gloomy letter from Edmund in Portsmouth. Fanny Price has naturally not been Jane Austen's favourite heroine among her readers; she was not meant to be. But the author made this remarkable denouement credible by painting Fanny and Sir Thomas, and their harsh moral code, in the most sympathetic possible way: so much so that many a discerning reader has taken it for granted that their code was also Jane Austen's; and the moral force of *Mansfield Park* is undeniable. Yet Jane's admiration of the morality of *Mansfield Park* seems tinctured with some very profound criticisms of it. Time and again she deceives or partly deceives us by appearing to make her characters' views her own.[11] I do not know what Miss Austen thought was a suitable punishment for adultery. I should be astonished if she took any but a severe view of it.[12] But I am convinced that this cannot be deduced from reading literally the text of *Mansfield Park*. For between the judgment on Maria composed (at latest) in 1813 and Mr Bennet's 'That is his notion of Christian forgiveness!' there is a gulf. It is true that Lydia's sin had been to live with a man before marriage; Maria was married to another. It is also very true that two of Jane's brothers – and her father above all – were clergymen and pastors. The author of *Mansfield Park* was not in any crude sense a preacher – her morality was much more subtle and artistic than that; but she was a parson's daughter – with all the subtle mingling of reverence and irreverence of the clergy and their standards which that implies.[13]

There is another problem in the moral world of *Mansfield Park*. Henry Crawford came near to success with Fanny.

> Could he have been satisfied with the conquest of one amiable woman's affections, could he have found sufficient exultation in overcoming the reluctance, in working himself into the esteem and tenderness of Fanny Price, there would have been every probability of success and felicity for him. His affection had already done something. Her influence over him had already given him some influence over her. Would he have deserved more, there can be no doubt that more would have been obtained; especially when that marriage had

[11] A good example is the moralising of Lady Bertram in *MP* III, c. 16. For Sir Thomas's laxity in his handling of church patronage, see p. 148.

[12] Cf. her comments on Mrs Powlett's elopement and the Countess of Oxford (*Letters*, L nos. 53, 82, pp. 131, 208; C nos. 52, 78.1, pp. 197, 504).

[13] See pp. 136–7.

taken place [between Mary Crawford and Edmund Bertram], which would have given him the assistance of her conscience in subduing her first inclination, and brought them very often together. Would he have persevered, and uprightly, Fanny must have been his reward – and a reward very voluntarily bestowed – within a reasonable period from Edmund's marrying Mary.[14]

This is a passage very hard to assess, since the reader is in considerable doubt whether Mary will agree to marry Edmund at all – on his modest income and in his clerical post. In part, it is the voice of Henry Crawford's conscience as much as of the author. But it very clearly and deliberately points to a possibility of a denouement in which the Crawfords may be happy as well as Edmund and Fanny – but with a happiness more superficial, one is bound to think, than that which Edmund and Fanny enjoy in Mansfield Parsonage. We are shown, as it were, two paths to a happy ending; the conclusion of the book, with all its element of tragedy, leads to the truer, deeper union. This is not to say that Jane wantonly destroyed the happiness of Maria to fashion that of Fanny; but rather, that – as so commonly in her books – she shows two worlds, one deeper in its values than the other.

In pursuit of a moral code, as of marriage and its modes, Jane Austen conducts a discussion, at a deep level; she does not pronounce dogmas.

It has often been taken for granted that she shared Sir Thomas Bertram's disapproval of private theatricals; she has sometimes been taken severely to task for her puritanical attitude, and even trounced for giving the domestic theatre a bad name among nineteenth-century moralists.[15] The language used in *Mansfield Park* is strong; even Tom Bertram comes in the end to feel that he was accessory to Maria's adultery because of 'all the dangerous intimacy of his unjustifiable theatre'.[16] But it had not been so clear to all the family that Sir Thomas would disapprove of theatricals as such: neither Lady Bertram nor Mrs Norris saw anything wrong in them – and it was the delicacy of Maria's situation, as a woman engaged, and of the whole family, with its master in peril on the sea, that made Edmund at first so determined against them; Fanny's terror of her uncle, and of acting, put an edge on her feelings and so on the reader's. It is indeed extremely improbable that Jane Austen was as firmly set against private theatricals as Fanny Price. There had been plays at Steventon in her childhood; her revered eldest brother James had written and directed parts of them; in her late twenties she wrote a short play, *Sir Charles Grandison*, for the family to perform.[17] There is no hint in her letters of the kind of prejudice represented in *Mansfield Park*. It is indeed possible that she had changed her view by the early 1810s; but the

---

[14] *MP* III, c. 17, p. 467.
[15] See, especially, Rosenfeld 1962 and cf. Lodge 1962–3.
[16] *MP* III, c. 17, p. 462.
[17] Southam 1980. On theatricals at Steventon, see *Memoir* (1870), pp. 43–4; (1871), p. 25.

burden of proof lies with those who deduce from the text of *Mansfield Park* that Jane Austen wished for a general ban on domestic theatres.

Much more revealing of her own views are the qualities she finds in her characters. All her books in some measure proceed at two levels: at a level of superficial error and misunderstanding, and at a deeper level in which true character asserts itself. Here one finds what Elinor and Marianne have in common; here one finds what Emma and Mr Knightley share. These are the qualities we may be sure Miss Austen admired.[18]

---

[18] To this we shall return in chapter 16.

4

Materials

Jane Austen is of special fascination to the historian, since we owe almost all we know of her to her own writings.[1] The memoirs and family reminiscences – valuable though they are for their fragments of genuine recollection – cannot compare with her own testimony in historical value. This is not, perhaps, unusual. It is true of many great poets that we know little of them apart from their writings, from Sappho to Wolfram von Eschenbach; and we know precious little of Shakespeare. The same is true of many notable thinkers: Duns Scotus is a striking example. But it is rare for a writer – who never attempted autobiography – to reveal herself in such enchanting fashion as Jane Austen.

A striking example of the contrast between her own evidence and family tradition is the story of her love affairs. She was a dependent female all her days, and a poor relation; she had no fortune, and for all her charm and wit and intelligence, she was not a desirable match for a suitor unprovided with means. This she doubtless knew – only too well – from her earliest days; and this, and her deep affection for her sister, and all the ties of family, may have made the spinster life more acceptable to her as time passed and no eligible suitor came. The strange mixture of irony and ease with which she imagines receiving proposals in some of her early letters can be interpreted in several different ways: they certainly read as if she was well protected against genuine romantic expectation or disappointment; but she may deceive us. In January 1796 Tom Lefroy – nephew of the close family friend Mrs Lefroy, wife of a neighbouring clergyman – called on her: 'he has but *one* fault, which time will, I trust, entirely remove – it is that his morning coat is a great deal too light.' A few days later she is preparing for a ball the next day: 'I look forward with great impatience to it, as I rather expect to receive an offer from my friend in the course of the evening. I shall refuse him, however, unless he promises to give away his white coat.' The day came – 'At length the Day is come on which I am to flirt my last with Tom Lefroy, and when you receive this it will be over – My tears flow as I write, at the melancholy idea . . .'[2] Tom Lefroy set off for Ireland,

[1] See Prologue, above.
[2] *Letters*, L nos. 1–2, pp. 1–4; C, nos. 1–2, pp. 1–6.

where many years later, he became Chief Justice, and reminisced (so we are told) on his boyhood love for Jane Austen: 'it was a boy's love', and, one fears, she and Cassandra laughed at him.[3] But there is another Tom in these letters, the Reverend Tom Fowle, Cassandra's fiancé, who was about to set sail with his patron for the West Indies – where he died, sadly and prematurely, of a fever.[4] In this context it is most unlikely that Jane was hiding a genuine passion for Tom Lefroy, but rather delighting her sister with a fantasy world in which she too would soon be engaged. There is an echo of the situation in *Pride and Prejudice*, when Jane, delighting in her engagement to Mr Bingley, laments that Elizabeth has no lover –

> 'If there *were* but such another man for you!'
>
> 'If you were to give me forty such men, I could never be so happy as you. Till I have your disposition, your goodness, I never can have your happiness. No, no, let me shift for myself; and, perhaps, if I have very good luck, I may meet with another Mr Collins in time.'[5]

In that case Elizabeth is hiding a secret: she is in love with Mr Darcy. In Jane Austen's, there is no reason to suppose any such secret – anyway, not in 1796. But romantic tradition abhors a vacuum, and later generations endowed Jane with three or four lovers. In the *Memoir* it is alleged that 'in her youth' she had refused an eligible suitor; and that late in life Cassandra told the story of a man they had met at a watering place, whom Cassandra thought suitable and 'likely to win her sister's love'. But soon after 'they heard of his sudden death'. The same story is told in the *Life* on Caroline Austen's authority: after the publication of the *Memoir* she was induced to note down the details as she recalled Cassandra telling them her.[6] In one version of the story, his name is given as Blackall, which suggests confusion with quite another suitor;[7] the story itself – written down after 1870 from a conversation with Cassandra before 1845 about an incident more than forty years earlier still – suggests the possibility of confusion with Cassandra's own unhappy love affair. At the very least we may suspect that Cassandra heightened the attraction between them out of a sense of its congruity with her own sorrow.

The date for such an incident may have occurred in any summer between 1801 and 1804, perhaps in 1802, when other evidence takes the family to Dawlish on the south Devon coast for a holiday. Caroline Austen also recalled being told by her mother Mary Austen, James's wife, who was involved, that on Friday 3 December 1802 Cassandra and Jane – who had

---

[3] *Life*, p. 89.
[4] Tom Fowle: see *FR* pp. 76, 93–4.
[5] *PP* III, c. 13, p. 350.
[6] *FR* pp. 126–7; for the summer of 1802, see *FR* pp. 121, 266 n. 20.
[7] See below, p. 29.

been visiting friends nearby, came suddenly back to Steventon Rectory, now James's home – demanding to be instantly transported to their parents in Bath. In due course the explanation came out: Jane had received an offer of marriage; it seemed eligible and she accepted it – but immediately repented; and the next morning cancelled her acceptance and fled the house in which it had been made. The story is so improbable that it has been universally accepted; and indeed, it has a good pedigree. It is hardly likely that James's wife or daughter would have invented a tale which portrays Jane behaving with so little dignity or consideration as to make her brother, a busy clergyman, miss his Sunday duty at very short notice. 3 December 1802, furthermore, *was* a Friday, so it seems almost certain that some kind of genuine tradition lies behind it. The abandoned suitor was 'the shy, stammering young Harris Bigg-Wither', brother of Jane's close friends Elizabeth, Catherine and Alethea Bigg – and himself five or six years younger than Jane.[8]

None the less, it was the work of a moment. It seems possible that the other involvement of her early years – the only one (Tom Lefroy apart) recorded in the *Letters* – was the least superficial – though because it is told us in Jane's own ironical, controlled, allusive prose, it has been the least regarded by most of her biographers.

The Reverend Samuel Blackall was a hereditary Emmanuel man who went up to Cambridge in 1787 and was 14th wrangler in the Mathematical Tripos in 1792. In 1794 he was ordained and elected a fellow of Emmanuel College; from 1803 to 1812 he was a tutor, instructing the young. As a fellow he was bound to celibacy; but in 1812 Dr John Askew, former fellow of Emmanuel and for many years rector of North Cadbury in Somerset – an Emmanuel living – died; and Blackall was able to take a country benefice and marry – even if his wife was not perhaps the first lady he had chosen. Jane herself sprang from the Oxford establishment and the only characters in her novels recorded as Cambridge men are Mr Wickham and Mr Crawford, among the most worthless of her young men. But she herself makes clear that she was not averse to one Cambridge man at least.

'That Samuel Blackall was' tempted to matrimony 'in 1798', writes Frank Stubbings – who brought Blackall to life in an enchanting article first published in 1965[9] –

we happen to know from the letters of Jane Austen. If Blackall was 'gay, gentlemanly, and classical' in 1811, at the age of 40, he can hardly have been less so at the age of twenty-seven; and when, visiting in Hampshire, he met among the unidea'd girls of the country

---

[8] *FR*, pp. 121–2 and 262 n. 21 for the source. The quotation is from *Letters*, L, pp. 497–8.
[9] Reissued in Stubbings 1984. What follows resumes passages from my own contribution to S. Bendall, C. Brooke and P. Collinson, *History of Emmanuel College* (1999), pp. 314–17.

rectories the charm and wit and perspicacity of Jane Austen, his delight in her company naturally led to a little wishful thinking.

On 17 November 1798 Jane wrote to her sister Cassandra:

Mrs Lefroy did come last Wednesday . . . Of her nephew [Tom Lefroy] she said nothing at all, and of her friend [Samuel Blackall] very little. She did not once mention the name of the former to *me*, and I was too proud to make any enquiries . . .

She showed me a letter which she had received from her friend [Samuel Blackall] a few weeks ago . . ., towards the end of which was a sentence to this effect: 'I am sorry to hear of Mrs Austen's illness. It would give me particular pleasure to have an opportunity of improving my acquaintance with that family – with a hope of creating to myself a nearer interest. But at present I cannot indulge any expectation of it.' This is rational enough; there is less love and more sense in it than sometimes appeared before, and I am very well satisfied. It will go on exceedingly well, and decline away in a very reasonable manner. There seems no likelihood of his coming into Hampshire this Christmas, and it is therefore most probable that our indifference will soon be mutual, unless his regard, which appeared to spring from knowing nothing of me at first, is best supported by never seeing me.[10]

'Our indifference will soon be mutual': we are reminded of Elizabeth's quip to Jane when Bingley had reappeared: 'if you persist in indifference, do not make *me* your confidante'. Perhaps even more, the whole passage has an echo – perhaps only a very distant echo – in Elizabeth's thoughts when she imagines the influence Lady Catherine de Bourgh may have on Darcy:

'If, therefore, an excuse for not keeping his promise [to return to Netherfield], should come to his friend within a few days . . . I shall know how to understand it. I shall then give over every expectation, every wish of his constancy. If he is satisfied with only regretting me, when he might have obtained my affections and hand, I shall soon cease to regret him at all.'[11]

A likely story; and we are free to interpret her maker's words in the same way, bearing in mind that in 1798 Jane Austen would be in no mood to sadden her sister, whose own love affair had come to a tragic end the year before, with her fiancé's death. It is an interesting speculation why Mr

[10] *Letters*, L no. 11, p. 19; C no. 11, pp. 27–8 (Stubbings 1984, pp. 79–80).
[11] *PP* III, c. 12, p. 343; c. 15, p. 361. It is perhaps worth noting that the first draft of *Pride and Prejudice* was completed not long before 1798.

Blackall had to wait so long for his country living. It seems likely that he had a particular affection for North Cadbury, and passed other opportunities over in its favour; he may have wanted time to forget Jane; or he may have savoured the opportunities for celibate conversation in the Parlour at Emmanuel.

In any event the story had an epilogue. On 3 July 1813 Jane wrote to her sailor brother Frank:

> I wonder whether you happened to see Mr Blackall's marriage in the papers last January. *We* did. He was married at Clifton to a Miss Lewis, whose father had been late of Antigua. I should very much like to know what sort of woman she is. He was a peice [*sic*] of Perfection, noisy Perfection himself which I always recollect with regard. – We had noticed a few months before his succeeding to a College living, the very living which we remembered his talking of and wishing for; an exceeding good one, [North] Cadbury in Somersetshire. – I would wish Miss Lewis to be of a silent turn and rather ignorant, but naturally intelligent and wishing to learn; – fond of cold veal pies, green tea in the afternoon, and a green window blind at night.[12]

How deeply Samuel Blackall touched her feelings we cannot say: enough, anyway, to be vividly remembered; enough perhaps too (as Frank Stubbings has suggested) to inspire some of the characteristics of Mr Tilney in *Northanger Abbey*, probably first drafted 'about the yeares [17]98 and [17]99'.[13] Mr Tilney is the first male character treated with all the sympathy which differentiates her later novels from the juvenilia – or rather, perhaps, the first to survive: we have no idea how Edward Ferrars and Mr Darcy fared in the 1790s. It is also the case that Henry Tilney marks a rare intrusion of an East Anglian name into the novels: Tilney All Saints is one of the loveliest churches in Norfolk; and Henry Tilney bears the name of a contemporary of Blackall's at Cambridge, an undergraduate at Caius who also became a country parson, and is the only Henry Tilney known to have studied at Oxford or Cambridge before 1850.[14] Like Jane Austen's Tilney, Mr Blackall was a lively, talkative, attractive young man, who took it for granted that the girls were less well read than he. And Mr Tilney provoked from Miss Austen some wry reflections. Catherine Morland

> was heartily ashamed of her ignorance – a misplaced shame. Where people wish to attach, they should always be ignorant. To come with

---

[12] *Letters*, L no. 86, p. 216; C no. 81, pp. 316–17 (Stubbings 1984, pp. 79–80); M F-259. This was the denouement of the letter as originally written, though she later added a postscript on other matters.

[13] See p. 45.

[14] Brooke 1985, p. 185 and n. 101. The quotation which follows is from *NA* I, c. 14, pp. 110–11.

a well-informed mind, is to come with an inability of administering to
the vanity of others, which a sensible person would always wish to
avoid. A woman especially, if she have the misfortune of knowing
anything, should conceal it as well as she can. . . . Catherine did not
know her own advantages; did not know that a good-looking girl
with an affectionate heart, and a very ignorant mind, cannot fail of
attracting a clever young man . . .

We may reasonably suppose that the *Letters* referring to Mr Blackall reveal
something of a relationship which – however brief – meant a good deal to
Jane; and we know more of her feelings about it than are accessible for the
other affairs distantly remembered by Cassandra and Caroline.

The Archive

The recorded materials from Jane Austen's pen survive either because she
published them or because Cassandra preserved them. A glance at what
does survive may suggest at first sight that Cassandra took pains to preserve
all her sister's remains that were available to her in 1817. *Northanger Abbey*
and *Persuasion* were soon to be published; but she carefully kept the suppressed chapters of *Persuasion* and the whole manuscript of *Sanditon,* so far
as it had been written.[15] That is to say, Cassandra preserved Jane's mature
literary production, except what had appeared in print. This is a very
striking fact, for it seems certain that she destroyed some, and likely that she
destroyed all the manuscripts of Jane's mature novels. They had been published; in her eyes – they were needed no more. As for earlier materials,
almost all the literary adventures Jane indulged in in her earliest years seem
likely to have been preserved in the three notebooks – Volumes the first,
the second and the third – from which our knowledge of the juvenilia
derives.[16] Early drafts of novels later published we have none: Jane herself
may have lost or destroyed them; or they may have fallen under the same
condemnation as the manuscripts of the later novels: what Jane wished to
see published was in print. But the letters tell a more complex and puzzling
story.

The Letters of Jane Austen

The historian who inspects Jane Austen's letters must tread delicately, like
Agag, king of the Amalekites, before Samuel hewed him in pieces before

---

[15] See pp. 6–7.
[16] See *MW*; and Southam 1964.

the Lord in Gilgal.[17] One fancies that Miss Austen would have regarded that as a reasonable punishment for prying into what was meant for her sister's – or other close friend's or relation's – eye *alone*. In *Persuasion* Anne Elliot was deeply shocked when she read one of Mr Elliot's letters highly disrespectful of her father and sister. 'She was obliged to recollect that her seeing the letter was a violation of the laws of honour, that no one ought to be judged or to be known by such testimonies, that no private correspondence could bear the eye of others . . .'[18] If there is safety in numbers, the historian may be excused: many thousands have read her most personal and intimate letters – those at least which escaped early destruction. But like all historical evidence – indeed, to a quite exceptional degree – they need care, consideration and imaginative insight in the interpreter.

The only one of Jane Austen's correspondents who systematically preserved her letters was her sister Cassandra.[19] Caroline Austen tells us that Cassandra herself destroyed many of the letters she had received, and their latest editor has shown with great care where missing letters can be discerned.[20] Although Cassandra had the run of all Jane's own papers, she left to posterity none of her own letters to her sister and only a tiny number of anyone else's.[21] Mercifully she handed over a great number of Jane's letters to her niece Fanny Knight, Lady Knatchbull – the daughter of their brother Edward, the rich relation who had inherited Godmersham Park in Kent and much else, including the cottage at Chawton where Jane and Cassandra lived with their mother from 1809. Of all her many nieces, Fanny was perhaps the closest to Jane, and so was an appropriate recipient of the treasure. Fanny lived until 1882, but was in very poor health latterly and could not sort her papers. Immediately after her death her son, Lord Brabourne, a distinguished Gladstonian politician, set to work to edit the letters in his possession – including all that he had of Jane's to Cassandra, five which alone survived of her many letters to Fanny, and some to Fanny's cousin Anna, which were made accessible to him.[22] Lord Brabourne published them in 1884; a few were sent by him to the sale room in later years; in 1893 he died, and most of the remaining originals were sent to the saleroom. The collection was dispersed, and a number have never reappeared. Thus his edition is a work of first-class importance,

---

[17] 1 Samuel (1 Kings) 15:33.

[18] *P* II, c. 9, p. 204.

[19] Though some of her occasional correspondents – e.g. her publishers – may have preserved all, or nearly all, they received.

[20] See below, p. 37; *Letters*, L, *passim*.

[21] Three of Cassandra's letters survive, preserved by Fanny Knight and Anne Sharp, to whom they were addressed: L nos. CEA/1–3, pp. 343–8.

[22] Brabourne 1884, repr. 1912. 'Edit' is a grand word: he cut out a few passages and a few names, and then (according to Chapman) 'sent the originals to the printer' (*Letters*, C p. vi). Details of Brabourne's sales, where known, are given in *Letters*, L, Notes.

which still has perhaps a few secrets to reveal. Its importance is reflected by statistics: of the 161 letters in Deirdre Le Faye's edition – or rather 154, if we omit tiny fragments and a set of verses – 94 were addressed to Cassandra, and of these 79 were from Brabourne's collection – which indeed comprised 96, if we add the five he included addressed to Fanny and twelve to her cousin Anna. Of all these, we still depend wholly on Brabourne for 15, 14 to Cassandra and 1 to Anna. Fortunately he was not an interfering editor: he cut a few passages out – as we know from those which can be compared with the originals – but sent the originals to the printer,[23] so a reasonably authentic text emerged, though naturally not free from errors.

In 1932 R. W. Chapman published the edition of the letters on which we all relied until very recently – especially in its revised form, the edition of 1952, now admirably revised and brought up to date by Deirdre Le Faye (1995).[24]

Chapman's edition was a labour of love, the work of a meticulous bibliographer; and it is provided with very valuable notes identifying some of the characters in the letters and the more obscure allusions, which abound; these have been improved, and his indexes made a great deal more accessible, by the latest editor. But they have both had such reverence for Miss Austen that they have insisted on putting all the notes at the back, where they can be difficult to find; and they kept them to a minimum. The careful reader of the letters, indeed, is well advised to have Lord Brabourne's edition to hand; for he gave quite a lot of useful commentary not repeated by his successors – and vital information from the diaries of his mother, Fanny Knight – which have indeed been used by Miss Le Faye, though not quoted as extensively as by Brabourne.[25]

Chapman and Le Faye have been equally economical in explaining the dates of the letters. Lord Brabourne was high-handed in his treatment of the dates, but rarely got them wrong. Thus he sometimes improved the dates on the letters before him. No. 2 (2) appears only to have been dated 'Thursday' and he added 'January 16' from the postmark – though this was actually the Saturday, two days later.[26] We know this because the original was sighted in 1931 and the postmark read as 16 January 1796. A slip occurs in no. 61 (60), which is of Jane's making, for it is dated 'Sunday Novr 21'. The letter was written when the move to Chawton was in prospect, and the year must be 1808, as Brabourne and Chapman correctly perceived: 21 November was never a Sunday between 1802 and 1813, much too early and too late for no. 61. The original has now turned up, and the date is

---

[23] See n. 22. The statistics are based on *Letters*, L and esp. Notes, pp. 353–469.

[24] *Letters*, C (edn. of 1952) and L (1995).

[25] Brabourne 1912, II, 260–4 (between Brabourne's letters 70 and 71), 287–91 (between nos. 75 and 76), 312–13 (between nos. 79 and 80).

[26] *Letters*, L p. 354. In what follows I give L's nos. with C's in brackets.

confirmed by the postmark, which reads NOV 21 1808: Jane wrote it on Sunday 20th and posted it on Monday 21st. Chapman, evidently using *The Book of Almanacs* or the like, checked all these dates, and noted where discrepancies occurred.[27] In doing so, he very rarely found it necessary to correct the year given by Brabourne. The puzzle remains, how Brabourne had dated the letters.

We can be reasonably sure that Lord Brabourne did not study *The Book of Almanacs*: if he had, he would not have let through the wrong year for three of his mother's five letters: nos. 151, 153, 155 (140–2), all early 1817, he dated to 1816. Nor did he correct the few which Jane herself had misdated. For many of the letters, he could have known the year from the postmark. But there is a large number with an illegible postmark or none at all; and though it is possible that some were legible in 1884, it can hardly have been so with most of them. With many, the circumstances help to confirm the date; but only the most minute research would prove this. Fortunately, all the letters known only from Brabourne's edition have month and week days which confirm the year he assigned – and for all but no. 141 (129) (to Anna) there is other evidence in the context or contents to confirm that the year is correct.[28] For the later years, we know from his own account that Lord Brabourne carefully compared the letters with his mother's diaries, and this still helps to confirm some of the dates. But for the majority, especially of the earlier ones, he must have had some other source of information. What this was can only be matter for conjecture. But the little note about the dates of the novels shows clearly that Cassandra was interested in dates and meticulous in recording them.[29] No one else but Cassandra could have dated the letters with such precision.

Brabourne described the letters as being preserved in

> a square box full of letters, fastened up carefully in separate packets, each of which was endorsed 'for Lady Knatchbull' in the handwriting of my great-aunt, Cassandra Austen, with which was a paper endorsed, in my mother's handwriting, 'Letters from my dear Aunt Jane Austen, and two from Aunt Cassandra after her decease,' which paper contained the letters written to my mother herself. The box itself had been endorsed by my mother as follows:- 'Letters from Aunt Jane to Aunt Cassandra at different periods of her life – a few to me – and some from Aunt Cassandra to me after At. Jane's death.'[30]

---

[27] A. de Morgan, *The Book of Almanacs* (1851 and often reprinted) was the classic source before C.R. Cheney, *Handbook of Dates* (1945).

[28] The letters known from Brabourne only are – L nos., with C, where they differ, in brackets – 1, 4, 9, 11–13, 18, 33, 46–7, 49 (48), 52 (51), 60 (59), 93 (88), 141 (C) (129).

[29] See below, pp. 44–5.

[30] Brabourne 1912, I, 204–5. The letters from Cassandra to Fanny are in *Letters*, L nos. CEA/1,3, pp. 343–8, C pp. 513–19.

Presumably the separate packets had slips of paper attached by Cassandra, giving the years to which they related. When Brabourne's collection of letters was dispersed, all evidence of this kind disappeared. It is a fundamental principle of record preservation that archive groups should be kept together, or vital evidence will be destroyed. I know of few examples of the ground for defending 'the sanctity of the archive group' more pressing or poignant than this. But one has to say that it does not seem that we have been left in ignorance of the correct date of more than a tiny handful of Jane Austen's letters, even so: the postmarks, the content, the context – and the almanac – have made it possible for Chapman, Le Faye and others to confirm the accuracy of Brabourne's dating of Jane's letters to Cassandra – and to correct the dating of her letters to his mother.

Lord Brabourne himself believed that the strays not in his collection, which he knew because they had been printed in the *Memoir*, had been separated from the rest at Cassandra's death, in 1845.[31] But it is noticeable that these letters – two of 1801, one of 1804, one of 1805, five of 1813 and one of 1814 – seem all to have been correctly dated by Mr Austen-Leigh in the *Memoir*, though only two now carry dated postmarks. He himself claimed that it was 'easy to ascertain their dates, either from the postmark, or from the contents',[32] but I am inclined to wonder if he did not have other aids. It seems to me likely that they were passed to his branch of the family by Cassandra herself, in dated bundles.[33]

In any case all the indications are that Cassandra preserved the Jane Austen archive with care and precision – and destroyed a part of it with equal precision. It is difficult to be sure precisely how the selection of letters which survived Cassandra's death came to be made. Here is the score, year by year, starting in 1796:

1796	7	1804	1	1811	6
1797	0	1805	5	1812	0
1798	8	1806	0	1813	15
1799	6	1807	3	1814	6
1800	5	1808	12	1815	4
1801	10	1809	4	1816	2
1802–03	0	1810	0	1817	0

It would be pleasant to find some rational criterion for this apparently random selection. Jane could only write to Cassandra when she was away

---

[31] Brabourne 1912, I, 207. The figures which follow relate to the letters to Cassandra *only*: L nos. 34, 38 of 1801; 39 of 1804; 44 of 1805; 78–81, 84 of 1813; 97 of 1814. In addition there are other letters from a variety of sources – most of them to Anna Lefroy (with some overlap in Brabourne) – in the *Memoir*; and two additional letters to Cassandra (L nos. 28, 43) in the second edition of the *Memoir*.

[32] *Memoir* 2nd edn. (1871) p. 57; this is an addition to *Memoir*, 1st edn. (1870), p. 80.

[33] Or set aside to be passed at her death.

from home without Jane, or Jane without Cassandra: perhaps they paid fewer or no separate visits in the years when no letters survive. Unfortunately, for the most part, the argument is circular: we rarely know of these visits unless there are letters.[34] Then again, the archive of a small house as of a large is most easily and commonly preserved if the occupants do not move – change of abode is perhaps the worst enemy private papers have to face. Thus, one might well expect the collection of all materials to be a great deal more complete after the move to Chawton Cottage in 1809 – for there Cassandra stayed until the end of her days. But the table shows no such pattern; on the contrary, most of 1809–10 are conspicuously blank.

Caroline tells us – little knowing, evidently, what *had* survived – that 'My Aunt [Cassandra] looked them over [the letters she had received from Jane, and kept] and burnt the greater part, (as she told me), 2 or 3 years before her own death.'[35] It has usually been supposed that Cassandra destroyed those which were particularly sensitive. Deirdre Le Faye, carefully monitoring series where there were only occasional gaps, has suggested that references to symptoms and illness and family failings were censored – though illness and irritation with even her closest family are by no means absent from the letters Cassandra preserved.[36] It is noticeable that none survive from 1797, the year of Cassandra's own personal tragedy, nor from 1802, the year (if the stories are true) when Jane lost one and rejected another suitor. But if Cassandra was reluctant to allow letters revealing Jane to disadvantage – or either of them crossed in love – it is surprising that so many letters were preserved; and especially surprising that the letters of 1796 should survive – letters full of Jane's Tom Lefroy and Mrs Lefroy's friend, Samuel Blackall – and delightful references to Cassandra's Tom Fowle. And if she wanted to preserve Jane's memory from the charge her brother Henry had so striven to counter, of being sharp-tongued, not to say shrewish – then a number more letters might have been consigned to the fire, including the famous references to Mrs Hall of Sherborne, who 'was brought to bed yesterday of a dead child, some weeks before she expected, oweing to a fright. – I suppose she happened unawares to look at her husband' – which elicited from E.M. Forster the comment that he heard 'the whinnying of harpies'.[37]

We seem to glimpse two Cassandras: the careful preserver of her sister's remains, keeping everything which she thought of value – weeding with

---

[34] See below, p. 207. In 1801–04 there were visits otherwise recorded (*Letters*, C Index I, s.v. Jane Austen s.a. 1802; *Life*, pp. 92–3; *FR* p. 126). But on these occasions Jane and Cassandra were together.

[35] Caroline Austen 1952, p. 10.

[36] *Letters*, L p. xv. In L no. 50 (49), e.g., she expresses marked irritation with James and his wife (1807).

[37] *Letters*, L no. 10, p. 17; C no. 10, p. 24; Forster's comment (Forster 1936, p. 156) is quoted in Chapman 1948, pp. 106–7.

precision, however mistakenly, Jane's literary manuscripts; and an anxious bewildered Cassandra, first tying the letters in tidy bundles, then laying about her among them – distributing a few to other members of the family, burning some of the bundles, thinning others – without a clear system or any deep understanding. It may well be this was the old lady of the 1840s, no longer in full control of all her faculties. Yet that may be quite wrong; for the letters must in any case have set her an acute problem. They were personal – meant only for her; Jane would have been horrified at their preservation for posterity. They were also striking memorials of one of the greatest writers of the English language; a part of the family heritage. Cassandra can be forgiven for not seeing them as part of the nation's heritage, as they are to us: she could indeed hardly have viewed them from that angle, even in 1845; but Lord Brabourne and his heirs who sent them to the sale room cannot be so forgiven: the archive group has been destroyed, presumably for ever.

The letters so lovingly edited have this value above all, that they reproduce the conversation of the sisters – and of other members of the family, and a number of friends, who also figure in them: they preserve the environment in which the novels were written. They sometimes tell us more, much more, than this: of her views and attitudes and prejudices; of her wonderfully charitable and uncharitable views of those about her – of the spirit of the woman who created Lady Bertram and Mrs Norris. Above all, they tell us from time to time a little about the progress of the novels, about the excitement of publishing them, of her dealings with publishers.[38] We can occasionally glimpse a novel in the making – especially *Mansfield Park*; but she never once reveals the work of the day – the hours spent in composition – and that seems to be Jane's fault, not Cassandra's. It cannot have been weeded out of the letters so haphazardly selected. They were her private hours, kept even from her sister.

There are none the less many points on which the letters and the novels reinforce one another. A striking example lies in her attitude to children. She has sometimes been accused of distaste for noisy children and lack of sympathy with harassed mothers. The truth clearly is that like many people she was alternately delighted and irritated by the behaviour of children – but had an exceptional gift in expressing her likes and dislikes. Caroline's moving description of Jane's skill with children and their devotion to her is clearly authentic and fits well the evidence of the novels – in which she often shows impatience with spoiled, ill-managed children, but firm, sensible and affectionate treatment of them is commonly a trait of her most amiable characters – Jane Bennet, Anne Elliot and even Emma Woodhouse. There are many delectable references to children in the letters,

---

[38] On links between letters and novels, see esp. pp. 46–7.

including the account of the nine-year-old Kitty Foote, daughter of a sailor colleague of Jane's brother Frank.

Our little visitor has just left us, and left us highly pleased with her; – she is a nice, natural, openhearted, affectionate girl, with all the ready civility which one sees in the best children of the present day; – so unlike anything that I was myself at her age, that I am often all astonishment and shame. – Half her time here was spent at Spillikins [Caroline Austen was to bear witness at Jane's skill at Spillikins]; which I consider as a very valuable part of our household furniture, and as not the least important benefaction from the house of Knight to that of Austen.[39]

In contrast, in February 1801, she wrote of a visit to the rector of Baughurst in Hampshire:

The place is not so pretty as I expected, but perhaps the season may be against the beauty of the country. The house seemed to have all the comforts of little children, dirt and litter. Mr Dyson [the rector] as usual looked wild, and Mrs Dyson as usual looked big

– she was expecting the seventh of her twelve children; they had been married somewhat over eight years and her eldest was about seven.[40] Somewhere between lay the pleasures of 'quiet cheerfulness' at Christmastime at Uppercross, after the Harville children had been brought 'to improve the noise of Uppercross, and lessen that of Lyme'.

The Juvenilia

Caroline Austen, at the age of 11, had imitated her aunt in writing verses and stories, which she read to Jane – who warned her in the kindest manner that at her age

it would be bad for me to be much taken up with my own compositions – Later still – it was after she got to Winchester [in May 1817], she sent me a message to this effect – That if I would take her advice, I should cease writing till I was 16, and that she had herself often wished that she had *read* more, and written *less*, in the corresponding years of her own life.[41]

---

[39] *Letters*, L no. 50, p. 120; C, no. 49, p. 179; on Spillikins, Caroline Austen 1952, p. 7.

[40] *Letters*, L no. 34, pp. 80–1; C no. 34, p. 121; on the Dysons, L p. 519. For Uppercross, see p. 133–4.

[41] Caroline Austen 1952, p. 10. Caroline's twelfth birthday fell on 18 June 1817, during Jane's final illness in Winchester (*Letters*, C, Index I).

Jane Austen's *Minor Works* certainly bear witness to her passion for writing, from precisely the ages of 11 and 12 that Caroline felt the urge. Jane was precociously clever, and the wit and shrewd comment on the literary absurdities of her age make even the earliest writings very entertaining reading. In some there is an ingenuity which offers something more. In 'The Three Sisters' (perhaps written when she was between 15 and 17),[42] Mary, Sophy and Georgiana are possible brides for Mr Watts. He proposes to Mary, who is undecided how to answer.

> He is quite an old man, about two and thirty, very plain *so* plain that I cannot bear to look at him. He is extremely disagreeable and I hate him more than anybody else in the world. He has a large fortune and will make great settlements on me; but then he is very healthy . . .

In the end she is stung into accepting him by the well-founded fear that he will propose to one of her sisters – who will be married before her and lord it over her – if she does not. The final letter – for most of the juvenilia take the form of letters – describes a quarrel between Mary and her betrothed. He complained to her mother,

> and she . . . persuaded him to think no more of it. He therefore met Mary with all his accustomed civility, and except one touch at the phaeton and another at the greenhouse [items in her more extravagant requirements], the evening went off with great harmony and cordiality

– phrases reminiscent of relations among the Ferrars family after Lucy had married Robert at the end of *Sense and Sensibility*:

> setting aside the jealousies and ill-will continually subsisting between Fanny and Lucy, in which their husbands of course took a part, as well as the frequent domestic disagreements between Robert and Lucy themselves, nothing could exceed the harmony in which they all lived together.[43]

The most celebrated of these early epistolary novels is *Love and Friend-ship*, composed at the advanced age of 14; but the most successful is perhaps

---

[42] It is entered in 'Volume the First' before compositions dated 1793 (*MW*, p. 2), and is dated 1792 in Southam 1964, p. 16; cf. pp. 34–5. It has to be remembered that the juvenilia survive in three volumes of transcripts made by Jane Austen over a period of years, sometimes in approximate chronological order, sometimes not. Southam 1964, cc. 1–2, seeks to sort out the order in which they were written – see esp. *ibid.* pp. 16, 21–44. For what follows, *MW*, pp. 57–71. The phaeton and the greenhouse were among Mary's unreasonable demands (p. 65).

[43] *SS* III, c. 14, p. 377.

Lesley Castle, probably written when she was 15 or 16.[44] It has a good deal of the absurdity which she enjoyed all her life, and something of the surrealist humour which broke through later on from time to time – as for example in the wit of Mr Bennet. In 'Letter the Second' Charlotte Lutterell writes in great indignation to Margaret Lesley that

> after having laboured both by Night and Day, in order to get the wedding dinner ready by the time appointed, after having roasted beef, broiled mutton, and stewed soup enough to last the new-married couple through the honey-moon, I had the mortification of finding that I had been roasting, broiling and stewing both the meat and myself to no purpose . . . I never remember suffering any vexation equal to what I experienced on last Monday when my sister came running to me in the store-room with her face as white as a whipt syllabub, and told me that Hervey [her betrothed] had been thrown from his horse, had fractured his scull and was pronounced by his surgeon to be in the most emminent danger. 'Good God! (said I) you dont say so? Why what in the name of heaven will become of all the victuals? . . .'

In a later letter she explains her tastes.

> I was always of the opinion that London and its amusements must be very agreeable for a while . . . I always longed particularly to go to Vaux-hall, to see whether the cold beef there is cut so thin as it is reported, for I have a sly suspicion that few people understand the art of cutting a slice of cold beef as well as I do: nay it would be hard if I did not know something of the matter, for it was a part of my education that I took by far the most pains with. Mama always found me *her* best scholar, tho' when Papa was alive Eloisa was *his*. Never to be sure were there two more different dispositions in the world. We both loved reading. *She* preferred histories, and I receipts. She loved drawing pictures, and I drawing pullets. No one could sing a better song than she, and no one make a better pye than I.[45]

This is immediately followed in 'Volume the Second' by 'The History of England from the reign of Henry the 4th to the death of Charles the 1st By a partial, prejudiced and ignorant Historian' – completed on Saturday 26 November 1791, a few weeks before her sixteenth birthday.[46] This is a

---

[44] It was transcribed between *Love and Friendship*, whose conclusion is dated 13 June 1790, and the *History of England*, whose 'Finis' was on Saturday 26 November 1791 (*MW*, pp. 109, 149) – but is dated 1792 in Southam 1964, p. 16; cf. pp. 32–4 from the dates of the letters in *Lesley Castle*, 3 Jan.–13 April 1792.

[45] *MW*, pp. 112–13, 128–9.

[46] *MW*, pp. 138–9, 149.

very lively trial run for *1066 and All That*, and parades opinions no doubt directly opposite to those of the books she was made to read.

> Richard the 3rd. The character of this prince has been in general very severely treated by historians, but as he was a *York*, I am rather inclined to suppose him a very respectable man. It has indeed been confidently asserted that he killed his two nephews and his wife, but it has also been declared that he did *not* kill his two nephews, which I am inclined to beleive true; and if this is the case, it may also be affirmed that he did not kill his wife, for if Perkin Warbeck was really the Duke of York, why might not Lambert Simnel be the widow of Richard . . .

– But he soon lost the throne to 'Henry Tudor E[arl] of Richmond as great a villain as ever lived' – and the Tudors get a bad press, especially Elizabeth; Jane's heroine is Mary queen of Scots. Later she introduces the Gunpowder Plot with words doubtless intended to shock (or entertain) her parents.

> As I am myself partial to the roman catholic religion, it is with infinite regret that I am obliged to blame the behaviour of any member of it; yet truth being I think very excusable in an historian, I am necessitated to say that in this reign the roman Catholics of England did not behave like gentlemen to the protestants . . .

Thus she makes rings round fashionable historical writing of her day – that is clear even if we do not know precisely what she read.[47] A gibe at James I suggests a more modern historical fashion. 'His Majesty was of that amiable disposition which inclines to Freindships, and in such points was possessed of a keener penetration in discovering merit than many other people' – she cites a 'sharade on a carpet', with reference to 'Car', earl of Somerset: 'My first is what my second was to King James the 1st, and you tread on my whole'.[48]

The most mature of these early works is *Lady Susan* of *c.* 1793–94 – that is when she was about 17 or 18.[49] This is a remarkably accomplished and cynical portrayal – in a series of letters, like almost all the juvenilia – of a heartless, scheming woman. There are also later fragments – *The Watsons* of *c.* 1804–05 and *Sanditon* of 1817 – which have aroused great interest from time to time, especially *Sanditon*, the work of her last months. But neither seems to contain the promise of a major novel. It is easy to see why *The*

---

[47] It has been supposed that her knowledge was based on Oliver Goldsmith's *History of England*; but Miss Tilney's favourite historians were 'Mr Hume [and] Mr Robertson' (*NA* I, c. 14, p. 109). Of these William Robertson wrote on Scotland, America and Charles V; but Hume's volumes on English history fit the pattern of Jane Austen's – both ending with Charles I.

[48] The quotations are from *MW*, pp. 141, 147–8.

[49] *MW*, pp. 243–313; for the date, see Southam 1964, chap. 3.

Watsons was never finished – even without the story told in the family that her father's death brought her work to a close. *Sanditon*, the beginning of a novel on the speculative development of a watering place, is too brief, or too affected by her illness, to deploy the major characteristics of the great novels.[50]

There is much more in the juvenilia and the fragments than this: the earliest works comprise a ferocious display of precocious wit and style. But they form the entertainment of an hour; the mature novels are very different.

In defining that difference it is easy to be too simple and superficial. Plainly the inspiration of the early works is literary: they are skits or parodies or even possibly satires;[51] they are hardly based on observation of human nature. It has sometimes been alleged that Jane Austen shows a deep lack of charity towards her fellow human beings – and her lash falls on many or most of the characters in her novels. But one difference which separates all the mature novels from what went before is the large element of sympathetic humanity in them: we are still in a world of literary art, yet one deliberately drawn from something like nature – human nature with its follies, crimes, failings and above all absurdities; but also with its ideals and aspirations. She never threw off entirely her literary inheritance. This has been shown very fully in the structure of her novels – by Marilyn Butler above all.[52] It is also apparent in the persistence of the scheming woman and the predatory male to the end of her days – Mrs Clay and Mr Elliot represent them still in *Persuasion*. But we must distinguish. The heroines of the juvenilia are mainly literary stereotypes cleverly handled. Mr Elliot and Mrs Clay also represent her observation – or belief, whichever one prefers to call it – that many men were predatory, many women scheming. But to go deeper, we must turn to the novels themselves.

---

[50] But it has been seen as a broadening of her interests to comprise a wider scene. I find the fragment too slight to draw such a conclusion. For the date of *The Watsons*, see Southam in *MW*, p. 314.

[51] But Marilyn Butler not unreasonably prefers to avoid these grand words: 'The great majority of these short fragments seem meant for nothing more ambitious than to raise a laugh in a fireside circle by that favourite eighteenth-century comic recourse, extreme verbal incongruity' (Butler 1987, p. 168).

[52] Butler 1987.

5

Chronology

Cassandra's Evidence

Jane Austen was born on 16 December 1775 at Steventon in Hampshire, where her father was rector; from his retirement in May 1801 till a few months after his death in 1805 she lived with her parents and her sister Cassandra in Bath; from 1806 to 1809 she and her mother and sister lived in Southampton; and finally, from July 1809 to May 1817, they were at Chawton Cottage in Hampshire – she only left Chawton in her final illness to spend her last few weeks and die, aged 41, in 8 College Street, Winchester, on 18 July 1817.[1]

Thus far the outline, it might seem, of an exceedingly uneventful life. These details are not in doubt: a succession of scholars led by R.W. Chapman and Deirdre Le Faye have elicited all that the external evidence of memoirs and reminiscences, and the internal witness of her correspondence, can tell us of her movements. But in these years Catherine Morland and Henry Tilney, Elinor and Marianne Dashwood, Elizabeth Bennet and Fitzwilliam Darcy, Fanny Price and Edmund Bertram, Emma Woodhouse and George Knightley, Anne Elliot and Frederick Wentworth – and a host of other immortal characters – sprang to life in her imagination and under her pen. The chronology of her imaginative life is much more interesting and a great deal more obscure than that of her life in the world.

A few months after Jane's death, so it seems, her sister Cassandra noted down the dates when the novels had been composed, and this brief memo has served as a fundamental guide to Jane's imaginative history ever since.[2] Here is the text, and I have noted dates of publication in square brackets.

'First Impressions begun in Oct. 1796. Finished in August 1797. Published afterwards, with alterations and contractions, under the

---

[1] For the chronological details of her life, see Appendix.

[2] See Facsimile in *MW*, facing p. 242. On its date, see Southam 1964, p. 54. He argues that the spelling 'North-hanger Abbey' suggests the list was made before publication; in any case the details seem to indicate that Cassandra had all the available materials to hand, and had not yet begun to destroy unwanted papers. For dates in square brackets, see *Letters*, C Index VI (unpaginated).

Title of Pride and Prejudice. [sold to Egerton Nov. 1812, publ. Jan. 1813]

'Sense and Sensibility begun November 1797. [Published by Egerton November 1811.] I am sure that something of this same story and characters had been written earlier and called Elinor and Marianne.

'Mansfield Park, begun somewhere about February 1811 – finished soon after June 1813. [published May–June 1814].

'Emma begun January 21st 1814, finished March 29th 1815. [published Dec. 1815 or early 1816].

'Persuasion begun August 8th 1815 finished August 6th 1816. [published posthumously 1818].

'North-hanger Abbey was written about the years [17]98 and [17]99 [published posthumously 1818].

C.E.A.'

The dates fall into three categories – the earliest entries, by months and years; those for the last novels, which give days as well as months and years; and 'North-hanger abbey' which is given only approximate years. Where the dates are very precise, it is evident that Cassandra had used notes by Jane herself on the original manuscripts – or copies made by Jane. Mercifully, Cassandra preserved the cancelled ending of *Persuasion* and all that was written of *Sanditon*. The original end of *Persuasion* is now Egerton MS. 3038 in the British Library; and *Sanditon* reposes in the Library of King's College, Cambridge. The close of *Persuasion* in the Egerton manuscript carries three dates in July 1816, the first two at the head of a page – the third, at what she supposed to be the conclusion itself, has 18 July 1816 at its foot. In *Sanditon* there is a series of dates between 17 January 1817 and 18 March 1817 – the last, as at the end of *Persuasion*, at the foot of the page.[3] When she abandoned *Sanditon* in her final illness – or in very understandable despair with a novel which she could not see her way to completing – she set down 18 March at the foot of the page. This entry in the original manuscript in her own hand is deeply moving: it marks the end of a wonderful career.

Furthermore, notes in Jane's own hand giving the dates of *Mansfield Park*, *Emma* and *Persuasion* also survive, to establish Cassandra's source and prove her notes accurate.[4] Jane's own sources for the dates she attached to *Mansfield Park* and *Emma* were almost certainly the notes she made on the original manuscripts of the books – as we know for sure in the case of *Persuasion*. We can accept these dates for the last novels, from *Mansfield Park* to *Sanditon*, with complete confidence. We may suppose that similar notes

---

[3] Cf. Southam 1964, pp. 87, 101–02.
[4] Jane's note on *MP*, *P* and *E* is in Chapman 1926, facsimile after p. 35.

had revealed to Jane or her sister the chronology of the early drafts of *Pride and Prejudice* and *Sense and Sensibility* written in 1796–97 and later, though these details cannot have the same authority as the later ones.

The dates of *Mansfield Park* fit happily the final stages of *Sense and Sensibility*. But they create an intriguing puzzle concerning the final revision of *Pride and Prejudice*, for they suggest that it took place while *Mansfield Park* was being written. It is noticeable, however, that *Mansfield Park* took well over two years to complete, whereas its successor, *Emma*, was completed in a year and two months. All this strongly suggests that, whereas the revision of *Sense and Sensibility* was complete before *Mansfield Park* was embarked on, *Pride and Prejudice* was revised and *Mansfield Park* written concurrently. This would seem an insuperable objection to any theory that there was some major development in her mind and outlook between the two, as has been suggested.[5]

The Evidence of the Letters

It is well known that Jane's letters throw a little light on *Mansfield Park* in the making. On 24 January 1813 she wrote to Cassandra: 'I learn from Sir J. Carr that there is no Government House at Gibraltar. I must alter it to the Commissioner's' – and so it is altered in the passage in which William Price observes with amazement the hairstyles of the women folk of the officers attending an assembly there.[6] A little later in the same letter Jane tells how she had asked Mrs Digweed about some pieces she had been reading, and expressing 'my hope of their having amused her. Her answer was "Oh dear yes, very much, very droll indeed – the opening of the house and the striking up of the fiddles!" – What she meant poor woman, who shall say?' We have moved on a few pages, and Mrs Grant is asking Lady Bertram about the game of speculation she is playing.

> 'I hope your ladyship is pleased with the game.'
> 'Oh! dear, yes. – Very entertaining indeed. A very odd game. I do not know what it is all about. I am never to see my cards; and Mr Crawford does all the rest.'[7]

We may wonder whether Mrs Digweed actually inspired Lady Bertram's inconsequential speech – or Jane's report of Mrs Digweed was somehow influenced by Lady Bertram. That she was at work on the passage seems clear; and is confirmed within the bounds of the same party.

5 See pp. 21–2, 51–2, 126.
6 *Letters*, L no. 78, p. 198; C no. 75, p. 292; M F-233; *MP* II, c. 6, p. 235; cf. Chapman's note.
7 *Letters*, L, no. 78, p. 199 (cf. p. 410); C no. 75, p. 293; M F-233-4; *MP* II, c. 7, p. 240.

'As soon as a Whist party was formed and a round table threatened, I made [the need to return to] my mother an excuse, and came away; leaving just as many for *their* round table, as there were at Mrs Grant's' – at which Lady Bertram was sitting at a table of six.[8]

On 29 January 1813 she wrote to Cassandra in high delight to describe the arrival of *Pride and Prejudice* from the publisher. 'I have got my own darling child from London'; and after some ecstasies which show how proud, how very reasonably proud she was of it, and especially of Elizabeth, she tries to strike a sober note.

'Now I will try to write of something else; – and it shall be a complete change of subject – ordination. I am glad to find your enquiries have ended so well. – If you could discover whether Northamptonshire is a country of hedgerows, I should be glad again.'[9] We seem still to be in the chapter in which Lady Bertram plays speculation, Mr Crawford describes the village and parsonage house of Thornton Lacey, Edmund's destined home – and Sir Thomas Bertram outlines the duty of a conscientious clergyman, to Miss Crawford's discomfort: Edmund's ordination looms over her.[10] In a sense, ordination was the theme of many parts of *Mansfield Park* – and if Cassandra could pick up a passing reference to Mrs Grant's table, she must have known this. But Jane is seeking a calmer frame of mind after the heady wine of the parcel of books; and there is nowhere in *Mansfield Park* more obviously suited to combine ordination and the Northamptonshire country-side than the description and discussion of Thornton Lacey. Chapman pointed out that Cassandra was staying with their eldest brother, the Reverend James, and may well have been enquiring about 'the disposal of livings'. These details suggest that she was a little over half way through the book in January 1813: it seems surprising that she was able to complete it in or soon after June; and it was not actually published until May–June 1814 – but we cannot know, of course, precisely in what order it was written.

The least authority evidently attaches to Cassandra's date for *Northanger*

---

[8] *Letters*, L no. 78, p. 199; C no. 75, p. 294; M F-234; *MP* II, c. 7, p. 240. The account of Mrs Grant's table shows that the passage in *MP* was in draft already – but Lady Bertram's speech may have been revised after this party.

[9] *Letters*, L no. 79, pp. 201–2; C no. 76, pp. 297–8. Cf. L no. 82, p. 208; C no. 78.1, p. 504.

[10] There are no hedgerows in Thornton Lacey – but there are no similar descriptions of country scenes for many chapters following to which this enquiry might obviously refer. Chapman conjectured (notes to *Letters* no. 76) that Jane Austen had had in mind a scene similar to that she later used in *Persuasion*, in which Anne Elliot overhears a conversation behind a hedgerow, but abandoned it owing to doubts about hedgerows in Northamptonshire. That may be, but the question itself indicates that Jane knew little about the shire, and that the vivid setting of Mansfield Park owed more to her imagination than to Cottesbrooke or its environs (on which see refs. in note to no. 78.1 in *Letters*, C, Addenda). The reference to Chapman on 'disposal of livings' below is from the same note.

Abbey, the most puzzling element in her list. For we have Jane's own word for it, in the author's preface, that *Northanger Abbey* was finished in 1803[11] – though some revision must have taken place much later, since Catherine Morland was still called Susan as late as 1809.[12] Now a great part of the action of the book takes place in Bath; and almost every chapter set in Bath reveals the intimacy of the author's knowledge of the place, its customs and its immediate environs. The Austens moved to Bath in 1801, and it seems extremely probable – though it has rarely been suggested – that *Northanger Abbey* was written in the years 1801–03. It is true that Jane had visited Bath before, and had relations there; and some of the most telling scenes in other books – the adventures at Lyme Regis in *Persuasion* for example – related to places Jane can only have visited briefly. Her question to Cassandra – 'If you could discover whether Northamptonshire is a country of hedgerows' she would be glad – may suggest that the setting of *Mansfield Park* owed more to her imagination than to any knowledge of the shire.[13] But with *Northanger Abbey* the case is different: it is closely based on genuine topography. It is very hard to believe that the novel took shape before 1801–03.

Yet we have Jane's own word in the same preface that it took 'many' years to complete; and Cassandra's belief that it was 'written about the years '98 and '99'. We know it underwent revision even after 1803. It may well be that a version of the story was written in the late 1790s, when Jane was in her early twenties: it is hard to believe that it had much in common with the book we now read – save that one major theme, the impact of Mrs Radcliffe's celebrated gothic novel, *The Mysteries of Udolfo*, would fit a date not much later than 1794, when it was published. *The Italian*, of 1797, is also mentioned, though its influence is not so deep; and Isabella's list of thrillers belonged to the years 1793–98.[14]

The relation of *Sense and Sensibility* and *Pride and Prejudice* to their earlier versions is even more problematic. There was a family tradition that *Sense and Sensibility*, like *Lady Susan* of *c.* 1793–4, had followed the common eighteenth-century pattern of a series of letters.[15] But it seems to rest on nothing more than Jane's niece Caroline's 'treacherous' memory – and she was only 12 when Jane died. B.C. Southam reckoned to find a trace of a lost correspondent for Elinor at Norland. He quotes the passage which reveals how little companionship Elinor found in her Devonshire friends:

[11] *NA* I, Advertisement, by the Authoress. It was delivered to a publisher in the spring of 1803, who returned it to Jane Austen in 1809: *Letters*, L no. 68(D), p. 174; C no. 67, p. 263.

[12] *Letters*, L. nos. 68 (D), 68 (A), pp. 174–5; C nos. 67, 67a, pp. 263–4. For the topography of Bath in *NA* (below) cf. Pevsner 1968, pp. 414–17.

[13] See above, nn. 9–10.

[14] *NA* I, c. 6, p. 38; cf. below, p. 60 n. 4.

[15] *Life*, p. 80; cf. Southam 1964, pp. 54–5, citing Caroline Austen in Chapman 1948, p. 42.

'they afforded her no companion that could make amends for what she had left behind, nor that could teach her to think of Norland with less regret than ever'.[16] But in the context Elinor's feelings are being contrasted with Marianne's, in the first flush of her love for Willoughby, and there seems little doubt that it was Edward Ferrars whom Elinor had left behind – with whom she did not correspond. The more one tries to picture the relationships within the Dashwood family on which the book is founded, the more difficult it is to imagine how it could ever have been written in letter form. But perhaps this is only to say that 'Elinor and Marianne' bore little resemblance to *Sense and Sensibility*. As a revelation of Jane Austen's mind, we have to take the book as we find it, as the product of the final revision completed in 1811.

The case is more perplexing still with *Pride and Prejudice*. There are a number of letters in the book as we have it – Mr Darcy's crucial letter to Elizabeth, explaining his conduct towards Bingley and Wickham, the correspondence of Mr Collins and Mr Bennet, the exchange between Elizabeth and Mrs Gardiner. But they are all an inherent part of a structure which depends, time and again, on features of Elizabeth's state of mind which she can only partially reveal to Jane – even less to Charlotte Lucas. No stretch of imagination will convert the book we know into a file of letters. If it started so – and this is pure conjecture[17] – *First Impressions* had little in common with *Pride and Prejudice*. Yet the original title presupposes something of the final story: the contrast between the first impressions of Jane and Bingley – as happy and favourable as at the end – and Elizabeth's strong dislike of Mr Darcy; and the breakdown of these first impressions to make way for a union between Elizabeth and Darcy. I have often, when reading *Pride and Prejudice*, tried to distinguish the more immature from the more refined elements in the book. Both are there, but the attempt to separate them always ends in lamentable failure. Mr Bennet's wit comprises some of Jane's subtlest humour – but much of him seems crude and immature. The scene at Pemberley – especially the progressive revelation to Elizabeth, within the context of his house and park, of Darcy's better nature – contains some of the subtlest effects in any of the novels. But without it, how could Darcy and Elizabeth be reconciled? The book is full of puzzles, and it is best to take it as we have it, as the published novel of 1813, which clearly includes a good deal of final revision, whatever Cassandra meant by 'alterations and contractions', or Jane herself by 'I have lopt and cropt' in preparing *Pride and Prejudice* for the printer.[18]

---

[16] *SS* I, c. 11, p. 54.

[17] Southam 1964, pp. 58–60.

[18] Cassandra, in her note quoted above; Jane, *Letters*, L no. 79, p. 202; C no. 76, p. 298. In *Letters* L no. 80, p. 203, C no. 77, pp. 299–300, M, F-238, she criticises *PP* in baffling fashion. 'The work is rather too light and bright and sparkling; – it wants shade; – it wants

The Use of Almanacs

Mr Collins' first visit to Longbourn began on Monday 18 November: Jane Austen had either drawn a bow at a venture, or looked up some calendar or almanac or work of reference to check the date. A modern historian reaches for Christopher Cheney's *Handbook of Dates* of 1945; its classic predecessor was Augustus de Morgan's *Book of Almanacs* of 1851. There have been other repositories, such as the mighty *Trésor de Chronologie* of the Comte de Mas Latrie (1889). In Jane Austen's day, almanacs for individual years were readily available, the only accessible source, indeed, for checking the vagaries of the Gregorian calendar. R.W. Chapman was convinced that in composing or revising many of her novels, Jane Austen used almanacs to fit the chronology together; and he and his friend Mr Mackinnon engaged in a delightful detective exercise to determine what almanacs she used – concluding that Mr Collins' visit took place in 1811, when 18 November was indeed a Monday.[19] They reckoned that *Pride and Prejudice* showed the use of almanacs of 1811–12, *Mansfield Park* of 1808–09. The almanacs attributed to *Pride and Prejudice* have a clear bearing on its date – or rather, on the extent of revision which took place shortly before it went to press. If we can be sure she arranged the chronology of the book to fit the almanacs of the years 1811–12, then we can be confident that she made substantial revision then: the book was first published in January 1813.[20]

There is a notable progression in the use of dates in her novels. She had made some use of them in the juvenilia. The letters in *Lesley Castle*, composed in 1792, bear dates starting 'January 3rd 1792' and progressing through 'February 12' and others to 'April 13th', which evidently represented, approximately, the dates of her own composition of the letters. Later in the year, she engaged in prophecy: the letters in *Evelyn* are dated between 14 July and 22 August, including 19 August 1809.[21] But other imaginary letters of about this time were not dated – and most notably,

---

to be stretched out here and there with a long Chapter – of sense it if could be had, if not of solemn specious nonsense – about something unconnected with the story; an essay on writing, a critique on Walter Scott, or the history of Buonaparte – or anything that would form a contrast and bring the reader with increased delight to the playfulness and epigrammatism of the general stile . . .' This may very slightly confirm her own indication that she had shortened the earlier version; but it can hardly aid us in determining the nature of the revision. She is playing with Cassandra who knew her mind; still more does she play with us, who know her not.

[19] Chapman's Appendices in *PP*, pp. 400–8; *MP*, pp. 554–7; *E*, pp. 497–8; *NA* and *P*, pp. 297–304.

[20] *PP*, p. xi.

[21] *MW*, pp. 110–38, 185–91, esp. 190 (*Evelyn*).

Lady Susan of *c.* 1793–94 comprises 41 letters with only one pretence of a date among them – the first is headed 'Langford, December'.[22] *Northanger Abbey* is almost devoid of precise dates: there is naturally some progress through the seasons from winter in Bath to spring in Northanger and a summer denouement; but the only dated letter is Isabella Thorpe's from Bath to Northanger, dated 'April'.[23] *The Watsons*, begun in or about 1804 and never finished, starts with a very precise date: 'Tuesday Octr ye 13th'; as no other dates follow it may be a bow drawn at a venture – or an extract from the almanac for 1801.[24] We cannot tell. But within *Sense and Sensibility*, in its final form, there is a certain progression, from a dateless start, through September, October and the autumn leaves – of which they talk at Barton when Edward visits them – to the much more numerous indications of date during their winter visit in London between January and March.[25] There are, however, no dates sufficiently precise to tempt the almanac hunter.

The most convincing evidence relates to *Pride and Prejudice*, for which Chapman posited the almanacs for 1811–12 – that is to say, for the years when the revision was under way. The most striking date records Mr Collins' first visit: he arrived on Monday 18 November. The Netherfield ball – by fitting together a firm statement that it was on a Tuesday with Mr Bingley's recollection, much later, that it was on 26 November – can be dated Tuesday 26 November. Both dates fit 1811. A highly ingenious reconstruction by Chapman and Mackinnon made the dates for the following year fit 1812, and no other year in the neighbourhood. It would perhaps be too ingenious were it not that it coincides so neatly with the evidence for 1811 – and makes a complete pattern for the book. There is, however, one date which will not fit these years, and that is Mr Gardiner's letter announcing the finding of Lydia and Wickham, which is dated 'Monday, 2 August'.[26] This fits 1802 and 1813 but no year between – nor in the late 1790s, when the book may have been first drafted.[27] Nor does it fit its own context, for the Gardiners and Elizabeth set off for Derbyshire in mid-July at earliest, and cannot have been back at Longbourn till the beginning of August. Mrs Gardiner's long letter of explanation to Elizabeth is dated 6 September, so her husband's letter must lie between, somewhere in mid-August. Here Jane Austen has clearly made a mistake. Chapman ingeniously suggested that the error was due to a confusion with another

---

[22] *MW*, p. 243.

[23] *NA* II c. 12, p. 216. From the first meeting of Henry Tilney and Catherine Morland to their marriage was less than twelve months (*NA*, p. 252).

[24] 13 October fell on a Tuesday in Jane Austen's adult life in 1795, 1801, 1807, 1812.

[25] *SS* I, c. 16, pp. 87–8; September is mentioned on p. 28, October on p. 53.

[26] See Chapman in *PP*, p. 401.

[27] The fall of leap years means that 2 August was a Monday in this period only in 1790, 1802 and 1813.

express sent to Longbourn – by Colonel Forster – whose date can be reconstructed as Saturday 2 August.[28]

The chronology of *Pride and Prejudice* is intricate, and it is hard for someone like myself who has often struggled with intricate chronological detail to imagine that it was planned without an almanac; that granted, the case for the use of almanacs of 1811–12 is strong. The case of *Mansfield Park* is more ambiguous. For here there is only one precise date offered in full form: a ball was held at Mansfield Park on Thursday 22 December. This fits 1808; and it is not by any means a stray date, but part of an intricate scheme involving Sir Thomas's calculations relating to the end of William Price's visit and Edmund's departure for Peterborough and ordination – both of which took place on the 23rd.[29] Chapman and MacKinnon were able once again to fit the rest of the chronology round this date, and suppose that she used almanacs for 1808–09. But the base of the evidence is slight in *Mansfield Park*, and there is one substantial difficulty, which has led some scholars to doubt that an almanac was used at all. In the final year of the story, Easter came 'particularly late' – 'as Fanny had most sorrowfully considered, on first learning that she had no chance of leaving Portsmouth till after it'.[30] The extreme limits of Easter are 22 March and 25 April, and in 1809 it fell on 2 April; so it has been held either that Jane Austen rode roughshod over her almanacs, or she failed to use them at all. But all this depends on assuming she used almanacs as historians would, so that a new one is needed when we pass 1 January. This would be natural when she was using those for current years, as with *Pride and Prejudice*; but not so if she happened to have an odd almanac for 1808 and used it for *Mansfield Park*. In that case she might traverse the same year twice, and Easter in 1808 fell on 17 April, which is indeed respectably late – though it was even later, on 18 April, in the year *Mansfield Park* was completed, 1813. We are in a world of conjecture, which mercifully does not weaken the case for dating a major revision of *Pride and Prejudice* in 1811–12.

But it is interesting to observe that in *Emma* and *Persuasion* – though the passage of the seasons is clear and important – there are few dates to tempt the almanac-hunter.

1800–1810

We need not doubt that Jane's early twenties, in the second half of the 1790s, were filled with creative writing which laid foundations for *Pride and*

---

[28] *PP*, pp. 401–2, 404.

[29] *MP*, pp. 253–6, 282; for what follows, see Chapman in *MP*, pp. 554–7; for Easter see ibid., pp. 430, 554.

[30] *MP* III, c. 14 ('xvi' in 1st and 2nd edns), p. 430.

Prejudice, Sense and Sensibility and perhaps *Northanger Abbey* too: what is much more obscure is what these drafts were like – in what measure if any they anticipated Jane's mature work. All that is clear is that *Northanger Abbey* of 1803 still rests in a world between the juvenilia and the mature novels of the 1810s. Much of it is a running commentary on the absurdities of the gothic novel – echoing the parody of current fashions which inspired so many of the juvenilia; and Catherine Morland is a kind of anti-heroine, evincing many of the qualities the exact opposite of those of more fashionable novels. But she is more than that. When she sets off for Bath, instead of preparing her for encounters with brigands and baronets, Mrs Morland tells her to wrap up warm at night and keep accounts.

> Every thing indeed relative to this important journey was done, on the part of the Morlands, with a degree of moderation and composure, which seemed rather consistent with the common feelings of common life, than with the refined susceptibilities, the tender emotions which the first separation of a heroine from her family ought always to excite.[31]

Here, stated far more bluntly than the later Jane Austen would have allowed, is the programme not only of *Northanger Abbey* but, in a considerable degree, of all her later novels. Undoubtedly her heroines lived in an imaginative world of her own creation; but she is the novelist par excellence who created the illusion that her world was ours. In that sense *Northanger Abbey* was a manifesto of her mature creative world. Catherine Morland is not only a moderately pretty *ingenue*; she is a voracious reader with a genuine love of books, however simple-minded. Her comments on the fashionable historical literature of the day – 'the men all so good for nothing, and hardly any women at all' – are a delectable mixture of naïveté and shrewd observation.[32]

It has often been thought that there was a gap in the creative life of Jane Austen between 1801, when she left Steventon, and 1809, when she settled at Chawton and returned to country life. No one need doubt that she preferred to live in the country, and drew inspiration from it; nor that the early notebooks reveal a constant stream of creative writing, of an ephemeral kind, yet compulsive too, from the age of 12 to the age of 20 or so. Cassandra's list, if we accept its general drift – and no one knew Jane more intimately throughout her life than she – suggests that Jane's early twenties, the late 1790s, were equally creative, issuing in the first drafts of *Pride and*

---

[31] *NA* I, c. 2, p. 19. I assume that only minor revision of *NA* took place after 1803. Since Jane Austen only recovered it in 1809, and it lacks many obvious features of the later novels, it is reasonable to suppose that what was published in 1818 was, in all essentials, the novel of 1803.

[32] *NA* I, c. 14, p. 108: see below, p. 60.

Prejudice and *Sense and Sensibility*, and possibly (in some sense) of *Northanger Abbey*. We have seen, however, that the years 1801–03 produced *Northanger Abbey* in something like its present form, and thus that the first two years at Bath were probably extremely active. *Northanger Abbey* was followed by *The Watsons*, an incomplete draft of *c.* 1804–05, which shows little promise of the great novels to come. It may have been abandoned partly because of her father's death: there is no doubt that that was a major trauma, bringing great disruption to the family. But it seems likely that the book's failure was already apparent to her, as it is to us. Meanwhile *Northanger Abbey* was in the hands of a publisher who had paid ten pounds for it and failed to publish it: this no doubt was a considerable discouragement. It may be that up till 1803 she had written for her own and her family's pleasure; but clearly after her father's retirement, and with a sense of declining resources and growing powers, she felt the urge to publish. After her father's death the family moved to Southampton; and as the Southampton era drew to its close early in April 1809, Jane made her first serious attempt to revive the idea of publication.[33] The years which followed were the most creative of her life. It may well be that so far from being fallow, unproductive years, the space between 1805 and 1809 had opened in her mind and imagination the path she was to follow: had revealed to her what was lacking even in *Northanger Abbey*, and what she might aim for.[34] There is a curious piece of advice reported by her niece Caroline that too much writing at an early age was not a good apprenticeship.[35] This has always seemed strange from Jane Austen, since her early notebooks show how much she wrote; and one cannot but think that the habit of writing steadily and continuously was crucial to the successes of the 1810s. But it may well reflect her own experience between 1805 and 1809, a kind of conversion to a new, more mature mode – owing much indeed to her earlier years, including the drafts of two of her best novels – but in essential ways marking a new beginning.

But this is conjectural; the dates when she finished the novels and published them – the dates when they achieved the nearest she could compass to perfection – are not.

[33] See n. 11.
[34] Mrs Q.D. Leavis in Leavis 1983, pp. 61–146, at p. 64, suggested that she had laid down the keels of several later novels in early life and was at work revising them in this period. Some of the links she proposed between early and late novels dwell in fantasy; but in some sense it may well be that Jane Austen was planning and revising towards the mature novels in these years.
[35] Caroline Austen 1952, p. 10.

6

Prelude to the Novels

At the outset of the *Code of the Woosters*, P.G. Wodehouse gave a definitive exposition of an all too familiar predicament. If one writes on a theme well known to some of one's readers – but less well known to others – how can one interest the cognoscenti while making oneself plain to the rest?

> A thing I never know, when I'm starting out to tell a story about a chap I've told a story about before, is how much explanation to bung in at the outset. It's a problem you've got to look at from every angle. I mean to say, in the present case, if I take it for granted that my public knows all about Gussie Finknottle and just breeze ahead, those publicans who weren't hanging on my lips the first time are apt to be fogged. Whereas, if before kicking off I give about eight volumes of the man's life and history, other bimbos, who were so hanging, will stifle yawns and murmur 'Old stuff. Get on with it.'
>
> I suppose the only thing to do is to put the salient facts as briefly as possible in the possession of the first gang, waving an apologetic hand at the second gang the while, to indicate that they had better let their attention wander for a minute or two and that I will be with them shortly.[1]

In a similar kind of way, serious discussion of the plots and structures of Jane Austen's novels depends on a knowledge of what happened. Many of my readers will have this to the full; many more will not. My own experience is that even after the thirtieth reading or so some details pass out of my memory; and when I read about other writers I am maddened by critics who assume that we have infallible memories. Furthermore, the more I read the literary critics on Jane, the more I find much that seems to depend on reading the novel differently – or reading a different novel from the one I read – or, quite simply, on not having read it at all. Such a statement invites nemesis; but one can only establish a view of what seems to be happening in the novels by a lucid description of the plot. 'Old stuff', say the bimbos – and if it is, let them skip it.

A more fashionable method in recent books on Jane Austen's novels has

---

[1] Wodehouse 1938, p. 15.

been to replace the plot of a novel with a series of penetrating snapshots – of perceptions of individual items in the novels, which too easily becomes a shopping list of the author's personal insights, throwing at best a fitful light on the novel as a whole.

Marilyn Butler argued that the structure of the novels was based on the conservative tradition of novel writing, and she produced overwhelming evidence of the truth of her contention.[2] Yet as one reads her interpretation of the individual novels, it becomes clear that she has explained too much. To put it very simply – much too simply – she has to make the novels much more didactic than they really can be. The influence is there, but helping, serving, not directing the artist's creation. There is also quite a different structure in them which is not political or didactic, but seems to go much deeper into the author's mind and convictions than her supposed toryism. It is a truism of any literary artists of merit that they work at a variety of levels. But it seems to be peculiarly the case with Jane Austen that she worked at two. This is most evident in *Emma*, which most critics have seen – in some form or other – as the most complete and self-conscious expression of her art.

The plot of *Emma* proceeds at a superficial level in which she lives in a world of fantasy and make-believe, and at a deeper level in which her better qualities – partly inculcated or encouraged by Mr Knightley – are preparing for the day when she marries him. At the end this deeper level is revealed, and the superficial set aside. That is much too simple and peremptory a summary: but it goes some way towards the heart of the matter.

Emma reveals this pattern to the fullest extent of any of the novels. But, in a measure, it is present in all. It seems to me that the failure of some critics to observe it has led them greatly to underestimate the sophistication and success of *Northanger Abbey* and *Sense and Sensibility* – in which, indeed, it takes a rather different form. The heroine of *Northanger Abbey* seems to be a staightforward, matter-of-fact young woman who is carried into a world of fantasy and folly by too much enjoyment of Mrs Radcliffe's *Mysteries of Udolpho*. A deeper reading suggests a quite different interpretation: for it is precisely the mingling of good sense and imagination – however ill assorted in her mind – that Henry Tilney finds so attractive – and he enjoys Mrs Radcliffe too, in his own way. *Udolpho* may be ridiculous, but the romantic imagination is not.

In *Sense and Sensibility* we are invited to see how preferable sense is to imaginative, over-zealous sensibility – or are we? That is about as far as many good critics have gone, and the moral is less inspiriting than the book. But I myself agree with Colonel Brandon in finding Marianne Dashwood more interesting than Elinor, and in the end no more deluded, no less admirable – however absurd.

---

[2] Butler 1987.

These fundamental features of the novels can only be made intelligible if we pursue the story of the novels and explore how relevant the pursuit of two approaches (as in *Northanger Abbey*) or two levels (as in *Emma*) is to their understanding. In historical enquiry the truth rarely lies in the obvious and well-known – but equally rarely in its opposite, in what is fashionably called revisionism. It lies in a subtle combination of the virtues of both: the rapier is a much more formidable weapon than the bludgeon. What the historian has above all to avoid is forgetting the obvious – for it may more often lead him to the truth than what is brilliant, original and in the end, obviously wrong. Perhaps it may not be so very different in some regions of literary criticism, in which a plain rehearsal of known facts can be more revealing than a bewildering series of penetrating snapshots.

7

Northanger Abbey

The first half of *Northanger Abbey* is set in Bath. The heroine, Catherine Morland, daughter of a country parson with 'a considerable independence, besides two good livings' – but a large family of ten children – is taken to Bath by well-to-do friends and neighbours, Mr and Mrs Allen.

> Every thing, indeed, relative to this important journey was done on the part of the Morlands with a degree of moderation and composure, which seemed rather consistent with the common feelings of common life, than with the refined susceptibilities, the tender emotions which the first separation of a heroine from her family ought always to excite.[1]

As in many of the juvenilia, the book pokes continuous fun at the sentimental novel and the gothic novel of its age; but this signature tune of the book also proclaims a central theme of the mature novels. 'The common feelings of common life': Jane Austen's imaginative world was clearly aimed – in some measure at least – to create the illusion of ordinary people behaving in ordinary ways. Catherine Morland is a kind of manifesto of what the heroine of such a book might be. She is in many respects a very run-of-the-mill young woman; by the advanced age of 17 she has grown quite pretty; but in mind and tastes she is just what one of a large contented family from a moderately prosperous parsonage might be. One special quality she has: she has become a keen reader; and while she is at Bath she reads Mrs Radcliffe's *Mysteries of Udolpho* (published in 1794) – supreme among the current horror stories of the gothic novels. Catherine is in part of her mind a down-to-earth young woman of 17, and in part absorbed in the imaginative adventures of *Udolpho*. *Northanger Abbey* is nicely poised between the presentation of a heroine drawn from common life, and a skit on the gothic novel. The second half of the book is set in Northanger Abbey, the mansion of General Tilney – whose son, Henry Tilney, she eventually marries. The house had been partly modernised in the eighteenth century and furnished to a modern taste. But it is built within the walls of a real abbey, with gothic arches and windows enough to feed

---

[1] *NA* I, cc. 1–2, pp. 1, 19.

Catherine's imagination – and to foster her naïve involvement in gothic adventure.

The modern reader tends to grow weary of Jane Austen's harping on the difference between Catherine and the proper heroine of a sentimental novel; and to find Catherine's imaginative adventures absurd. But the threads are woven together with extraordinary skill; most striking of all is her skill in saving Catherine from being dull.

More than that, in an arresting anticipation of the structure of the mature novels, Jane Austen shows the way in which the union of warmth, matter-of-factness and wild imagination combine to captivate Henry Tilney. *Udolpho* is not just absurd: it helps to make Catherine more than commonplace.

The visit to Bath enables her to encounter two new friends who help to mould her views and interests. The first is Isabella Thorpe, a pretty, lively, friendly daughter of an old friend of Mrs Allen. But her charms and standards are all skin deep; she is first and last a flirt. Her brother John Thorpe is an Oxford friend of Catherine's brother James; and the two men come to Bath, James in search of Isabella. James and Isabella even become engaged for a time, but in the heady world of Bath she cannot keep her attention on one man, and is presently flirting with a rival. John Thorpe is equally superficial: a boastful, tedious rattle. For a while they all get on well enough together, old and young alike: Mrs Thorpe (a trial run for the subtler portrait of Mrs Musgrove in *Persuasion*) and Mrs Allen 'spent the chief of [the day] . . . in what they called conversation, but in which there was scarcely ever any exchange of opinion, and not often any resemblance of subject, for Mrs Thorpe talked chiefly of her children, and Mrs Allen of her gowns'.[2]

A chance encounter at a ball introduces Catherine to Henry Tilney, the second son of General Tilney, an Oxford graduate and a clergyman; soon after, he brings his sister Eleanor to Bath, and they meet often – in spite of John Thorpe's crude efforts to keep them apart. There is a vivid scene in which Thorpe boasts that he has told the Tilneys that Catherine has a prior engagement with himself and his family next day, and so cannot keep her promise of going for a walk with them. Catherine rushes off to the Tilneys' lodgings and into the house just as they are entering – speeds past the footman and finds her own way into their presence to deny Thorpe's invention in words which are quite unintelligible, but in a manner perfectly clear.

Henry Tilney is a clever, sophisticated young man, who talks over Catherine's head – and she rapidly comes to worship him. It is a theme frequently harped on in Jane Austen's novels that husband and wife can mould and reshape each other's characters: the fate of Mr Elton in *Emma*, after his

[2] *NA* I, c. 5, p. 36.

marriage, is a striking example. Already, in *Northanger Abbey*, Jane plays this tune, but in a different key.[3] Talking books with Isabella Thorpe had been very superficial; for the best that Isabella can do is to trot off a list of improbable, but genuine thrillers.[4] Henry has read *Udolpho* too – and all Mrs Radcliffe's books, and admires most of them. But his real tastes are much wider, and so are his sister's, who rapidly provides a model for Catherine.

When Catherine sets out on her walk with the Tilneys she utters her raptures on *Udolpho*.

> 'You are fond of that kind of reading?' [Eleanor observes.]
> 'To say the truth, I do not much like any other.'
> 'Indeed!'
> 'That is, I can read poetry and plays, and things of that sort, and do not dislike travels. But history, real solemn history, I cannot be interested in. Can you?'
> 'Yes, I am fond of history.'
> 'I wish I were too. I read it a little as a duty; but it tells me nothing that does not either vex or weary me. The quarrels of popes and kings, with wars or pestilences, in every page; the men all so good for nothing, and hardly any women at all – it is very tiresome; and yet I often think it odd that it should be so dull, for a great deal of it must be invention. The speeches that are put into the heroes' mouths, their thoughts and designs – the chief of all this must be invention, and invention is what delights me in other books.'

Catherine may have been naïve, but she is revealed here – as elsewhere, by slight touches – to have a good deal of native shrewdness of a forthright kind. Miss Tilney's response is hardly convincing.

> '. . . I am fond of history – and am very well contented to take the false with the true. In the principal facts they have sources of intelligence in former histories and records, which may be as much depended on, I conclude, as any thing that does not actually pass under one's own observation; and as for the little embellishments you speak of, they are embellishments, and I like them as such. If a speech be well drawn up, I read it with pleasure, by whomsoever it may be made – and probably with much greater, if the production of Mr Hume or Mr Robertson, than if the genuine words of Caractacus, Agricola, or Alfred the Great.'
> 'You are fond of history! – and so are Mr Allen and my father; and I

---

[3] Contrary to Butler 1987, p. 177.

[4] *NA* I, c. 6, p. 40. See A.D.M. Killop, 'Jane Austen's Gothic titles', *Notes and Queries*, 12th Series, 9, 5 Nov. 1921, pp. 361–6. All seven novels listed were published between 1793 and 1798.

have two brothers who do not dislike it. So many instances within my small circle of friends is remarkable! At this rate I shall not pity the writers of history any longer.'[5]

There follows a lively discussion between Henry and Catherine on the torments of learning; and then the subject changes to one of which Catherine has no notion – the Tilneys are viewing the landscape 'with the eyes of persons accustomed to drawing, and decided on its capability of being formed into pictures, with all the eagerness of real taste'. Catherine

> was heartily ashamed of her ignorance. A misplaced shame. Where people wish to attach, they should always be ignorant. To come with a well-informed mind, is to come with an inability of administering to the vanity of others, which a sensible person would always wish to avoid. A woman, especially, if she have the misfortune of knowing anything, should conceal it as well as she can.[6]

One is reminded of Jane herself on Samuel Blackall, when many years after his meetings with her, she read of his marriage to a Miss Lewis. 'I would wish Miss Lewis to be of a silent turn and rather ignorant, but naturally intelligent and wishing to learn.'[7] Whether or not (as has been supposed) Jane had Mr Blackall in mind when she created Henry Tilney, she had shrewdly observed the way to attach such men. Henry gives Catherine a first lesson in landscape drawing, to which she listens with enthusiasm.

> Catherine was so hopeful a scholar, that when they gained the top of Beechen Cliff, she voluntarily rejected the whole city of Bath, as unworthy to make part of a landscape. Delighted with her progress, and fearful of wearying her with too much wisdom at once, Henry suffered the subject to decline, and by an easy transition from a piece of rocky fragment and the withered oak which he had placed near its summit, to oaks in general, to forests, the inclosure of them, waste lands, crown lands and government, he shortly found himself arrived at politics; and from politics, it was an easy step to silence.[8]

Henry Tilney, for all his virtues, does not escape Jane Austen's sharp eye for assertions of male superiority.

Unlike his two younger children, General Tilney is a man of doubtful temper and dedicated to worldly prosperity. He encounters John Thorpe in idle, boasting mood: John at the time was hoping for Catherine's hand himself – and he gives a lavish picture of her family fortune and prospects. The General observes that a friendship has been formed between Catherine

---

5 *NA* I, c. 14, pp. 108–9.
6 *NA* I, c. 14, pp. 110–11.
7 *Letters*, L no. 86, p. 216; C no. 81, p. 317; M, F-259. On Blackall, see pp. 31–2.
8 *NA* I, c. 14, p. 111.

and Henry and Eleanor, and encourages it: at his behest, Eleanor invites her to Northanger Abbey – where Jane delights to complete the deconstruction of the gothic novel.

As they travel towards Northanger, Henry amuses himself by feeding Catherine's mind with romantic terrors; and although Northanger proves by no means the rambling mansion of her dreams, she finds enough to disturb a lively imagination nourished on *The Mysteries of Udolpho*. In her room she encounters a chest which she has to struggle to open – which yields nothing but a white cotton counter-pane, neatly folded. Later, at night, she observes an ebony cabinet strangely similar to one Henry had described in his imaginary narrative as they travelled: she cannot rest till she has explored it. With a storm howling round the Abbey, she struggles with it, and finds, in an inner recess, a pile of manuscript sheets – at which moment her candle goes out. By the light of day it turns out to be a laundry list, accidentally left by a recent visitor. Her third ordeal comes from an urge to visit the chamber where Mrs Tilney died, for she has built up a picture of the General – in spite of his polite, indeed excessively polite behaviour to herself – as a cruel husband. Her favourite reading even leads her to imagine for a time that Mrs Tilney may still be alive, concealed somewhere in the building. She succeeds in finding the room which had been Mrs Tilney's chamber – but it is not the ancient, terrifying chamber she had pictured, but a comfortable modern room built by the General's father. Her dreams dissolve; but at that moment she encounters Henry, who with remarkable penetration – after a few hasty words of explanation – guesses a little of what she has suspected, and gently rebukes her. 'Dearest Miss Morland, what ideas have you been admitting?'

This is a crucial moment in the book. Catherine flees to her room

> with tears of shame . . . The visions of romance were over. Catherine was completely awakened . . . Charming as were all Mrs Radcliffe's works, charming even as were the works of all her imitators, it was not in them perhaps that human nature, at least in the midland counties of England, was to be looked for.[9]

This is a most important truth, but it is not the whole truth. Her imagination is evidently a part of Catherine's charm in Henry's eyes; and her readiness to be moulded by his taste equally so. 'The visions of romance' in another sense were far from over: we are only five chapters from Henry Tilney's proposal. But for a while, her illusions have been shattered: she is chastened; she returns to the ordinary world, soon much enhanced by a visit to Henry's parsonage at Woodston, twenty miles away.[10] Not long after, the General goes to London for a week; while there he encounters

---

[9] *NA* II, cc. 9–10, pp. 198–200.
[10] *NA* II, c. 11.

John Thorpe again – who has now abandoned hope of marrying Catherine, and as Isabella and James have parted, is disaffected with the Morland family. He lies as freely to the General as before, but in a different sense: he diminishes their wealth and enlarges the family; he is certain after all that she will not be heiress to the Allens. 'The General needed no more. Enraged with almost everybody in the world but himself, he set out the next day for the Abbey'[11] – where he makes Eleanor turn Catherine out of the house with the shortest possible notice, and send her back to her parents by post coach, without even a servant to look after her.

The Morlands welcome her to their home, but are naturally baffled and resentful at the General's treatment; and they advise her to forget the Tilneys. Catherine, however, finds it hard to settle to her old pursuits: she is restless, listless – has all the traditional signs of being in love. Her state is a kind of trial run for the more portentous predicament of Mr Darcy. Her mother reads her a lecture against allowing the grander world she has visited to disaffect her with her own home.

> 'There is a very clever essay in one of the books up stairs upon much such a subject, about young girls that have been spoilt for home by great acquaintance – "The Mirror", I think. I will look it out for you some day or other, because I am sure it will do you good.'

But Catherine soon lapses again 'into languor and listlessness' and her mother hastens upstairs in search of the book 'anxious to lose no time in attacking so dreadful a malady'.[12] After some minutes of search and other distractions, she returns downstairs to find that Henry Tilney has called. They engage awhile in conversation; then Henry asks if Mr and Mrs Allen are at home and proposes to visit them – and asks Catherine to show him the way. As they go, he asks her to marry him.

> She was assured of his affection; and that heart in return was solicited, which, perhaps, they pretty equally knew was already entirely his own; for though Henry was now sincerely attached to her, though he felt and delighted in all the excellencies of her character and truly loved her society, I must confess that his affection originated in nothing better than gratitude, or, in other words, that persuasion of her partiality for him had been the only cause of giving her a serious thought.[13]

Gratitude is commonly in Jane Austen's novels the first stage towards a secure and lasting love.

Henry was acting in direct opposition to his father's will; and Catherine's

---

[11] *NA* II, c. 15, pp. 246–7; cf. II, c. 13 for the consequences.
[12] *NA* II, c. 15, p. 241.
[13] *NA* II, c. 15, p. 243.

parents, while welcoming the prospect of their union, withold consent until some show of relenting from the General is forthcoming. So 'Henry returned to what was now his only home [his parsonage] . . .; and Catherine remained at Fullerton to cry.'[14] They did not have to wait long: after a few months the young man in Eleanor Tilney's life inherited an estate and a peerage; and 'never had the General loved his daughter so well . . . as when he first hailed her, "Your Ladyship!" '[15] In this moment of euphoria Eleanor can speak up for Henry and Catherine; General Tilney can learn that Thorpe's denigration of the Morlands was as false as his first enhancement of their fortune; and the General's consent can be despatched to the Morlands.

> Henry and Catherine were married, the bells rang and every body smiled; and, as this took place within a twelvemonth from the first day of their meeting, it will not appear, after all the dreadful delays occasioned by the General's cruelty, that they were essentially hurt by it. To begin perfect happiness at the respective ages of twenty-six and eighteen [Jane is characteristically precise about their ages] is to do pretty well; and professing myself moreover convinced, that the General's unjust interference, so far from being really injurious to their felicity, was perhaps rather conducive to it, by improving their knowledge of each other, and adding strength to their attachment, I leave it to be settled by whomsoever it may concern, whether the tendency of this work be altogether to recommend parental tyranny, or reward filial disobedience.[16]

[14] *NA* II, c. 16, p. 250.
[15] *NA* II, c. 16, p. 251.
[16] *NA* II, c. 16, p. 252.

8

Sense and Sensibility

Between Barton [the home of Mrs Dashwood, mother of Elinor and Marianne] and Delaford [where Elinor was the parson's wife, Marianne the squire's] there was that constant communication which strong family affection would naturally dictate; – and among the merits and the happiness of Elinor and Marianne, let it not be ranked as the least considerable, that though sisters, and living almost within sight of each other, they could live without disagreement between themselves, or producing coolness between their husbands.[1]

These are the last words of *Sense and Sensibility*. They remind us of the sharp edge of Jane's mind: doubtless her sister Cassandra, her constant companion and closest of friends, enjoyed the joke. But they also bring together – in a novel full of selfish, self-seeking, artificial, unattractive characters – four or five of the warmest and most attractive of Jane's creations: Elinor and her husband, Edward Ferrars, Marianne and Colonel Brandon, and their mother, Mrs Dashwood; the third sister, Margaret, is too young to play a leading role – indeed, she is a cipher. Elinor and Marianne have been painted in strongly contrasting colours, and most critics have exaggerated the distance between them. Elinor, aged 19 at the outset of the story, is a model of good sense, practical, thoughtful, generous and kind – mature beyond her years. Marianne is 16 at the outset, soon 17, intensely romantic, and dogmatic in her sensibility.[2]

In the contrast between the surface and the depths of the story *Sense and Sensibility* – not surprisingly – marks a stage on the path that will lead us to *Emma*. On the surface Elinor and Marianne are markedly different in character; but at a deeper level – in background, personality, convictions and destiny – they are much more alike. At the same time, we are not far from *Northanger Abbey*: Marianne's imaginative sensibility and romantic absurdity make a large part of her charm in her future husband's eyes.

Marianne's views on marriage are most fully expounded, with true

---

[1] *SS* III, c. 14, p. 380; cf. above, c. 3 n. 3.

[2] Elinor was 19 at the outset (*SS* I, c. 1, p. 6), Marianne 16 (*SS* I, c. 3, p. 18), but soon 17 (c.8, p. 37; cf. III, c. 14, p. 378) – 17 still as the book nears its conclusion (III, c. 13, p. 369), but 19 when she married (III, c. 14, p. 379).

dramatic irony, in conversations – first about her future husband Colonel Brandon, then between the Colonel and Elinor.

Marianne to her mother:

'I know very well that Colonel Brandon is not old enough to make his friends yet apprehensive of losing him in the course of nature. He may live twenty years longer. But thirty-five has nothing to do with matrimony.'

'Perhaps,' said Elinor, 'thirty-five and seventeen had better not have anything to do with matrimony together. But if there should by any chance happen to be a woman who is single at seven and twenty, I should not think Colonel Brandon's being thirty-five any objection to his marrying *her*.'

'A woman of seven-and-twenty,' said Marianne, after pausing a moment, 'can never hope to feel or inspire affection again; and if her home be uncomfortable, or her fortune small, I can suppose that she might bring herself to submit to the offices of a nurse, for the sake of the provision and security of a wife. In his marrying such a woman therefore there would be nothing unsuitable. It would be a compact of convenience, and the world would be satisfied. In my eyes it would be no marriage at all, but that would be nothing. To me it would seem only a commercial exchange, in which each wished to be bene-fited at the expense of the other.'[3]

Not long after, Elinor and the Colonel are in conversation – he has fallen in love with Marianne, who reminds him all too vividly of his own first love.

'Your sister, I understand, does not approve of second attachments.'

'No,' replied Elinor, 'her opinions are all romantic.'

'Or rather, as I believe, she considers them impossible to exist.'

'I believe she does. But how she contrives it without reflecting on the character of her own father, who had himself two wives, I know not. A few years however will settle her opinions on the reasonable basis of common sense and observation; and then they may be more easy to define and to justify than they now are, by any body but herself.'

'This will probably be the case,' he replied; 'and yet there is some-thing so amiable in the prejudices of a young mind, that one is sorry to see them give way to the reception of more general opinions.'

To this Elinor does not say heartily amen: for all her affection for her sister, she finds that her 'enthusiasm and ignorance of the world . . . have all the

---

[3] *SS* I, c. 8, pp. 37–8. Cf. pp. 79, 174–5 for the view of marriage of a woman of 'seven-and-twenty', Charlotte Lucas.

unfortunate tendency of setting propriety at nought; and a better acquaintance with the world is what I look forward to as her greatest possible
advantage' – a sentiment the reader may share when contemplating
Marianne's exaggerated grief at the checks and sorrows she encounters.[4]

Their father, Mr Dashwood, married twice: from the first marriage came
one son, John, whose wife, Fanny Ferrars, has converted him into a selfish
money-seeking young man, devoted only to his and her advancement: they
are a thoroughly united couple, a striking instance of a common theme in
Jane Austen, of the influence husband and wife may have on each other.
Fanny and John Dashwood enhance each other's vices to the point of cari-
caturing each other. Up to a point John means well; and on his father's
deathbed he promises to look after his stepmother and half-sisters. But the
grandfather, the elder Mr Dashwood's father, had left all but a trifling
legacy to John Dashwood and his and Fanny's son. It is a characteristic Jane
Austen situation: as in *Pride and Prejudice* and *Persuasion* the estate must go to
a male relation; the women must fend for themselves – find husbands or
live on charity or starve. It was a situation not wholly unfamiliar to the
unmarried daughter of a parson of modest means. In one of the most
famous of Jane's set-pieces, John and Fanny Dashwood debate what is to be
done to help the girls. He starts by proposing three thousand pounds – a
thousand each to his sisters; but after much eloquence from Fanny, 'he
finally resolved that it would be absolutely unnecessary, if not highly
indecorous, to do more for the widow and children of his father, than such
kind of neighbourly acts as his own wife pointed out' – 'looking out for a
comfortable small house for them, helping them to move their things, and
sending them presents of fish and game, and so forth, whenever they are in
season'.[5] In fairness to John Dashwood, Jane rounds off this portrait of
immortal selfishness by showing that he was distinctly uncomfortable when
circumstances prevented him from helping them even in these excessively
modest ways.[6]

For a cousin of Mrs Dashwood, Sir John Middleton, invites them to take
a cottage on his estate, and they move away from Norland in Sussex, now
the home of the John Dashwoods, to Barton near Exeter. The Middletons
are one of the ill-matched pairs who litter Jane Austen's pages: he the
bucolic country squire, hearty, noisy, extrovert, she elegant, cold and
refined – only really stirred to life when spoiling her children. They are
nicely balanced by Lady Middleton's mother, Mrs Jennings, as vulgar as her
son-in-law, but redeemed in Jane's eyes, and eventually in the Dashwoods'
too, by a warm heart and sincere good feelings.

Before leaving Norland, Elinor had developed an attachment to Edward

---

[4] *SS* I, c. 11, pp. 55–6.
[5] *SS* I, c. 2, pp. 12–13.
[6] *SS* I, c. 5, pp. 25–6; II, c. 11, esp. p. 222.

Ferrars, brother of Mrs John Dashwood, a quiet well-meaning witty young man – as unlike his sister as possible. Their mother, Mrs Ferrars, is a widow immensely rich – by a savage irony, she is unlike Mrs Dashwood in having total control of her family fortune, and grievously abusing her opportunity – ambitious for her children, but anxious to avoid 'that reproach which she always seemed fearful of incurring, the reproach of being too amiable'.[7] Edward is an Oxford graduate and has a leaning for the church; it is hard to call it a strong vocation – though it may well become such. Mrs Ferrars wishes to see him shine in politics or, failing that, the army – the two professions for which he is most completely unfitted. Happily for her, she can console herself by advancing her other son, Robert, and her daughter, Fanny Dashwood, who are close rivals for the crown as the most selfish character in any of Jane's novels. Even for Edward, she retains the hope of a rich marriage: the late Lord Morton's daughter, rich and highly born, and apparently without any will of her own – but somehow at Mrs Ferrars' beck and call – is frequently offered him as a bait. Such was Mrs Ferrars' idea of marriage, a commercial transaction indeed, in which profit and social advancement should if possible be combined; poor woman, she has in the end to make do with Elinor.

If Edward was amiable, he was also weak: his best hope of improvement and happiness lies in marriage with Elinor; but at an earlier age he had become entangled with a young woman of tolerably good looks and manner, but ignorant and penniless, Lucy Steele. Edward had studied as a boy with a tutor in Devon; Lucy was his tutor's niece and they were thrown much together. At eighteen, 'I was . . . entered at Oxford and have been properly idle ever since'[8] – that is, had nothing better than Lucy to think of. But we are also reminded that Jane Austen sprang from the Oxford establishment, and that her father and eldest brother had been fellows of St John's; her books are lightly scattered, as it were with rose prunings blowing in the wind, with barbed references to Oxford – and her family's professions. But there was an affectionate touch to them too, a hint that Oxford was at least preferable to Cambridge, for to Cambridge she sent George Wickham and Henry Crawford.[9]

Lucy Steele is a relation of Mrs Jennings and so of Lady Middleton; and she and her sister are invited to stay with the Middletons. Lucy, with malice aforethought, makes Elinor her confidante – tells her of her engagement to Edward – and seeks her advice. For many months, till the denouement of the book, Elinor lives with the miserable knowledge that Edward is betrothed to another – and at first her tender conscience forbids her to take even her closest family into her confidence.

---

[7] *SS* III, c. 14, p. 373.
[8] *SS* I, c. 19, p. 103.
[9] See p. 139.

Marianne, meanwhile, had had a nasty fall and been carried home by an amiable, handsome, lively young man called Willoughby. They have a lightning romance together: they have many tastes in common, and he in his turn finds her extremely attractive. Willoughby proves to be a characteristic Austen character, admirable on the surface, but beneath it a predatory male. He is everything a romantic hero should be, save that he is spurious, rotten at the core. Such were to be proved Wickham, Crawford and Mr Elliot. Willoughby's villainy comprises the seduction and desertion of Colonel Brandon's ward – the daughter by another man of his own first love. This discovery (not revealed to the reader till many pages later) takes Colonel Brandon away in haste from Barton – and he and Willoughby subsequently fight a duel in which neither is hurt. A hint of the story comes to Willoughby's rich aunt, on whom his future prospects depend; and she dismisses him from her favour and her house. He is far from rich and deep in debt; and so he hastily marries an heiress to save himself from want.

These events are unfolded in London, where Elinor and Marianne stay with Mrs Jennings. Marianne had consented to go in the hope of meeting Willoughby; and she does – and is coldly repulsed. She writes to him, writes twice; then they meet in a crowded party, under the eye of his wife to be. His cold and formal acknowledgement of her presence is followed by a letter even colder. In due course Lucy's engagement to Edward is revealed to the Ferrars, and Fanny has hysterics: Edward retires to Oxford, steadfastly refusing to abandon Lucy; and Elinor is compelled to reveal to her family all that she has already suffered.

Thus Elinor and Marianne leave London in like misery. They stay briefly with Mrs Jennings' other daughter, Mrs Palmer, in Somerset – the subject of one of Jane's most remorseless portraits of a silly woman, but happy and cheerful in spite of it; Marianne is taken seriously ill, and there are even fears for her life. Colonel Brandon is with them and offers to fetch Mrs Dashwood to her daughter's sick-bed; and while he is away Willoughby – who has been told of Marianne's condition – drives furiously from London to Somerset. In a very powerful scene between Willoughy and Elinor, he is able to win her sympathy to a limited extent – even to exculpate some of the worst of his faults – but not to change his character. It is a noteworthy feature of *Sense and Sensibility* that two of the most mature, effective and memorable scenes in the book – the debate between John and Fanny Dashwood at the outset, and the dialogue between Elinor and Willoughby near the end – are so varied in tone: the first satirical, the second emotional and dramatic.

Marianne is now on the mend. The vain, foppish Robert Ferrars, Edward's elder brother, has attempted meanwhile to talk Lucy out of her engagement to Edward. But after a time, 'instead of talking of Edward, they came gradually to talk only of Robert, – a subject on which he had always more to say than on any other' – and the conclusion was, that he and Lucy were married.[10] A garbled account of the marriage leads the Dashwoods to believe that she and Edward have married, and when he comes to call, they try hard to receive him with their usual warmth. Here Jane permits herself a touch of melodrama – for Edward has really come to ask Elinor to marry him; and in a brilliant portrayal of a man driven to deep absence of mind by love and embarrassment, the truth slowly emerges – and so eventually does his proposal.[11]

Edward now prepares for ordination: he can enjoy the modest living of Delaford, to which Colonel Brandon has presented him; but more is needed to support his married state – and so he proposes to visit Fanny and 'intreat her good offices in his favour' – that is, to help him to reconciliation with his mother, who has not yet forgiven him for his first betrothal – let alone for another almost equally imprudent. Marianne has been purged by suffering – by the loss of Willoughby, by her illness, most of all by the discovery of what Elinor has suffered. ' "And if they really *do* interest themselves", said Marianne, in her new character of candour, "in bringing about a reconciliation, I shall think that even John and Fanny are not entirely without merit." '[12] However that may be, Edward is restored to modest favour and all is well; but he and Elinor are not insulted by becoming favourite children of his mother; that is reserved for Robert and Lucy, whose faults are in the long run almost wholly forgotten.

> They settled in town, received very liberal assistance from Mrs Ferrars, were on the best terms imaginable with the Dashwoods [Fanny and John]; and setting aside the jealousies and ill-will continually subsisting between Fanny and Lucy, in which their husbands of course took a part, as well as the frequent domestic disagreements between Robert and Lucy themselves, nothing could exceed the harmony in which they all lived together.[13]

Elinor and her mother are now fully apprised of Colonel Brandon's devotion to Marianne.

> With such a confederacy against her – with a knowledge so intimate of his goodness – with a conviction of his fond attachment to herself, which at last, though long after it was observable to everybody else – burst on her – what could she do?
>
> Marianne Dashwood was born to an extraordinary fate. She was born to discover the falsehood of her own opinions, and to counteract, by her conduct, her most favourite maxims. She was born to overcome an affection formed so late in life as at seventeen, and with

[10] *SS* III, c. 14, p. 376.
[11] *SS* III, cc. 12–13, pp. 358–62.
[12] *SS* III, c. 13, p. 372.
[13] *SS* III, c. 14, p. 377.

no sentiment superior to strong esteem and lively friendship, voluntarily to give her hand to another! – and *that* other, a man who had suffered no less than herself under the event of a former attachment, whom, two years before, she had considered too old to be married, – and who still sought the constitutional safeguard of a flannel waistcoat!

'But so it was . . . She found herself at nineteen, submitting to new attachments, entering on new duties, placed in a new home, a wife, the mistress of a family,[14] and the patroness of a village. . . . That Marianne found her own happiness in forming his, was equally the persuasion and delight of each observing friend. Marianne could never love by halves; and her whole heart became, in time, as much devoted to her husband, as it had once been to Willoughby.'[15]

These two marriages form a kind of contrast not unusual in Jane Austen – in a certain measure reminiscent of the marriages in *Pride and Prejudice*. Elinor and Edward have much in common, in feelings, interests and outlook; their devotion to one another is none the less deep for having been so long hardly expressed. Colonel Brandon is an older, experienced, man who has had adventures and sufferings over a long period of years. But in the end he proves to have much in common with Marianne – more than is quite fully expounded in the carefully understated denouement – too much understated for some tastes; admirably so to mine. He has a passionate devotion to young women of Marianne's beauty and temperament; he has feelings – however he may cloak them in gentlemanly behaviour – which lead him to the duelling field. They have a common experience of suffering. The end of *Sense and Sensibility* comes as a series of shocks: Lucy's marriage, Edward's freedom and proposal, Marianne's discovery of her love for the Colonel. They are shocks, that is, on the surface of the book: at the deepest level the two marriages are wholly appropriate.

The contrast between Elinor's sense and Marianne's (and their mother's) sensibility is a very obvious and vital element in the book. So admirable is Elinor in her good sense and restraint and self-command that many critics have supposed Elinor to present the author's ideal – even though Elinor allows herself to fall in love with a man as deeply entangled, in his way, as Willoughby. But the more I read and reread the book, the more impressed I am by the sympathy Jane lavished on Marianne. A good deal of this is put into Colonel Brandon's mouth, naturally enough, and what he says of the matter is highly *sympathique*. It is true that Marianne, especially in the earlier chapters, is perverse, thoughtless and exaggerated. But she is also extremely young. When Jane revised the book, she was much the same age as Colonel

---

[14] In the eighteenth-century sense of 'a household' – it does not necessarily imply children. See Naomi Tadmor's forthcoming *Household, Kinship and Patronage in Eighteenth-Century England* (Cambridge, 1999).
[15] *SS* III, c. 14, pp. 378–9.

Brandon, and with the mature wisdom of 35 she put the final touches to the absurdity – and the fresh vigour and life and charm – of 17.

Some readers have found the extreme of romantic dottiness in Marianne's fondness for fallen leaves.

> 'And how does dear, dear Norland look?' cried Marianne [to Edward, who has just left Norland to visit them at Barton].
>
> 'Dear, dear Norland', said Elinor, 'probably looks much as it always does at this time of year. The woods and walks thickly covered with dead leaves.'
>
> 'Oh!' cried Marianne, 'with what transporting sensations have I formerly seen them fall! How have I delighted, as I walked, to see them driven in showers about me by the wind! What feelings have they, the season, the air altogether inspired! Now there is no one to regard them. They are seen only as a nuisance, swept hastily off, and driven as much as possible from the sight.'
>
> 'It is not every one', said Elinor, 'who has your passion for dead leaves.'[16]

The dead leaves of autumn and winter are among the supreme beauties of nature; it is abundantly clear that Elinor does not have the argument all her own way. Marianne's rhapsody, to one reader at least, has a truer ring, less trace of literary study in it than Fanny Price's in *Mansfield Park*.

> 'The evergreen! – How beautiful, how welcome, how wonderful the evergreen! – When one thinks of it, how astonishing a variety of nature! – In some countries we know the tree that sheds its leaf is the variety, but that does not make it less amazing, that the same soil and the same sun should nurture plants differing in the first rule and law of their existence. You will think me rhapsodising; but when I am out of doors, especially when I am sitting out of doors, I am very apt to get into this sort of wondering strain. One cannot fix one's eyes on the commonest natural production without finding food for a rambling fancy.'[17]

Jane drew Fanny with a subtlety exceptional even for her; and the comparison gives food for thought.

Nor is Marianne's love of the picturesque uninstructed or unreflected, as emerges a little later in Edward's visit.

> 'It is very true' said Marianne, 'that admiration of landscape scenery is become a mere jargon. Every body pretends to feel and tries to describe with the taste and elegance of him who first defined what

[16] *SS* I, c. 16, pp. 87–8.
[17] *MP* II, c. 4, p. 209.

picturesque beauty was. I detest jargon of every kind, and sometimes I have kept my feelings to myself, because I could find no language to describe them in but what was worn and hackneyed out of all sense and meaning.'[18]

Nor is it the case that her tastes and attitudes are always at variance with Elinor's; very much the contrary. They are alike in finding the vulgarity of Sir John Middleton tiresome – and though Elinor is much readier to feel and express gratitude for his very real kindness to them, she cannot pretend to enjoy his rough and ready wit or playing with Lady Middleton's spoiled children – nor can she enter into Lucy Steele's insincere raptures over them. As the book goes on, we are made to see more and more in common between Elinor and Marianne – not only in their situation and their sufferings, but in their ideals and convictions; we are prepared with many subtle strokes to see that they are painted as warm, civilised young women of understanding and conscience, surrounded by a world peopled with fools and knaves.

Thus the story proceeds, as so often in Jane's mature novels, at two levels: on the surface, Elinor and Marianne are utterly at variance in their tastes and outlook. Deep down, they have much more in common, centred in the warmth of a deeply united family.[19]

---

[18] *SS* I, c. 18, p. 97.
[19] See pp. 19–20, 65, esp. n. 1.

9

Pride and Prejudice

A fundamental theme of *Pride and Prejudice* is the problem of how a man and a woman get to know one another before marriage. Jane Austen solved the difficulty in her next two novels by creating hero and heroine who had known each other from the childhood of one or the other or both. In *Pride and Prejudice* it is assumed that Mr and Mrs Bennet hardly knew one another before he proposed – and he only discovered what a silly, tiresome woman she was after the event. Even Jane and Bingley fall in love very rapidly after only a few evenings together; but in their case a natural sympathy and likeness of temperament and tastes makes the prognostic happier than it might have been. But Elizabeth and Darcy have to batter their way through an almost impenetrable screen of misunderstanding and misrepresentation. Darcy's first proposal comes almost exactly halfway through the book. In the first half, the misunderstandings steadily grow. They come to a crescendo on the eve of his proposal, when she receives from Colonel Fitzwilliam confirmation that it was Darcy who had deliberately separated Bingley from Jane. In Elizabeth's eyes that was all in character, for she had already accepted from Wickham's lips his account of Darcy's heartless, cruel treatment of himself. Nor are the misunderstandings all on one side. For all that Darcy dotes on her, he sees her as an inferior creature from a world lower than his; he sees all the objections to a man of his standing marrying into a family with such vulgar connections as Mrs Bennet and her family – and so uncouth in behaviour as most of the family were, even on occasion Mr Bennet himself. Elizabeth has to clear away a fog of illusion; Mr Darcy has to learn a deeper lesson. He has to learn to respect his future wife and everything about her; to see her family as she sees them; to acknowledge that in some aspects of mind and character she is his superior – in most ways they are equals. That she is raised above her natural station by marriage to Mr Darcy of Pemberley is simply not the case: and that is for him a very puzzling, difficult, salutary lesson.

In order to see them both learning their lessons, Jane Austen had to reveal more of Mr Darcy than of any of her earlier heroes. It is obvious in a superficial sense that Jane shows us more of the female mind at work than the male: she never pursues the men into their bedrooms. But it is not true that Darcy is left remote and undeveloped, as some have asserted. First of all, she is freer with hints of his devotion than with any of her earlier or later heroes: she shows him falling in love step by step. Then she takes him to Hunsford where he stays on week after week growing ever more listless as lovers often do. But she reveals his mind most fully by the simple but powerful device of making him write a long letter of explanation of his attitude to Bingley and Jane, and of his relations with Wickham. In this letter dignity, self-reliance, arrogance, insight, intelligence and sound human feeling are displayed strangely mingled – and he invokes God's blessing on a woman who had insulted him a few hours before with all the eloquence Elizabeth and her creator could command. Elizabeth is prepared a little, and the reader a good deal more, for the encomium of the house-keeper at Pemberley a few months later. Although the latter part of the book is more and more written from Elizabeth's point of view – the suspense she must suffer in order fully to realise her change of feeling towards him dictated that it should be so – the reader is never really left in much doubt of Darcy's continuing devotion. He is Jane's first outstanding male portrait: Edward Ferrars and Colonel Brandon are lightly sketched in comparison. Of later heroes, only Mr Knightley is painted in deeper, richer colours. Mr Darcy begins with a contrasting pattern of different attributes and assumptions, and they are gradually modified under the influence of Elizabeth until he is a worthy partner for her. She changes too – less, on the surface, for from beginning to end she is the wittiest and most charming of Jane's heroines; but her judgments at the outset are sharp and superficial. Her impressions of Wickham bring nemesis and make her look deeper; and it is in the depths of personality and principle that she and Darcy are most alike. The final commendation comes from her aunt and uncle Gardiner, of all her relations the closest to her in outlook and the most congenial as companions. Thus Mrs Gardiner: 'His behaviour to us has, in every respect, been as pleasing as when we were in Derbyshire. His understanding and opinions all please me; he wants nothing but a little more liveliness, and *that*, if he marry *prudently*, his wife may teach him.'[1]

At the superficial level the marriage of Elizabeth Bennet and Fitzwilliam Darcy united two remarkably different characters: he stiff, proud, formal, she lively, witty, playful. Nor are they alike in background or fortune. He, at 28, has been for five years master of a great estate, worth £10,000 a year; on his mother's side he is descended from the peerage. Elizabeth's father is a gentleman indeed, and she has been brought up in his comfortable house. But her father's estate is entailed to a cousin, and she has only a very modest fortune of her own. Her mother's family are in trade, or country attorneys, not, by lineage, gentlefolk; and her mother in particular is a silly, flighty, vulgar woman. Worst of all, Elizabeth's youngest sister, Lydia, by the end of the book, is married to a former protégé of Mr Darcy's father, George

---

[1] *PP* III, c. 10, p. 325. For Mr Darcy's age, see *PP*, pp. 200, 369.

Wickham – a scapegrace, a gamester, always in debt; a man of surface charm, rotten at the core – who has actually tried to seduce Darcy's sister. It is a shockingly unequal marriage.

Not all of this was foreseen by Darcy when he first realised that he had fallen in love with Elizabeth; but enough to shock and horrify him. 'In vain have I struggled. It will not do. My feelings will not be repressed. You must allow me to tell you how ardently I admire and love you.'[2] The attentive reader is prepared for his declaration, not only by a series of carefully planted hints, but by a picture of a normally self-possessed, articulate man rendered hopelessly distrait and absent by being head over heels in love. Elizabeth has missed all the hints, and has had a different preparation – for several reasons she is angry with him, and instantly rejects him.

In the second half of the book (which I – unlike many readers – find the better of the two) we are shown in a variety of ways why the marriage (when it eventually comes) is not so unequal. There is social comment here, for social equality of a kind is gradually asserted; but it is Elizabeth's view of equality, or compatibility, not Jane's or ours or anyone else's, which is revealed; and at the deepest level, they are shown to be partners in a different sense – with common interests and outlook, and complementary personalities. Superficially, *Pride and Prejudice* is yet another tale of the moderately poor girl who wins a very rich husband – and that aspect of the story is emphasised, so that deeper regions may be the more fully explored.

Thus Elizabeth's sister Jane, on hearing of their engagement:

> 'Will you tell me how long you have loved him?'
> 'It has been coming on so gradually, that I hardly know when it began. But I believe I must date it from my first seeing his beautiful grounds at Pemberley'

– Darcy's country house in Derbyshire.[3] To Elizabeth's celebrated jest we shall presently return.

The social comment comes closest to the surface when Darcy's aunt, Lady Catherine de Bourgh – who has been deeply incensed by a report that Elizabeth and Darcy are to marry – visits the Bennets in order to bully Elizabeth out of any such monstrous pretension.

After angry exchanges, Lady Catherine comes to the point: she intends Darcy to marry her own daughter, and it is intolerable that she should be frustrated by

> 'the upstart pretensions of a young woman without family, connections, or fortune. Is this to be endured! But it must not, shall not be. If

2 *PP* II, c. 11, p. 189.
3 *PP* III, c. 17, p. 373. See pp. 81, 177.

you were sensible of your own good, you would not wish to quit the sphere, in which you have been brought up.'

'In marrying your nephew I should not consider myself as quitting that sphere. He is a gentleman; I am a gentleman's daughter; so far we are equal.'

Thus Elizabeth utters the classic expression of the eighteenth-century doctrine of the equality of all gentlemen.

'True. You *are* a gentleman's daughter. But who was your mother? Who are your uncles and aunts? Do not imagine me ignorant of their condition.'[4]

It is a pleasant irony in this extraordinary scene that Lady Catherine behaves with greater vulgarity than Mrs Bennet. When Darcy first declared his love for Elizabeth, she had retorted on him that the mode of his declaration 'spared me the concern which I might have felt in refusing you, had you behaved in a more gentleman like manner'.[5] Behaviour is as important as birth to any reasonable definition – in Elizabeth's eyes – of a gentleman.

Over the months which followed his first declaration, these words of hers tortured him, for – although a man of deep pride – he was also highly intelligent and brought up to believe in, and attempt to live by, good principles. He slowly learns the truths which underlie what she has said: he cannot treat his wife as an inferior; Elizabeth's conduct and character more than compensate for her less admirable relations – nor are they all beneath his notice. When they are engaged Elizabeth is still much embarrassed by the vulgar behaviour of some of her circle of friends and relatives – and looks forward 'to all the comfort and elegance of their family party at Pemberley'[6] – and it is made clear that Mrs Bennet is not invited there. 'Happy for all her maternal feelings was the day on which Mrs Bennet got rid of her two most deserving daughters.' 'Got rid' is nicely phrased. 'With what delighted pride she afterwards visited Mrs Bingley [Jane, her eldest daughter], and *talked of* Mrs Darcy, may be guessed.'[7] Elizabeth's father delighted in visiting Pemberley 'especially when he was least expected', as fits his whimsical humour.[8] Other sisters are occasional visitors, and it is a special delight to Elizabeth and Darcy when Jane and Mr Bingley settle within thirty miles of Pemberley. But their first, and most welcome visitors of all, are Elizabeth's aunt and uncle from the City – who in spite of living by trade are the most elegant of Elizabeth's relations, and who played a crucial role in bringing the Darcys together. On this note the book ends:

[4] *PP* III, c. 14, p. 356. See pp. 159–60.
[5] *PP* II, c. 11, p. 192.
[6] *PP* III, c. 18, p. 384.
[7] *PP* III, c. 19, p. 385. Italics mine.
[8] Ibid.

we see that there is social comment here, but that it is Elizabeth's. Her view of society is not egalitarian in a modern sense; only gentlemen are equal – and well-bred men and women. True elegance is a matter of attitude and outlook and inner conviction. The aristocrat can be vulgar, the rich land-owner can behave in ungentlemanly fashion.

The book takes its title from Darcy's pride and Elizabeth's prejudice; and so far we have dwelt on aspects of their relationship alone – and on some of the deeper, more sombre colours of the book. But Jane herself claimed to think 'the work . . . rather too light and bright and sparkling' – though she revelled in it too[9] – and it is also the wittiest of her novels.

'It is a truth universally acknowledged, that a single man in possession of a good fortune, must be in want of a wife.'[10] Little as Mrs Bennet knew of the philosophies of the Enlightenment, the sentiment expresses her philosophy – and the lighter side of the book. It is about three or four mar-riages, not one. Mr Bingley has just come to settle near the Bennet's home, and he soon meets and falls in love with Jane Bennet. But Bingley is deeply dependent on the counsel of Darcy, his closest friend, who has seen him often in love before; and after a very promising start to the romance, Darcy and Bingley's two sisters carry him off to London and safety. The sisters, though fond of Jane, are mercilessly portrayed as heartless snobs – and yet we are left in no doubt that their father made his fortune in the north of England by trade. One of them is married, but the other, Caroline, has set her cap at Darcy – and grows jealous of Elizabeth and more hostile to the Bennets as the plot develops; till in the end she is compelled to pretend affection for Jane as her sister-in-law, and pay 'off every arrear of civility to Elizabeth' so as to be able still to visit Pemberley.[11]

Meanwhile the Bennet's cousin, the Reverend Mr Collins, has come to stay: a pompous, obsequious clergyman of grandiloquent verbosity – who physics Mr Bennet's humour delightfully, if taken in very small doses. He is the heir of the property, and comes to apologise that one day he will have to turn them all out – and to propose marriage to one of them to make amends. Jane is the eldest and most beautiful, and he plans to propose to her; but at a hint from Mrs Bennet that Jane has prospects already, he rapidly changes from Jane to Elizabeth – 'and it was soon done – done while Mrs Bennet was stirring the fire' – and proposes to her.[12] When Elizabeth, who has seen enough of him to know how absurd he is, rejects him, Mrs Bennet rushes to her husband, demanding that he insist that Elizabeth change her mind.

'I understand that Mr Collins has made you an offer of marriage. Is

---

[9] *Letters* L, no. 80, p. 203; C, no. 77, p. 299.
[10] *PP* I, c. 1, p. 3.
[11] *PP* III, c. 19, p. 387; for the origin of Mr Bingley's fortune, see *PP* I, c. 4, p. 15.
[12] *PP* I, c. 15, p. 71.

it true?' [says Mr Bennet.] Elizabeth replied that it was. 'Very well – and this offer of marriage you have refused?'

'I have, sir.'

'Very well. We now come to the point. Your mother insists upon your accepting it. Is not it so, Mrs Bennet?'

'Yes, or I will never see her again.'

'An unhappy alternative is before you, Elizabeth. From this day you must be a stranger to one of your parents. – Your mother will never see you again if you do *not* marry Mr Collins, and I will never see you again if you *do*.'

– a denouement characteristic of Mr Bennet's humour, and of his treatment of his wife.[13]

But Mr Collins has been instructed by his patroness, who is no less than Lady Catherine de Bourgh, that he should marry; and marry he does. He finds Elizabeth's close friend and neighbour, Charlotte Lucas, more amenable, for Charlotte is 27 and seeks a home: her philosophy of marriage is very different from Elizabeth's.[14] So to Hunsford Rectory she departs, the wife of Mr Collins.

Much of the plot turns on the means by which Elizabeth and Mr Darcy become, first more, and then better, acquainted with one another. He had seen enough of her in her homeland to be greatly attracted. He next meets her at Hunsford, proposes and is rejected; then at Pemberley – where a new dawn breaks for them both; finally at her home, where he proposes again and successfully.

Elizabeth is induced by Mrs Collins to pay her a visit: we are shown how a sensible woman can make a reasonably comfortable home for herself in spite of having Mr Collins for husband. We are shown how one kind of clergyman behaves – especially in obsequious flattery of his patroness; we are taken to Lady Catherine's palace of Rosings, whose furnishings match her wealth and vulgar taste. Elizabeth meanwhile has been told by George Wickham – and naïvely believes him – that he has been scandalously ill-treated by Darcy. While at Hunsford, Darcy's cousin, the agreeable Colonel Fitzwilliam, inadvertently reveals to Elizabeth that Darcy has boasted to him of separating Bingley from Jane – he has not been told the names, but the circumstances of the case leave no doubt in Elizabeth's mind to whom Darcy had referred. As she nurses her wrath in the wake of this latest shock, Mr Darcy calls at the parsonage and proposes to her – and is sent on his way angry but chastened.

Next morning she meets him on the edge of the park and he gives her a long letter in which he explains his treatment of Bingley and Jane – he was

[13] *PP* I, c. 20, pp. 111–12.
[14] See pp. 174–5. For Charlotte's age, see *PP* I, c. 22, p. 123.

genuinely convinced that Jane's feelings were cooler than Elizabeth knew them to be, and tried to save Bingley from what he imagined a passing infatuation. But he also explains his relations with Wickham – who not only received much help from him and vilified him entirely without foundation, but had also tried to seduce his young sister Georgiana. The letter is a very powerful revelation of Darcy's mind, and the fulcrum on which the story turns. It is very hard to believe that even in this extremity Darcy would have given his sister away – though he clearly suspected that Elizabeth might be in love with Wickham, and needed urgent warning; and it is hard to imagine how he could have hoped to convince her with less cogent evidence. In any case, the story naturally startles Elizabeth into a slow but steady realisation that he must be telling the truth.

After Hunsford, Elizabeth's next outing is a holiday with her uncle and aunt from the City, Mr and Mrs Gardiner. To her immense delight, the original plan had been a visit to the Lakes – but Mr Gardiner's business engagements abbreviate the tour, and Elizabeth sadly discovers that they can go no further than Derbyshire. Between Bakewell and the imaginary small town of Lambton – where Mrs Gardiner had once lived – lies Pemberley;[15] and with much hesitation – after ascertaining that Mr Darcy himself is not there – Elizabeth agrees to pay a visit to Pemberley. They are shown round the house by the elderly housekeeper, Mrs Reynolds, who tells them that Mr Darcy is a model master and landlord – greatly to the surprise of all three visitors. They then take a turn in the park under the gardener's guidance – but as they leave the house Darcy himself appears. At first both he and Elizabeth are too much surprised and embarrassed for more than a brief encounter; but as their walk progresses, he joins them again and asks to be introduced to the Gardiners – and though not at ease he is at his most courteous. He has come back early, ahead of a party which will include his sister and Bingley; and he asks to be allowed to bring Georgiana to meet her. The very next day – when Georgiana has had hardly a moment to recover from her journey – they come to call, and this visit and his manner reveal to the Gardiners – what had been as far as possible from their thoughts before – that he is in love with Elizabeth. Georgiana, aged 16 and almost too shy to show how pleased she is to meet Elizabeth, none the less (under her brother's instruction) invites them all to dinner at Pemberley. But before they can come, news of a catastrophe reaches them: Lydia and Wickham have eloped. As Elizabeth reads the letters from Jane which give this terrible news, Darcy calls alone – it is never explained (or perhaps it is carefully not explained) what he came for –

---

[15] Clearly Jane Austen conceived Pemberley as near Bakewell, and it has often been supposed that Chatsworth was the model for Pemberley. She had no first-hand knowledge of Chatsworth (so far as we know), and it seems likely that it provided only the approximate site. On the fashion for visiting the Lakes, see Moir 1964, c. 11.

and learns what has happened. Jane had sent two letters, the first ill-directed and so delayed; if it had not been delayed, Elizabeth would not have gone to Pemberley at all.

The visit to Pemberley reveals to Elizabeth – what she had hardly imagined possible before – that Darcy has conquered her. When she later said to Jane of her love for him 'I believe I must date it from my first seeing his beautiful grounds at Pemberley', she spoke in jest – but she spoke the truth.[16] The park, indeed, has symbolic value: it seems to reflect a natural habitat. The wooded slopes of the park, the housekeeper's testimony, his own polite reception of them – the warmth of his attentions: all this began to change her view of him – and as she tells him of Lydia's fate, which he will understand as no one else could, she instantly believes that it must be a barrier between them – and that fear opens her eyes to her feeling for him.

Darcy's reaction is very different. Having gathered from Elizabeth that the couple are thought to be in hiding in London, he makes haste to search for them – in order to do everything he can to see them safely married, Wickham freed from his debts and set on a possible career. In all this he succeeds, and then calls on the Gardiners to explain what he has done – and insist that no word passes to the Bennets that it is his doing. Mr Bennet, after some days of fruitless search, has meanwhile returned to his sorrowing family. They soon learn that Lydia and Wickham are to be married and Mrs Bennet looks happily round for a home for them.

> 'Mrs Bennet, before you take any, or all of these houses, for your son and daughter, let us come to a right understanding. Into *one* house in this neighbourhood, they shall never have admittance. I will not encourage the imprudence of either, by receiving them at Longbourn.'

– And he went on to make clear that he 'would not advance a guinea' for Lydia to buy wedding clothes – even though Mrs Bennet 'could hardly comprehend' how 'his anger could be carried to such a point of inconceivable resentment, as to refuse his daughter a privilege, without which her marriage would scarcely seem valid'.[17]

But Jane and Elizabeth argue with him, and he relents – not on the clothes but the visit – and is subsequently encouraged by receiving a rebuke from Mr Collins on that account. In the course of her giddy, tumultuous chatter, Lydia reveals to Elizabeth that Darcy had been present at her wedding. Elizabeth cannot rest till she understands how this improbable, impossible circumstance can be explained, and writes in haste to her aunt. The Gardiners are by now clearly apprised of Darcy's devotion to Elizabeth – though he has never confessed it to them; and so Mr Gardiner had accepted, however reluctantly, an arrangement which gave him all the

---

[16] See p. 76.
[17] *PP* III, c. 8, p. 310.

credit which was really due to Darcy. Darcy has blamed himself for what had occurred: he had failed to apprise the world of Wickham's character. 'He called it, therefore, his duty to step forward, and endeavour to remedy an evil, which had been brought on by himself.' – Thus Mrs Gardiner.

> If he *had another* motive, I am sure it would never disgrace him. . . . Our visitor was very obstinate. I fancy, Lizzy, that obstinacy is the real defect of his character after all. He has been accused of many faults at different times; but *this* is the true one. Nothing was to be done that he did not do himself . . .

After the wedding, Mr Darcy

> dined with us the next day . . . Will you be very angry with me, my dear Lizzy, if I take this opportunity of saying (what I was never bold enough to say before) how much I like him. His behaviour to us has, in every respect, been as pleasing as when we were in Derbyshire. His understanding and opinions all please me; he wants nothing but a little more liveliness, and *that*, if he marry *prudently*, his wife may teach him. I thought him very sly; – he hardly ever mentioned your name. But slyness seems the fashion. Pray forgive me, if I have been very presuming, or at least do not punish me so far, as to exclude me from P. I shall never be quite happy till I have been all round the park. A low phaeton, with a nice little pair of ponies, would be the very thing . . .[18]

The denouement is not far off: Lydia's marriage speeds her sisters' on their way, little as they would have relished the thought. Mr Darcy has compelled Wickham to become Elizabeth's brother-in-law – and so his own, if his hopes may be fulfilled; and this scenario completes the humbling of his pride. He encourages Bingley to return to Jane and they are quickly engaged; he still hesitates for himself, seeking reassurance that Elizabeth's feelings are truly different from those she had expressed that evening, not many months before, in Hunsford parsonage.

The *deus*, or *dea*, *ex machina* takes the improbable form of Lady Catherine

---

[18] *PP* III, c. 10, pp. 322–5. Lydia's wedding (so she tells us) took place at St Clement's church at 11 a.m. (*PP* p. 318). Since they breakfasted at 10 and had time for a carriage ride to the church after it, this cannot be St Clement Danes, well over a mile to the west through the most crowded part of the City: it must refer to St Clement Eastcheap (see Brooke and Keir 1975, pp. 123–5). Wickham lodged in the parish. The marriage evidently took place on the Monday after the banns had been called on three Sundays: they could not be married in the Gardiners' parish church since Lydia had only resided there a fortnight. (For the rules, see Cripps 1850, pp. 653–5; for the rule that marriage had to be celebrated between 8 a.m. and 12 noon, Cripps 1850, p. 676.) None the less, St Clement's is quite close to Gracechurch St., and it is curious to find that Wickham and Lydia had been in hiding not all that far from the Gardiners.

de Bourgh. Having failed in her attempt to secure Elizabeth's refusal to be Mrs Darcy, she calls on Darcy to disclose their conversation,

> dwelling emphatically on every expression of [Elizabeth], which, in her ladyship's apprehension, peculiarly denoted her perverseness and assurance, in the belief that such a relation must assist her endeavours to obtain that promise from her nephew, which *she* had refused to give. But, unluckily for her ladyship, its effect had been exactly contrariwise.
>
> 'It taught me to hope', said [Darcy to Elizabeth], 'as I had scarcely ever allowed myself to hope before. I knew enough of your disposition to be certain, that, had you been absolutely, irrevocably decided against me, you would have acknowledged it to Lady Catherine, frankly and openly.'
>
> Elizabeth coloured and laughed as she replied, 'Yes, you know enough of my *frankness* to believe me capable of *that*. After abusing you so abominably to your face, I could have no scruple in abusing you to all your relations.'[19]

Thus Lady Catherine's intervention brings them at last together — though before Darcy has begun to propose again, Elizabeth has set another powder trail in motion by revealing that she knows how much they owe him for Lydia's marriage. Not all the obstacles to happiness are yet removed, however. Elizabeth has not yet revealed, even to Jane, the change in her view of Mr Darcy; and she spends two uncomfortable evenings, convincing first Jane, then her father, that she loves him. She is not even sure how her mother will react, who has never ceased to refer to him as 'that disagreeable Mr Darcy'. When she tells her the news

> Its effect was most extraordinary; for on first hearing it, Mrs Bennet sat quite still, and unable to utter a syllable. Nor was it under many, many minutes, that she could comprehend what she heard; though not in general backward to credit what was for the advantage of her family, or that came in the shape of a lover to any of them. She began at length to recover, to fidget about in her chair, get up, sit down again, wonder, and bless herself.
>
> 'Good gracious! Lord bless me! only think! dear me! Mr Darcy! Who would have thought it! And is it really true? Oh my sweetest Lizzy! how rich and how great you will be! What pin-money, what jewels, what carriages you will have! Jane's is nothing to it — nothing at all. I am so pleased — so happy. Such a charming man! — so handsome! so tall! — Oh, my dear Lizzy! pray apologise for my having disliked him so much before. I hope he will overlook it. Dear, dear

---

[19] *PP* III, c. 16, p. 367.

Lizzy. A house in town! Everything that is charming! Three daughters married! Ten thousand a year! Oh, Lord! What will become of me, I shall go distracted.'[20]

Thus Elizabeth is able at last to answer her aunt's letter.

I would have thanked you before, my dear aunt, as I ought to have done, for your long, kind, satisfactory detail of particulars; but, to say the truth, I was too cross to write. You supposed more than really existed. But *now* suppose as much as you chuse; give a loose to your fancy, indulge your imagination in every possible flight which the subject will afford, and unless you believe me actually married, you cannot greatly err. You must write again very soon, and praise him a great deal more than you did in your last. I thank you, again and again, for not going to the Lakes. How could I be so silly as to wish it! Your idea of the ponies is delightful. We will go round the Park every day. I am the happiest creature in the world. Perhaps other people have said so before, but not one with such justice. I am happier even than Jane; she only smiles, I laugh. Mr Darcy sends you all the love in the world, that he can spare from me. You are all to come to Pemberley at Christmas.[21]

[20] *PP* III, c. 17, pp. 374, 378.
[21] *PP* III, c. 18, pp. 382–3.

10

Mansfield Park

The Poor Relation

The heroine of *Mansfield Park*, Fanny Price, is a poor relation. She has been rescued from a down-at-heel home in Portsmouth at the age of ten and brought up by her uncle, Sir Thomas Bertram, and her aunts Lady Bertram and Mrs Norris, in the great house, Mansfield Park, among her cousins, two boys and two girls. She is subjected by most of them to frequent reminders, usually inadvertent but sometimes deliberate, of her lowly status and dependence. She is by nature timid and sensitive, and feels some of the affronts most bitterly – but is indeed so modest that many of them she expects and takes for granted. And the conclusion? – After she has married the second son of Sir Thomas, who is ordained and becomes rector of Mansfield, 'the parsonage there . . . soon grew as dear to her heart, and as thoroughly perfect in her eyes, as everything else, within the view and patronage of Mansfield Park, had long been'.[1]

The portrait of Fanny is the most deeply sensitive presentation of a poor relation known to me; but it is also full of ironical touches, which rob Fanny of the attributes of moral perfection and heroism which have some-times been attributed to her. The one member of the family who never forgets her needs, and helps and instructs and forms her tastes and her mind, is her cousin Edmund, whom she eventually marries. She falls in love with him at the age of ten, and her devotion – though it matures and deepens – never fluctuates from that time on. She slowly realises that it is so; she knows (or thinks she knows) that it is wrong and that marriage with him is something which cannot be. Though cousins, they are far apart: she is dependent, he is a son, even if a younger son – and a son is a very different person from a poor niece; she must not think of him, but she constantly does. Indeed, it never occurs to Edmund until the very end of the novel, when he himself is trying to recover from an unhappy love, that he might marry Fanny: by then she is a sister to him; she has been eight years in love

---

[1] *MP* III, c. 17, p. 473.

with him before he begins to think of her as a wife. This underlines the ambivalence of her role: she is a poor relation, and so cannot marry into the inner family; she is Sir Thomas's niece, and so she can – in the end – aspire to a closer link.

Fanny's devotion to Edmund was the first of her loves at Mansfield: slowly, she becomes equally devoted to everything peaceful and secure in the house and gardens and park, and especially Lady Bertram. Aunt Bertram is one of Jane's supreme creations – a delectable vision of amiable indolence; everyone who has had to work hard in life should love Aunt Bertram, even if only with the love of hopeless envy. Thus she is a perfect foil to Fanny – who could hardly have found peace and contentment if she had worked for anyone less kind or more energetic. In return for her quiet, steady, unquestioning, unremitting help to Lady Bertram in arranging her cushions, getting her over all the little difficulties in her needlework and running all her errands, the aunt becomes as dependent on the niece as the niece is on the aunt.

The role of the poor relation is deeply shocking to a modern audience; Fanny seems little better than a slave. Yet there was a critical difference. Sir Thomas Bertram doubtless had slaves on his Antiguan estates; but Fanny in his eyes is first and foremost a niece – and in the end a daughter and more than a daughter. Even for someone so nervous as Fanny, there were compensations. Rather one should say that Fanny was especially rewarded, after many hardships, with a devotion to Mansfield Park and everything and almost everyone connected with it – all the greater because she was not born to it, and so did not take it for granted.

The exception was Mrs Norris, her other aunt, widow of a former incumbent of Mansfield, the most relentless of Jane Austen's unpleasant characters. 'Not even Fanny had tears for Aunt Norris – not even when she was gone for ever' at the end of the book.[2] Yet it was Aunt Norris who had first suggested Fanny's adoption into the family at Mansfield; but that was the end of her kindness. At a moment, when the family thought Sir Thomas was far away, they amused themselves in acting a play; and Fanny – who very strongly disapproved of the play, of private theatricals altogether indeed – while candidly enjoying such good acting as she witnessed – refused to join in. Presently her cousin Tom, the eldest son and heir of Sir Thomas, urged on her that she was needed for one small part. All except Edmund joined in pressing her, and

> Mrs Norris completed the whole, by thus addressing her in a whisper at once angry and audible: 'What a piece of work here is about nothing, – I am quite ashamed of you, Fanny, to make such a difficulty of obliging your cousins in a trifle of this sort, – so kind as they

[2] *MP* III, c. 17, p. 466.

are to you! – Take the part with a good grace, and let us hear no more of the matter, I entreat.'

Edmund intervenes on her behalf:

'Do not urge her, madam . . . Let her choose for herself, as well as the rest of us. Her judgment may be quite as safely trusted. Do not urge her any more.'

'I am not going to urge her,' replied Mrs Norris sharply; 'but I shall think her a very obstinate, ungrateful girl, if she does not do what her aunt and cousins wish her – very ungrateful indeed, considering who and what she is.'

Tormenting words, which bring a sharp reaction of better feeling from friends and relations about Fanny, and in the end rescue her from acting; but not before she has felt very deeply the humiliation of being charged with 'obstinacy and ingratitude . . . enforced with such a hint at the dependence of her situation'.[3] Later on, when Sir Thomas is back, Fanny is invited out to dinner at the parsonage, to the indignation of Aunt Norris.

'The nonsense and folly of people's stepping out of their rank and trying to appear above themselves, makes me think it right to give *you* a hint, Fanny, now that you are going into company without any of us; and I do beseech and intreat you not to be putting yourself forward, and talking and giving your opinion as if you were one of your cousins . . . *That* will never do, believe me. Remember, wherever you are you must be the lowest and last . . .'[4]

Words which serve to point the very striking contrast between the utter dependence of Fanny's position – and her deep love for everything and everyone about her, except Mrs Norris. The reader will recall that Mrs Norris herself was dependent for such status and income as she had on Sir Thomas's patronage of her husband and Lady Bertram's complacent acceptance of an energetic helper near at hand. No one but she talks so unkindly to Fanny; but they often say or do things unconsciously to remind her 'who and what she is'.

Now all this is very scandalous, and Jane doubtless means us to be shocked; but it is also very interesting, and very sensitively and shrewdly portrayed. It reflects a social world which will never perhaps entirely pass while dependent relatives, of any age, exist – though utterly remote from most folk's experience today. Yet I can recall tea at the house of a rich great-uncle when I was a small boy, when as a child I took my place in the servants' hall – and by chance with his grandson and eventual heir, a boy of about my age – and even to a small boy the difference with which we were

[3] *MP* I, c. 15, pp. 146–7; c. 16, p. 150.
[4] *MP* II, c. 5, p. 322.

treated was sufficiently apparent. My mother was a parson's daughter, and as a young woman enjoyed much kindness and hospitality from the same rich uncle, a wealthy barrister, landowner and politician – and a like hospitality from another, a surgeon and businessman, but a less congenial character – whose hospitality the young nephews and nieces also rejoiced in, little as they cared for the uncle. My mother greatly enjoyed the opportunities offered by having rich relations – without any illusions (in Edwardian days) of equality with her better-off relations. More to the point, Jane herself was a parson's daughter, whose knowledge of great houses came from her brother's adoption by a rich country gentleman – in whose house she felt happily at home, but whose family never ceased to regard her as coming from a lower world.[5]

Fanny Price's character, warm and affectionate, timid and nervous, came to be formed and developed, naturally enough, by her cousin Edmund – and so she was prepared to be an admirable parson's wife. But if we ask the question, was Fanny by nature good – or only so out of love for her cousin? – we shall receive no very clear answer. When Fanny and her brother William are together, we are invited to presuppose a background in which cheerful, good natured, warm-hearted brother and sister can grow up in close affection; though when we visit Portsmouth later in the book we wonder how. Jane never allows Fanny to present her principles in any positive way without some touch or hint or louder emphasis that love of Edmund is a powerful motive. There are moments when her priggishness almost makes one sympathise with Aunt Norris; it is a profound mistake to see in her Jane's ideal of young womanhood. But the portrait never ceases to be sympathetic.

The Play within the Play

As in *Hamlet*, the plot of *Mansfield Park* is set off against a cruder version of some of its themes, a play within the play. August von Kotzebue (1761–1819), a popular German playwright now justly forgotten, save by students of the German theatre and of Jane Austen, wrote many plays, of which *Das Kind der Liebe* – *The Child of Love* – was perhaps the most popular in England. The indelicacy of the theme and the title were slightly disguised in Mrs Inchbald's immensely popular translation, as *Lovers' Vows*.

One's appreciation of the nuances of those chapters in *Mansfield Park* in which the play is chosen and rehearsed can undoubtedly be enhanced by knowledge of the play. Yet it is not true, as has often been alleged, that they are 'not fully intelligible' without such knowledge.[6] With great cunning,

[5] See p. 154.
[6] Chapman in *MP*, p. 474.

and careful use of the technique of progressive revelation, enough of *Lovers' Vows* is revealed to show the links – though hardly enough, perhaps, to show what an inferior play it was – how richly it deserved to be banned by Sir Thomas.

Long before the epoch of the play, Baron Wildenhaim had seduced the young lady of inferior status whom his mother had delighted to bring up as a companion – thus Mrs Inchbald; in the original she was a chambermaid. The Baron returned to his regiment; Agatha, found to be pregnant, was turned away from the castle; and when the play opens many years later she is destitute and encounters her son Frederick, also now a soldier, but a poor one. The Baron meanwhile has married and lost his wife – but there is a daughter, Amelia, of the marriage, who has been instructed by a young pastor, Mr Anhalt, her tutor. The Baron, following the conventions of his kind, proposes to marry Amelia to Count Cassel – who turns out to be a minor Don Juan and a fop with lovers in every land. The Baron sends Anhalt to instruct Amelia in the nature and duties of marriage, and in particular on her duty to marry Count Cassel.[7] But Anhalt and Amelia are in love, and Amelia retorts by instructing Anhalt that she will only marry *him*. The Baron is horrified when she breaks this news to him; yet he is not wholly without good feeling, and has long striven to find Agatha and provide for her. When she appears – and Frederick, not knowing who the Baron is, tries to rob him to provide for his mother – the truth is quickly revealed; under Anhalt's firm direction, the Baron agrees to marry Agatha – Amelia and Anhalt are united – and the tragic tale of seduction and penury ends in a blaze of sentimental happiness.

The Plot of Mansfield Park

The central themes of *Lovers' Vows* are seduction and marriage; and both play a crucial role in *Mansfield Park*. *Lovers' Vows* affects the actors, and enables Jane Austen to sail close to the wind with impunity: Kotzebue, not Jane, was its author. But the balance – and the role – are profoundly different. We shall see on another page how central to the book are the discussions of the nature of marriage and how one should enter it.[8] In the denouement, Edmund, the parson, who took the part of Anhalt in the play, marries his lady love – but not the same lady who had played Amelia. For Mary Crawford, with whom Edmund was in love – and who fittingly took the role of Amelia – is estranged from him at the end of the book. Her brother, Henry Crawford, has seduced Edmund's sister Maria. Count Cassel in the play is a fop and a nitwit, and is played by Mr Rushworth,

[7] See p. 91.
[8] See pp. 178–83.

similarly rich and equally nitwitted – he is the victim of one of Jane Austen's most cruel portraits of an idiot male, 'an inferior young man'.[9] Maria in the part of Agatha has very touching scenes with her son Frederick, Henry Crawford, with whom she is in love – though the love is not returned and she is engaged to Rushworth. Thus a delicate net is spread over the characters of the play and the book, entangling them.

Sir Thomas and Lady Bertram have four children, Tom, the heir – idle and expensive, soon running deep into debt – Edmund, who is to be a clergyman, Maria and Julia; to these they add Fanny, their niece, adopted into the family at the age of ten. Before Mr Norris died, Tom's extravagance had made 'necessary' the sale of the next vacancy at Mansfield – hitherto intended for Edmund – to Dr Grant, a flagrant act of simony of which Sir Thomas is ashamed – but essentially because it robbed Edmund to pay Tom.[10] Soon after their arrival, Dr and Mrs Grant were visited by her half-brother and half-sister, Mary and Henry Crawford. Hitherto they had lived with their uncle Admiral Crawford, a sailor not noted (in spite of Jane's closing words on the navy in *Persuasion*) for his domestic virtues: when his wife died, he brought his mistress to live with him, and even Mary Crawford reckoned she had to find another home. The Crawfords indeed bring a breath of the laxer air of London to the stricter climate of Mansfield. Sir Thomas, though never doubting the Mansfield living was his property, and mercenary in its disposition when need arises, is extremely strict in all matters of sexual propriety and convention; and Dr Grant, though first and foremost an indolent *bon viveur*, can preach an effective sermon, and his curate can reduce Lady Bertram to tears.[11] Henry Crawford enjoys flirting with both the Bertram girls, and Maria in particular is soon in love with him. When Sir Thomas is called away to Antigua to restore the ailing fortunes of his estates there, the Bertrams and the Crawfords meet often, and in particular meet and mingle in two of the great set pieces of the book. First of all at Sotherton, the seat of Mr Rushworth, to whom Maria has become engaged – the first suitor who appears with a larger income than her father's; and Mr Rushworth, though innocent of any ideas of his own, has been enthused by a friend who has hired Mr Repton[12] with a zeal to improve. Mr Crawford had already made all the improvements possible on his own, lesser estate, in his early twenties; and so it is decided that almost the whole family – including Fanny, in spite of a routine attempt by Mrs Norris to prevent her going – shall visit the Rushworth seat at

[9] *MP* II, c. 3, p. 200.

[10] *MP* I, c. 3, pp. 23–4: see p. 148.

[11] *MP* I, c. 11, p. 111; cf. *MP* III, c. 16, p. 453: by the date of the 'affecting sermon' Dr Grant was in Bath, so it was presumably the work of his curate.

[12] *MP* I, cc. 6, 9–10. Jane Austen characteristically confuses us by introducing a real person, Humphrey Repton, the most celebrated 'improver' of the day.

Sotherton and advise Mr Rushworth how to improve his park. They are shown round the grand Elizabethan house, including the disused chapel,[13] by Mr Rushworth's prosing mother; and then they wander aimlessly in the grounds – in a scene of confusion a little reminiscent of the antics of the lovers in the forest in *A Midsummer Night's Dream*. The day of pleasure brings only dissatisfaction and jealousy: jealousy to Rushworth of Henry Crawford; jealousy between Maria and Julia, both in a fair way to falling in love with Crawford; jealousy to Miss Crawford, who is much attracted to Edmund, of the profession he is to enter – she first learns in the chapel that he is to be ordained; jealousy to Fanny of Miss Crawford.

Their next major entertainment is the theatre. The Hon. Mr Yates arrives from the ruins of a performance of *Lovers' Vows* in a country house in the south west – cancelled at the last moment owing to bereavement in the family there. The Bertrams, led by Tom, are fired with a zeal to act; and after long deliberation they set out, with Mr Yates' enthusiastic help, and warm support from the Crawfords – and even Aunt Norris – to perform *Lovers' Vows* themselves. Like the visit to Sotherton, the rehearsals bring many trials in their train. The first act reveals Frederick and Agatha hand in hand – son and mother, yet as acted by Henry Crawford and Maria – his chosen Agatha – a kind of love scene. His choice of Maria seals the fate of both sisters: here the play within the play is seen at its most powerful. Julia, deeply jealous, determines to rid herself of her feeling for Crawford, and begins to allow the attentions of Mr Yates – whom she will ultimately marry. Maria is henceforward deeply in love with Crawford: his choice of her as a theatrical partner leads to her undoing in the end.

Edmund and Fanny, meanwhile, refuse to act. They know that Sir Thomas disapproves of theatricals, and would especially disapprove of his daughter, an engaged woman, acting on the stage with another man; and they reckon it especially disrespectful when he is in the midst of a hazardous crossing of the Atlantic. But there is a second pair to be chosen – of real lovers; and when Miss Crawford accepts the part of Amelia – and resents Tom's threat to find an Anhalt from outside their circle – Edmund, out of consideration for Miss Crawford (in various senses of the word), accepts the part. Fanny is torn between horror at Edmund's inconsistency, envy of Mary Crawford, terror at what Sir Thomas will think – and embarrassment when Edmund and Mary both consult her. She is also, in spite of herself, attracted by the better acting. But before the rehearsals can proceed much further, they are halted by drama of another kind. Sir Thomas returns from Antigua – earlier than has been expected and hoped – and the whole scheme is rapidly dismantled.

But not the feelings it has roused: when Henry Crawford also leaves Mansfield, and Maria has to face the sorry truth that her love is not

[13] See pp. 145–6. For Sotherton, see Pevsner 1968, p. 407.

returned, she determines to seek the only path to freedom she can see from the tediousness of life at Mansfield Park, under its dull and dignified master. She assures Sir Thomas that she really wishes to marry Mr Rushworth, and married they are. The Rushworths set off on their honeymoon with Julia in their train, for a life of pleasure in Brighton – 'every public place was new to Maria, and Brighton is almost as gay in winter as in summer', as Jane observes with characteristic *double-entendre*[14] – and subsequently in London, where such marriages were very much the norm.

Thus Fanny is left the sole young woman in the family circle in Mansfield Park, to enjoy enhanced attention from all about her, and a growing intimacy with Miss Crawford, towards whom her feelings are increasingly ambivalent. When Henry Crawford comes again he finds Fanny the only woman to flirt with; but his attentions are more coldly received than he has ever experienced before – and he decides on a more serious attack. This has little positive effect on Fanny – none on her judgment of him, none on her feeling for him, since her heart is wholly Edmund's, but a little in her enjoyment of his more sensitive and cultivated behaviour towards her. But in the process Crawford himself falls in love, and determines to make her his wife.

The happiest days of Fanny's early life came in the rare visits of her brother William, who shares her heart with Edmund. William, after seven years as a midshipman, spends a happy fortnight at the Park, admiring and admired – especially by Crawford, who almost wishes he had been a sailor and enjoyed the heroic exploits William describes. If Jane's sailor brothers looked sourly at the portrait of Admiral Crawford, they were well rewarded in William Price; and he in his turn came to be much beholden to the Admiral. For after a fortnight of talking to Fanny and hunting with Crawford, culminating in a ball at the Park arranged in Fanny's honour by Sir Thomas, who has observed Crawford's attentions to his niece with pleasure and approval, William is taken by Crawford to meet the Admiral. The outcome is that the Admiral, on Henry's insistence, procures at last William Price's promotion to Lieutenant. William is made – and by Henry's endeavours.

Armed with this news Henry Crawford comes to the Park to tell Fanny the good news – and to propose to her. To everyone's stupefaction she refuses him. She does not like him well enough; she cannot love him. Well and good, says Crawford – give me time. Sir Thomas is not so patient, indeed is flabbergasted by her refusal of so desirable an establishment – beyond what he could himself have ever hoped to procure for her. We are given a very piquant vision of differing viewpoints on entry to marriage, rendered the more telling because Fanny cannot possibly reveal her true motives – she cannot tell Sir Thomas how Crawford behaved with Maria

[14] *MP* II, c. 3, p. 203.

and Julia; still less can she admit that she is in love with Edmund. On this point she tells her uncle, in effect, a moderately innocent lie – she forms a 'no' with her lips, but says nothing.[15]

Everyone was against her. Even Lady Bertram, who often declared she could not manage without Fanny, was inspired by the one idea which had made her own life prosperous – that a handsome woman of little fortune might attract a rich suitor – 'her uncle, the lawyer, himself,' we are told at the outset of the book, 'allowed her to be at least three thousand pounds short of any equitable claim to' marriage with Sir Thomas. So Lady Bertram thought that she

> 'could do very well without you, if you were married to a man of such good estate as Mr Crawford . . .' Lady Bertram was quite talkative. 'I will tell you what, Fanny . . . I am sure he fell in love with you at the ball, I am sure the mischief was done that evening. You did look remarkably well . . . And you know you had Chapman [Lady Bertram's maid] to help you dress. I am very glad I sent Chapman to you [though she had arrived after Fanny's preparations were complete]. I shall tell Sir Thomas that I am sure it was done that evening.' – And still pursuing the same cheerful thoughts, she soon afterwards added, – 'And I will tell you what, Fanny – which is more than I did for Maria – the next time pug has a litter you shall have a puppy.'[16]

A concession showing the exceptional warmth of her feeling on the occasion, but very confusing to Jane Austen scholars, who have supposed on other grounds that pug was male. We may conclude, if we like, that Jane was more interested in portraying Lady Bertram than in pet dogs – in marked contrast to Van Dyck, who commonly put much more character into his dogs than into their owners.

Even Edmund – though deeply sympathetic to Fanny – hopes she will accept Crawford in the end, for this would help to bring closer to him the two women he loves most in the world, Mary Crawford and Fanny herself. To speed the process, Sir Thomas proposes that Fanny revisits her old home in Portsmouth, to take the measure of the difference between the Price home and what Crawford might offer. Fanny is delighted at the prospect, especially as it will enable her to see William in his Lieutenant's uniform. But the visit is full of disappointment. Her mother gives her a momentary welcome, but soon shows how little she really cares for her – not by any positive unkindness, but by her preoccupation with household cares and children she loves more. Her father, a one-time Lieutenant of Marines, has become a coarse-spoken idler. She quickly learns to long for Mansfield; and even (in some measure) to welcome a visit from Mr

---

[15] *MP* III, c. 1, p. 316.
[16] *MP* III, c. 2, p. 333; for the lawyer's opinion, I, c. 1, p. 3.

Crawford as a diversion from the distressing dullness of life in Portsmouth. That apart, she finds some compensation in helping her sister Susan to learn her taste in books, and her standards in life: timidly, diffidently, Fanny becomes a teacher, and even a subscriber to a circulating library. Meanwhile, there is no news of any plan to fetch her back to Mansfield: Aunt Bertram talks of Fanny almost every hour – but Sir Thomas plans to fetch her himself, after Easter.[17] Thus Edmund, in a letter outlining his hopes and fears in his pursuit of Miss Crawford, still unreconciled to being a parson's wife – but still attracted to him.

Before Easter came news that Tom was seriously ill, and all in confusion at Mansfield as a result. Then 'Easter came – particularly late this year' – to the convenience of Miss Austen in dragging out Fanny's visit, but to the distress of some of her critics, who have difficulty in finding a plausible year in which it happened so.[18] Easter was followed, not by Sir Thomas, but by two letters from Miss Crawford – the first making it all too abundantly clear that she hoped Tom would die and Edmund become the heir; the second, written in haste, hinting at scandal. Fanny was deeply alarmed, yet also baffled, for it gave no precise indication of what had happened; but enlightenment came from a newspaper her father was reading. 'It was with infinite concern the newspaper had to announce to the world, a matrimonial *fracas* in the family of Mr R. of Wimpole St.' – although only initials were given, the street and the details, and Miss Crawford's letter, made it all too clear to Fanny that Maria Rushworth and Henry Crawford had eloped. She was filled with all manner of alarm.[19]

But soon after there came a letter from Edmund, couched in terms of deepest gloom, adding news of Julia's elopement with Yates, but announcing that he himself was coming next day to take Fanny back to Mansfield. Jane makes no bones about Fanny's reaction. 'She was, she felt she was, in the greatest danger of being exquisitely happy, when so many were miserable. The evil which brought such good to her!'[20] – she could go home without any further delay; and she could guess that Edmund was delivered for ever from his infatuation with Miss Crawford. It is one of the most exquisite moments in the novel, and Fanny is not spared. But she has to endure Edmund in his grimmest mood before they reach the park – where 'her eye fell everywhere on lawns and plantations of the freshest green' – we have been delayed till spring is at its height for a purpose –

> and the trees, though not fully clothed, were in that delightful state, when farther beauty is known to be at hand, and when, while much is

---

[17] *MP* III, c. 13, p. 423, in a letter from Edmund to Fanny.
[18] *MP* III, c. 14 ('xvi' for 'xiv' in 1st and 2nd editions), p. 430; cf. Chapman's note, p. 554; and see p. 52.
[19] *MP* III, c. 15, p. 440.
[20] *MP* III, c. 15, p. 443.

actually given to the sight, more yet remains for the imagination. Her enjoyment, however, was for herself alone. Edmund could not share it. She looked at him, but he was leaning back, sunk in a deeper gloom than ever, and with eyes closed as if the view of cheerfulness oppressed him, and the lovely scenes of home must be shut out.

It made her melancholy again; and the knowledge of what must be enduring there, invested even the house, modern, airy, and well situated as it was, with a melancholy aspect.

By one of the suffering party within, they were expected with such impatience as she had never known before. Fanny had scarcely passed the solemn-looking servants, when Lady Bertram came from the drawing room to meet her; came with no indolent step; and, falling on her neck, said, 'Dear Fanny! now I shall be comfortable.'[21]

As in the denouement of *Emma*, the beauty refreshed of gardens, lawns and trees prepares us for a happier dawn. But there has first to be a day of judgment. Henry Crawford had encountered Maria Rushworth and found her cold and aloof: in a moment of folly he determined to break down her coolness – only to find that he was trapped by her genuine affection for him; flirtation led to entanglement – and in the end he found himself compelled to elope with her, regretting Fanny as he went. As in *Sense and Sensibility*, the catastrophe in *Mansfield Park* is dramatic and unexpected; and so is Maria's punishment. Henry indeed loses Fanny and his best hopes of lasting happiness; but that – for him – is all. Maria is exiled to a distant home, where Mrs Norris – whose devotion to dear Mrs Rushworth seems if possible enhanced by her fall – volunteers to live with her. Sir Thomas's standards are extremely strict: on no account would he receive Maria back to Mansfield, or give any countenance to vice; he would support her in every comfort, but afar. These were his views, not Jane's: we need not suppose her lax in her attitudes, nor need we suppose her to condone such harsh treatment of a daughter.[22] The establishment of Maria and Aunt Norris was 'remote and private . . .: shut up together with little society, on one side no affection, on the other, no judgment, it may be reasonably supposed that their tempers became their mutual punishment'.[23] But for the rest, things were a little better. Sir Thomas is rid of Mrs Norris – 'to be relieved from her . . . was so great a felicity, that had she not left bitter remembrances behind her, there might have been danger of his learning

---

[21] *MP* III, c. 15, pp. 446–7.

[22] *MP* III, c. 17, pp. 461–5. For the moral judgment, see pp. 23–4, 193. Cf. the throwaway line in *PP* III c. 8, p. 309, after Lydia Bennet's marriage: 'To be sure it would have been more for the advantage of conversation, had Miss Lydia Bennet come upon the town; or, as the happiest alternative, been secluded from the world, in some distant farm house' – but at least, though married, she must be miserable with such a worthless husband.

[23] *MP* III, c. 17, p. 465.

almost to approve the evil which produced such a good' – and the reader is left almost feeling sorry for Mrs Norris, after such treatment from her creator.[24] Julia and Yates are, after all, married, and Yates proves to have a little more sense and a good deal more substance than had been feared; above all, he looks up to Sir Thomas, and seeks guidance and forgiveness from him. Tom recovers and is reformed – even more shocked by the effect of his theatre on Maria than by his illness.

But what of Edmund? He falls victim to some of Jane Austen's sharpest and most affectionate irony.

> I purposely abstain from dates on this occasion, that everyone may be at liberty to fix their own, aware that the cure of unconquerable passions, and the transfer of unchanging attachments, must vary much as to time in different people. – I only intreat every body to believe that exactly at the time when it was quite natural that it should be so, and not a week earlier, Edmund did cease to care about Miss Crawford, and became as anxious to marry Fanny, as Fanny herself could desire.[25]

And so they marry and settle in Thornton Lacey, the inferior – but very presentable – living, with which Edmund has to be content for the present. But this will not do for long. Dr Grant has already departed to a prebend at Westminster – leaving Mansfield, presumably, to a curate – at a time when it was highly desirable that no relations of the Crawfords should be in the neighbourhood of Mansfield Park; and Miss Austen presently carries him off with an apoplexy – after 'three great institutionary dinners in one week';[26] Mrs Grant and her sister continue to live together elsewhere – and the parsonage at Mansfield can be Edmund's at last. The death of Dr Grant occurred 'just after they had been married long enough to begin to want an increase of income, and feel their distance from the paternal abode an inconvenience'.[27] At the end of *Framley Parsonage*, Trollope evidently wished to drop a delicate hint that there were children of the marriage of Lucy Robarts and Lord Lufton – and he accomplished this by telling us where the nursery was. Jane almost never carries her heroine so far; but *Mansfield Park* ends with just such a hint – and a clear statement of how Fanny came to have the same devotion to Mansfield Parsonage as she had long had for Mansfield Park.[28]

---

[24] *MP* III, c. 17, p. 466.
[25] *MP* III, c. 17, p. 470.
[26] *MP* III, c. 17, p. 469.
[27] *MP* III, c. 17, p. 473. Marianne's 'family' at the end of *SS*, does not necessarily imply children: see p. 71 n.14.
[28] See p. 11.

11

Emma

The Two Levels

It is sometimes said that Emma was a vain, self-willed, selfish young woman who fell in love and so was converted and purged of her faults. But this is not the story that Jane Austen told. It is indeed true that when Emma grows aware of her love for Mr Knightley, she struggles much harder to be worthy of him. But she has been learning – and resisting – his lessons all her life, and he claims to have been in love with her since she was thirteen.[1] These are not random ideas, nor the fantasies of lovers. Mr Knightley never ceases to say – even at the height of his infatuation with her – that she was a spoilt child. But she has learned, not always consciously, not always painlessly, the lessons he has to teach. Emma is self-willed and self-deluding, at times an insufferable snob – 'a heroine whom no one but myself will much like', as Jane herself is reputed to have said.[2] On a first reading it is hard to like her; and to a young reader Mr Knightley, 'a sensible man about seven or eight-and-thirty', seems much too old to be a hero – and so he would have seemed to Marianne Dashwood.[3] Nor is Mr Knightley the paragon he has sometimes been supposed; he would be very much less interesting if it were so. He is an open-minded, open-hearted country squire, wonderfully free from snobbery and cant; candid to a fault. He tells Emma's devoted and beloved ex-governess, Mrs Weston, to her face how ill she performed her task. The offence is only a little mitigated by his telling her in the same breath that her failings as a governess make her all the better suited to be a wife.[4] Knightley is also quickly drawn to jealousy: the young Frank Churchill, even as a rumour, arouses his envy – and when Frank arrives in Highbury, Mr Knightley is exceedingly jealous of him. For this the reader forgives him in the end, for it is due to his deep, long-seated devotion to Emma. It is a strange love affair in many ways,

---

[1] *E* III, c. 17, p. 462.
[2] *Memoir* (1870), p. 204; (1871), p. 148 – said by the author to be Emma, though Jane Austen might also have said it about Fanny Price.
[3] *E* I, c. 1, p. 9.
[4] *E* I, c. 5, p. 38.

for he is almost a father to her: when she was thirteen he was already about thirty.[5] But that is a part of its point: from the start Emma and he share many basic qualities which prepare them both for the denouement – and justify (if it can be justified) the tamest of Jane's endings. 'But, in spite of these deficiencies [the absence of finery and show], the wishes, the hopes, the confidence, the predictions of the small band of true friends who witnessed the ceremony, were fully answered in the perfect happiness of the union.'[6] None the less, Emma – however unwittingly – has her revenge on his endless criticisms of her, for none of her failings save him from falling hopelessly in love.

Emma is in two respects the perfect expression of Jane Austen's art. It is written on a 'little bit (two inches wide) of ivory on which I work with so fine a brush'[7] – all the action, all the characters, meet in a small town and its surrounding villages and hamlets; the furthest they normally travel is to London – only 16 miles away;[8] and Emma has never been to the sea till she goes there, briefly, for her honeymoon. Even more striking is the contrast of the two levels at which the plot moves.

In some sense all Jane Austen's novels proceed at two levels: at a superficial level of shallow sentiment or self-deception – and a deeper level at which real convictions and deepest feelings are revealed. In *Emma* the contrast of the two levels enters into every corner of the structure of the novel. Emma lives a part of her life in a world of fantasy – she is romantic, 'imaginist' to use the word Emma herself coined:[9] she befriends the beautiful young illegitimate Harriet Smith and imagines a gentlemanly origin for her and a series of lovers – doing great harm, which is happily superficial, in the process; she toys with a romance between herself and Frank Churchill, pretending to fall in and out of love with him. But in the end it is revealed that Harriet is still really in love with the young farmer Robert Martin; that Frank Churchill has been engaged to Jane Fairfax for months; that Emma herself and Mr Knightley have the deepest bonds of affection, and that she has always acknowledged his superiority to Frank and everyone else. The progressive revelation of their common qualities and of their love for one

---

[5] See p. 14n. At the opening of the book, Emma has 'lived nearly twenty-one years'; Mr Knightley is 37 or 38 (*E* I, c. 1, pp. 1, 9).

[6] *E* III, c. 19, p. 484.

[7] 'as produces little effect after much labour' – in jest to her nephew, Edward: *Letters* L, no. 146, p. 323; C, no. 134, p. 469, 16 December 1816, about a year after the publication of *Emma*, when *Persuasion* was in the making.

[8] *E* III, c. 13, p. 424. For various conjectures on the site of Highbury, see *Life*, pp. 302–3 and 303 n. 1. Leatherhead seems the most likely – and it had a house near it called Randalls and a notable eighteenth-century worthy called Mr Knightley; but Cobham, Esher and Dorking have had their supporters. Very likely, as with Lambton (see p. 80), she deliberately planted an imaginary town in a real landscape.

[9] *E* III, c. 3, p. 335; cf. *Oxford English Dictionary*, s.v. imaginist.

another brings the deeper levels of the novel to the fore – and the superficial deceptions fade away.

The means by which the various deceptions are uncovered give *Emma* a certain likeness to a modern detective novel: the analogy has often been observed, but it is none the less revealing for that. It is a well known technique of Agatha Christie and her kind to scatter their pages with clues which they know, or hope, their readers will not pick up at first reading. Jane applied this technique in *Emma* with great skill and subtlety. In due course we shall see how she applies it to Emma herself and to Mr Knightley – both of them, and the reader, are given hints of growing affection which they are slow to grasp – and few readers, perhaps, have detected them at first reading. But the same technique is much more widely used in the novel.

It has also often been noted that *Emma* and *Persuasion* contain relatively less dialogue and more internal musing than the earlier novels – I say relatively, since *Emma* in particular is amply stocked with Jane Austen's ripest and subtlest dialogue, especially in the conversations of Mr Knightley and Mrs Weston and in the monologues of Miss Bates. But the difference is real and has been explained in all sorts of rarefied ways. Yet in both cases the plot would collapse were it not so. In *Emma* the plot can only be kept afloat – the reader can only be in the dark – if we see most of the action only through Emma's mistaken vision. In *Persuasion* a much slighter plot depends on suspense: on the reader not knowing – as Anne Elliot does not know – whether and when Captain Wentworth's affection for her will revive. Only by seeing everything through Anne's eyes can the suspense be sustained.

Emma opens with the marriage of Emma's companion and friend Miss Taylor to Mr Weston; and to fill some of the gap left by her departure, Emma seeks the friendship of Harriet Smith. Harriet is the chosen wife of Robert Martin; but in Emma's eyes he will not do: she must find her own special friend a husband of better breeding. Emma is highly intelligent, but self-willed and self-deluding, too accustomed to having her own way, too attached to her own opinions; and in the early stages of the book at least, an insufferable snob. So she chooses the young vicar, Mr Elton, for Harriet and cultivates his friendship for Harriet's sake – not for a moment realising that Mr Elton has set his sights on Emma herself, nor that she is deceived in regarding him as a sound and sensible young man. When Mr Elton destroys Emma's illusions by proposing to her, Emma forswears all match-making for the future – soon to be equally deceived into supposing a possible union between Harriet and Frank Churchill.

Frank Churchill is the hero of the sub-plot. He is Mr Weston's son by a former marriage but has been brought up – like Jane's brother Edward Knight – to be quasi-son and heir to a rich uncle and aunt, Mr and Mrs Churchill of Enscombe in Yorkshire. He is very dependent on the whims of Mrs Churchill, and has no illusion when he falls in love with Jane Fairfax on a holiday in Weymouth that Mrs Churchill will approve a match with a young woman – however elegant, accomplished and well educated – who has neither family, position, nor dowry. Her grandmother, Mrs Bates, widow of a former Vicar of Highbury, is now 'a very old lady, almost past everything but tea and quadrille'.[10] Her daughter, Miss Bates, is the immortal gossip of the book, loved and tolerated by all in spite of her poverty and ceaseless talk – save by Emma, who finds her a bore.[11] 'Jane Fairfax was an orphan, the only child of Mrs Bates's youngest [as we should say, younger] daughter.'[12] What hope have they of ever marrying? – Only the sanguine temper and easy charm of Frank Churchill could imagine a happy outcome; but the more cautious, high-principled Jane Fairfax is too much in love to refuse. By a happy chance they can meet. She has been brought up to be the companion and close friend of Miss Campbell, and educated at the expense of Miss Campbell's father – Colonel Campbell, himself formerly friend and commanding officer of Jane's father, who had died in action. Miss Campbell marries and goes with her husband to Ireland – and Jane is urged to accompany the whole family thither for a stay of several months. But this gives her the excuse to go to her own home – to her aunt and grandmother in Highbury, the seat of the novel. To Highbury Frank can also go – when Mrs Churchill allows him – to visit his father and his newly wed stepmother.

'My heart was in Highbury', as Frank confessed to his stepmother when all had been revealed, 'and my business was to get my body thither as often as might be, and with the least suspicion.'[13] Frank Churchill was a lively young man, none too serious. 'That young man . . .' said Mr Woodhouse,

> is very thoughtless. Do not tell his father, but that young man is not quite the thing. He has been opening the doors very often this evening, and keeping them open very inconsiderately. He does not think of the draught. I do not mean to set you against him, but indeed he is not quite the thing![14]

Emma takes a different view. – 'I am sure it was a source of high entertainment to you' she says to Frank, 'to feel that you were taking us all in . . . I think it might have been some amusement to myself in the same situation.'[15]

The secret engagement of Frank and Jane is not revealed till very late in the novel; but Jane Austen distributes clues meanwhile with a lavish hand.

[10] *E* I, c. 3, p. 21.
[11] See pp. 12–13.
[12] *E* II, c. 2, p.163.
[13] *E* III, c. 14, p. 439.
[14] *E* II, c. 11 [c.13, by an error, in the edition of 1816], p. 249.
[15] *E* III, c. 18, p. 478.

It is far too late for me to recall at what point – if at any – I began in my first reading of the novel to suspect this denouement; but few first readers, I fancy, pick up the earlier hints.

First of all, Mr Knightley tells us most emphatically that Frank Churchill could and should have come to wait on his stepmother as soon as she was married.

> It is on her account that attention to Randalls [the Westons' home] is doubly due, and she must doubly feel the omission. Had she been a person of consequence herself, he would have come I dare say; and it would not have signified whether he did or no. Can you imagine your friend [Mrs Weston] behind-hand in these sort of considerations?[16]

However much Emma may defend him on the ground of Mrs Churchill's whims, the fact remains: he does not come till after Jane Fairfax is settled in Highbury. This – the loudest hint till near the end – we are conditioned not to pick up, for we have no reason to suppose any liaison between Frank and Jane at this point. Yet we are set a very decided puzzle: why does Jane come to the humble house of her family rather than stay in all the comfort of the home of her closest friends? Emma sees this as a real problem, and propounds a romantic solution to it – that Jane Fairfax is in love with her friend's husband Mr Dixon, and stays away from their home out of tact and consideration.[17] It is a curious twist in the story that Emma may have hit on the wrong – on an absurd – solution; but she is quite right to seek a romantic explanation.

Her fancy is heightened by learning that Mr Dixon had saved Jane from falling overboard at Weymouth – and Emma learns in due course that Frank Churchill had been at Weymouth at the same time. But all she learns from this discovery is that Jane is extremely cautious in what she says of him, and 'suspiciously reserved' in what she says of Mr Dixon.[18] In January Frank Churchill has still not come; but in February – very shortly after Jane's arrival – he is there at last, after travelling with extraordinary speed.[19] Once Frank Churchill is among them, hints which carry meaning for a reader who knows or suspects his first interest in Highbury are scattered with some abandon. Every time he is visiting in Highbury he contrives to find a reason to go to the house where Mrs and Miss Bates and Jane Fairfax live – and to stay longer than he intended. On one occasion his excuse is the endless chatter of Miss Bates which gives him no pause in which to make his escape; on another he is an unconscionable time screwing a rivet

---

[16] *E* I, c. 18, p. 149. This conversation takes place in January (p. 145); the wedding was in the previous September (see *E*, p. 496).

[17] *E* II, c. 1, p. 160.

[18] *E* II, cc. 1, 2, pp. 160, 169.

[19] February: *E* II, c. 18, p. 309. For his speed of travel, *E* II, c. 5, pp. 190–1.

into Mrs Bates's glasses. Sometimes he makes elaborate pretence of not wanting to go there – or forgetting them. But the consequence is always that he sees as much of Jane as he can without arousing suspicion.[20] On one occasion he takes his stepmother there – though she has quite forgotten she had promised to go; on another a piano mysteriously appears from London for Jane – a very accomplished pianist – to play on, shortly after Frank has paid a visit to London (16 miles distant) to have his hair cut. Again, Emma detects him in the act of contemplating Jane at a party very intently – and he excuses himself by observing the oddity of Jane's hairstyle.[21]

The hints multiply; yet Emma is totally deceived. In order to cover his true position, Frank pretends to make Emma the object of his attentions, greatly to his father and stepmother's delight. Emma is much taken up with wondering if she is or is not in love with him – and decides on the whole that she is not; but that he is in love – or in danger of falling in love – with her. It is the greatest of all her fantasies. She has some excuse: he deliberately flirts with her, and she is flattered and attracted to him – and might have been seriously entangled, but that, deep down, she already owns Mr Knightley his superior.

When Frank comes again in May, Mr Knightley, inspired by a deep dislike of Frank and anxiety on behalf both of Emma and of Jane, of whom he thinks highly,

> began to suspect him of some double dealing in his pursuit of Emma . . . Mr Knightley began to suspect him of some inclination to trifle with Jane Fairfax . . . There were symptoms of intelligence between them . . . – symptoms of admiration on his side, which, having once observed, he could not persuade himself entirely void of meaning, however he might wish to escape any of Emma's errors of imagination.

His doubts culminate in a meeting at Hartfield, the home of the Woodhouses: Emma, Jane and Mr Knightley had fallen in with the Westons, including Frank, and Miss Bates and her niece, who 'had accidentally met'. Frank enquired of his stepmother whether Mr Perry, the apothecary, had set up his carriage yet? The question puzzles her – she had never heard of the idea; but Miss Bates throws light on it by admitting that Mrs Perry had told her of the scheme as a great secret – and she might have mentioned it – 'I am a talker, you know; I am rather a talker.' Frank had made a slip – for it was Jane who had told him; and he instantly seeks a way of communicating with her. Emma has prepared alphabets for her young nephews to play with – and Frank asks if they can be found so that he can play a word game. After a while he sends a group of letters to Miss Fairfax which make up 'blunder'

---

[20] See esp. *E* II, c. 6, pp. 198–9; c. 9, esp. p. 236.

[21] *E* II, cc. 7–8; c. 8, p. 222. There are also a number of reminiscences of Weymouth (where Frank and Jane first met) and carefully contrived duets with Miss Fairfax.

– but Mr Knightley sees them, and sees in them confirmation of his suspicions. He stays behind at Hartfield after all the rest have gone, to warn Emma; but of any understanding between Frank and Jane she is utterly incredulous: she thinks that what Mr Knightley has seen is related to her own suspicion of affection between Jane and Mr Dixon. 'She spoke [her incredulity] with a confidence which staggered, with a satisfaction which silenced, Mr Knightley' – and he went sadly home fearful of the outcome.[22]

But the greatest skill and subtlety in distributing clues is applied to Emma's growing absorption in Mr Knightley. When Mrs Weston suggests that Mr Knightley might be in love with Jane Fairfax, Emma reacts very sharply; when she is dancing at the Westons' ball at the Crown, she is disturbed to see that he is not dancing – and looks at him and his figure with great admiration. A little later, of an incident in which both were involved: 'I do remember it . . .' said Emma to Harriet. 'Stop; Mr Knightley was standing just here, was not he?' – a fact Harriet does not remember.[23] Later, when Emma and Mrs Weston are discussing Frank Churchill's deception, she cries out ' "So unlike what a man should be! – None of that upright integrity, that strict adherence to truth and principle, that disdain of trick and littleness, which a man should display in every transaction of his life." '[24] The words are Emma's, but the voice is Mr Knightley's – whose image she has clearly in mind – who very characteristically commented on the same events: ' "My Emma, does not every thing serve to prove more and more the beauty of truth and sincerity in all our dealings with each other?" '[25]

Mr Woodhouse

In an early chapter Mr Knightley and Mrs Weston dissect Emma's character. 'With all dear Emma's little faults', asserts Mrs Weston, 'she is an excellent creature. Where shall we see a better daughter, or a kinder sister, or a truer friend? No, no; she has qualities which may be trusted.'[26] She is indeed a model daughter.

> She dearly loved her father, but he was no companion for her . . . Having been a valetudinarian all his life, without activity of mind or body, he was a much older man in ways than in years; and though everywhere beloved for the friendliness of his heart and his amiable temper, his talents could not have recommended him at any time.[27]

[22] *E* III, c. 5, pp. 343–51.
[23] *E* II, c. 8, pp. 224–30; III, c. 2, pp. 325–6; c. 4, pp. 339–40.
[24] *E* III, c. 10, p. 397.
[25] *E* III, c. 15, p. 446.
[26] *E* I, c. 5, pp. 39–40.
[27] *E* I, c. 1, p. 7.

Very early in the book Emma helps him to entertain a small party of old friends – Mrs and Miss Bates, and Mrs Goddard, the local school mistress, and her own particular friend-to-be and Mrs Goddard's charge, Harriet Smith.

Emma did

> then do all the honours of the meal, and help and recommend the minced chicken and scalloped oysters with an urgency which she knew would be acceptable to the early hours and civil scruples of their guests. Upon such occasions poor Mr Woodhouse's feelings were in sad warfare. He loved to have the cloth laid, because it had been the fashion of his youth; but his conviction of suppers being very unwholesome made him rather sorry to see any thing put on it; and while his hospitality would have welcomed his visitors to every thing, his care for their health made him grieve that they would eat. Such another small basin of thin gruel as his own, was all that he could, with thorough self-approbation, recommend, though he might constrain himself, while the ladies were comfortably clearing the nicer things, to say:
>
> 'Mrs Bates, let me propose your venturing on one of these eggs. An egg boiled very soft is not unwholesome. Serle understands boiling an egg better than any body. I would not recommend an egg boiled by any body else – but you need not be afraid – they are very small, you see – one of our small eggs will not hurt you. Miss Bates, let Emma help you to a *little* bit of tart – a *very* little bit. Ours are all apple-tarts. You need not be afraid of unwholesome preserves here. I do not advise the custard. Mrs Goddard, what say you to *half* a glass of wine? A *small* half-glass, put into a tumbler of water? I do not think it would disagree with you.'
>
> Emma allowed her father to talk – but supplied her visitors in a much more satisfactory style . . .[28]

Mr Woodhouse is the delight of all but a handful of the readers of *Emma*: those for whom he has no relish are lost souls. Yet the magic web Miss Austen has woven round him cannot, or should not diminish his daughter's credit for being so constantly kind and attentive to him. That she might have been tempted to treat him less kindly is only too apparent from her rudeness on a much later page to Miss Bates: all the more credit for her constant patience with Mr Woodhouse.[29] With such preparations – and with Mr Woodhouse never far from the stage – the deeper qualities in Emma are securely laid before us. It is interesting to compare his role with Lady Bertram's in *Mansfield Park*: she is totally indolent, fails in most of the

[28] *E* I, c. 3, pp. 24–5.
[29] See p. 107.

duties of a mother and a chatelaine – yet the peaceful affection with which she treats Fanny Price is fully as important to making Mansfield Park a true home to the nervous, sensitive girl as the support of Edmund himself.

Almost equally admirable is Emma's behaviour as sister and friend. Her closest friend is Mrs Weston, who is utterly devoted to her and has forgotten any disagreements they had when Emma was a child. Emma's sister Isabella is very like Emma, 'differing only in those striking inferiorities, which always brought the other in brilliancy before him' as Mr Knightley observes when he visits Isabella and her husband, his brother John, in their London home.[30] Isabella is a devoted wife and mother, yet with a good deal of her father in her – slow in mind and utterly dependent on her apothecary, her doctor, as we would say. John is a clever barrister, very fond of his wife, but impatient too – sometimes ill-tempered, especially when expected to attend dinner parties during short visits to Hartfield, the Woodhouse home. In helping to mind their children, in keeping the peace between John Knightley and her father, in making Isabella comfortable, Emma shows endless patience and good will.

She is remarkably intelligent: 'she inherits her mother's talents' says Mr Knightley in one of the very rare references to Mrs Woodhouse, long since departed – and in saying this answers (as much as can be answered) the reader's natural amazement that Mr Woodhouse could have fathered such a child.[31] But Mr Knightley also says, perhaps a little harshly: 'I have done with expecting any course of steady reading from Emma. She will never submit to any thing requiring industry and patience, and a subjection of the fancy to the understanding.'[32] Self-will, self-approbation and fancy inspire the plot of the book, at the more superficial level. Most of Emma is about her fantasies and failings.

Harriet Smith

Emma indulges in a series of dreams. She befriends Harriet Smith, a beautiful, illegitimate and naïve young woman already more than half in love with Mr Knightley's principal tenant farmer, Robert Martin. Emma imagines that Harriet is a gentleman's daughter – and anyway thinks the protégée of Miss Woodhouse of Hartfield worth something less rustic than Mr Martin. So she fixes on Mr Elton, the vicar of Highbury, quite unaware that he is after Emma herself, a possibility which never occurs to her – such are her notions of social order – until she is warned by John Knightley, and has a slightly tipsy proposal from Mr Elton himself. Emma feels the deeper

[30] E III, c. 13, p. 433.
[31] E I, c. 5, p. 37.
[32] E I, c. 5, p. 37.

shame, since but for her Harriet would never have imagined Mr Elton in love with her. So she forswears all such matrimonial schemes for the future; and keeps her oath for a few chapters. But she is soon imagining love between Harriet and Frank Churchill – and even deceives herself into believing Harriet shares her view, only to discover that it is Mr Knightley, not Mr Churchill, that Harriet has fallen for. This double deception at last awakens Emma from her dreams, for her horror at the thought reveals to her her own true feelings: 'that Mr Knightley must marry no one but herself!'[33] It is a while before she learns that he is of the same mind, and all the dreams and nightmares can be laid to rest. But Emma's illusions are rapidly stripped away, and with them some of the real differences between her and her lover. Thus she ceases to view Robert Martin with disdain, and rejoices whole-heartedly when Harriet after all becomes engaged to him. She takes some convincing that it is so, for Harriet has been in love with two other men and spoken disparagingly of Mr Martin: 'I hope I know better than to care for Mr Martin.' 'It really was too much to hope even of Harriet, that she could be in love with more than *three* men in one year.' Emma even accuses Mr Knightley of not understanding what Mr Martin has said to him – ' "It was not Harriet's hand that he was certain of – it was the dimensions of some famous ox" ' – but she believes him in the end, and is deliciously happy. For she had bitterly repented leading Harriet astray, and it was an immense relief to find she had done no permanent harm.

> Serious she was, very serious in her thankfulness, and in her resolutions; and yet there was no preventing a laugh, sometimes in the very midst of them. She must laugh at such a close! Such an end of the doleful disappointment of five weeks back! Such a heart – such a Harriet![34]

The Denouement

Before the death of Mrs Churchill enables Frank to make his engagement known, the secret presses on Jane Fairfax. Her conscience troubles her; they fall out over what he regards as her excessive precautions. Finally, they both join in an expedition to Box Hill – a day of pleasure which turns out even more disastrous than the visit to Sotherton in *Mansfield Park*. Frank and Jane have quarrelled, and he shows his displeasure by flirting with Emma more openly than ever – and Emma is carried away, not by affection for him, but just by the excitement of the event, to encourage him. His final ploy is to demand of the company on Emma's behalf

---

[33] *E* III, c. 11, p. 408.
[34] *E* III, c. 11, p. 411; c. 15, p. 450; c. 18, pp. 473, 475.

'either one thing very clever, be it prose or verse, original or repeated – or two things moderately clever – or three things very dull indeed . . .'

'Oh! very well,' exclaimed Miss Bates, 'then I need not be uneasy. "Three things very dull indeed." That will just do for me . . .'

Emma could not resist. 'Ah! ma'am, but there may be a difficulty. Pardon, me – but you will be limited as to number – only three at once'

– which 'could not anger, though a slight blush shewed that it could pain her'.[35] This is a deeply painful moment – and Emma is swiftly rebuked by Mr Knightley, but she fails on the spur of the moment to explain her penitence to him, and goes home depressed. The evening is even more dreadful for Jane Fairfax, who spends it with Mr and Mrs Elton. The vicar, spurned by Emma, has found a cheerful, lively partner in Bath, and furnished Miss Austen with her most devastating portrait of a vulgar, interfering woman. Mrs Elton has found a place for Jane where she may be governess – in the home of someone near Maple Grove (her old home) who moves in the first circles – and Mrs Elton has pressed and urged her to take it. Hitherto, Jane has firmly refused, evidently because she wishes to stay in Highbury while Frank can visit her there. But now she accepts – and writes to Frank breaking the engagement.

By chance her letter reaches him at Richmond in Surrey (where the Churchills are staying) almost at the moment when Mrs Churchill – who has been often ill and equally often supposed to invent her illnesses – suddenly justifies her maladies by dying. It is a catastrophe of a kind beloved by Jane Austen: first, Frank is in such confusion he fails to post his letter to Jane attempting reconciliation; then – when she promptly returns all his letters and gives her future address near Bristol – he makes a gambler's throw and confesses to his uncle. The poor man, who had been a devoted even if a bullied husband, none the less soon consents – and Frank can ride to Highbury, be reconciled to Jane – and reveal his engagement to a small circle of family and friends.

Emma is already depressed by the shame of her behaviour at Box Hill; and she is yet more deeply ashamed to have been thus deceived and betrayed into thoughtless behaviour to Jane by his subterfuge; and her discomfiture is complete when she discovers that Harriet believes Mr Knightley to be in love with her. Mr Knightley, meanwhile, distressed by Emma's open encouragement of Frank at Box Hill – and not knowing yet of Frank's engagement to Jane – rides off to stay with his brother in London to escape from the sorrows of Highbury. 'But he had gone to a wrong place. There was too much domestic happiness in his brother's house;

---

[35] *E* III, c. 7, pp. 370–1.

woman wore too amiable a form in it' and Isabella reminded him constantly of Emma.[36]

Through a stormy evening Emma feels the depression which the weather enhances and in a measure symbolises – and finds it difficult even to give comfort to her father which he needs when the weather is bad.

> The weather continued much the same all the following morning; and the same loneliness, and the same melancholy, seemed to reign at Hartfield – but in the afternoon it cleared; the wind changed into a softer quarter; the clouds were carried off; the sun appeared; it was summer again. With all the eagerness which such a transition gives, Emma resolved to be out of doors as soon as possible. Never had the exquisite sight, smell, sensation of nature, tranquil, warm, and brilliant after a storm, been more attractive to her . . .

Many readers have noticed how the brightening of the weather comes as the prelude to a happier future for Emma – though there is nothing crude or simple about Miss Austen's effects: a brilliant sun had shone mercilessly on the slopes of Box Hill. Mr Perry, the apothecary, is with Mr Woodhouse, and he is happy – so she can leave him and wander in the garden – where she is soon joined by Mr Knightley. He has heard that morning in London of Frank's engagement; 'he had ridden home through the rain; and had walked up directly after dinner, to see how this sweetest and best of all creatures, faultless in spite of all her faults, bore the discovery'. In one of the most justly celebrated scenes in the book, the errors and misunderstandings on the surface of the tale are stripped away, and their affection for each other revealed in all its fullness.

> He had found her agitated and low. – Frank Churchill was a villain. – He heard her declare that she had never loved him. Frank Churchill's character was not desperate. – She was his own Emma, by hand and word, when they returned into the house; and if he could have thought of Frank Churchill then, he might have deemed him a very good sort of fellow.[37]

They go in and join Mr Woodhouse for tea. 'Poor Mr Woodhouse' – who hates change, and execrates marriage above all as the most notable harbinger of change

> little suspected what was plotting against him in the breast of that man whom he was so cordially welcoming, and so anxiously hoping might not have taken cold from his ride. – Could he have seen the heart, he would have cared very little for the lungs; but without the most

[36] *E* III, c. 13, pp. 432–3.
[37] *E* III, c. 13, pp. 424, 433.

distant imagination of the impending evil, without the slightest perception of anything extraordinary in the looks or ways of either, he repeated to them very comfortably all the articles of news he had received from Mr Perry, and talked on with much self-contentment, totally unsuspicious of what they could have told him in return.[38]

But it cannot be kept from him long; nor can he be expected to rejoice as Emma and Mr Knightley – and the readers of the book – rejoice. He must once have looked on marriage with a kindly eye, and keeps fond memories of his wife, long dead. But for the present and future, he sees nothing but evil in marriage, which has taken 'poor Isabella' and 'poor Miss Taylor' – Mrs Weston – from him. Everyone is much better off as they are.

Emma's kindness to her father never falters, and it soon emerges that Mr Knightley is truly an eligible partner for her, since he is prepared to marry her without breaking up her home – that is, he will move into Hartfield and stay there while Mr Woodhouse lives. Gradually their persuasions, and the soothing words of relatives and friends, reconcile Mr Woodhouse to accepting that it will happen – and even to seeing it as possibly, one day, far in the future, a happy event. Then one night 'Mrs Weston's poultry-house was robbed . . . of all her turkies – evidently by the ingenuity of man. Other poultry-yards in the neighbourhood also suffered. – Pilfering was *housebreaking* to Mr Woodhouse's fears. – He was very uneasy' – and so came to realise the value of having Mr Knightley always in the house. At the moment of terror, John Knightley and his family were staying at Hartfield; but he would soon be gone. 'The result of this distress was, that, with a much more voluntary, cheerful consent than his daughter had ever presumed to hope for at the moment, she was able to fix her wedding-day.'[39]

Whether the need for protection really changed Mr Woodhouse's philosophy of marriage, we cannot tell. At an earlier moment, Emma had declared: ' "I wish I may not sink into 'poor Emma' with him at once. – His tender compassion towards oppressed worth can go no farther." '[40] All that we can say is that when Jane Austen exploits the old man's timidity to further her ends she puts a crowning touch on this most ingenious of novels.

[38] *E* III, c. 14, p. 434.
[39] *E* III, c. 19, p. 483–4.
[40] *E* III, c. 17, pp. 464–5.

12

Persuasion

The Two Levels

Persuasion is the last and the slightest of the completed novels: it is slight in scale and conception, not in depth or subtlety. Whether because she was aware of failing strength or because she had an idea which fitted a *Novelle* not a full-length novel, it is conceived at all points on a less ambitious scale than its immediate predecessors. An exceptionally high proportion of its characters are fools or knaves. The fools include Sir Walter Elliot and his daughters Elizabeth and Mary; Louisa and Henrietta Musgrove; the dowager Lady Dalrymple and her daughter. The knaves are Mr William Elliot and Mrs Clay. There is indeed an intermediate layer of characters of sense and depth, lightly sketched: Admiral and Mrs Croft and the other sailors, and above all Lady Russell. Lady Russell plays a crucial part in the development of the story; she is in her way as important to its structure as Mr Woodhouse in *Emma*. Her strength is that she has some of the intelligence, good sense and sound feeling of her closest friend, Anne's mother, long since departed; her weakness, that she shares a good deal of the snobbery, and something of the superficiality, of the Elliots; her redeeming feature, that 'she loved Anne better than she loved her own abilities' and so could be quickly reconciled to Captain Wentworth as Anne's husband in the end.[1] Yet she is much more slightly developed, more lightly sketched than Mr Woodhouse. Depth and force of character, intelligence, insight, perceptiveness: these qualities are only developed to the full in Anne Elliot and Captain Wentworth. *Emma* is seen in large measure through the heroine's eyes, since the reader must not know too much about the state of mind of Frank Churchill or Mr Knightley. By the same token the story of *Persuasion* is the hidden revival of Captain Wentworth's understanding and admiration of Anne – and so of his love for her – and its suspense depends on knowing only her side of the story till very near the end. That is not quite the whole truth: the visit to Lyme which reveals to him – and so to the reader – that Anne is still very pretty and a great deal more intelligent, resolute and effective than most of the characters about her – comes only

---

[1] *P* II, c. 12, p. 249, cf. p. 270.

half way through. The story might have ended there; but it is sustained with great skill and conviction through a second volume and another setting: in the artificial society of Bath Mr Elliot woos Anne and arouses Captain Wentworth's jealousy. Only when he sees her in the company, not of Mr Elliot but of his sailor colleagues, is he convinced that she can still love him and that the reconciliation can be complete. *Persuasion* has two endings: in the first, which the author set aside, the crucial meeting takes place in the lodgings of Admiral and Mrs Croft; in the second, definitive ending in a hotel sitting room where Anne is overheard by Wentworth deep in speech with his friend Captain Harville. In both cases, the naval setting rescues her from the world of the Elliots and Lady Russell which had inhibited him.

As in *Sense and Sensibility*, the contrast between the depth of character of the leading characters and the shallowness of most of those about them is particularly striking. Above all, the shallowness of Louisa Musgrove, with whom Captain Wentworth nearly entangles himself, and the depth of Anne Elliot, reveal – or symbolise – the two levels at which the story unfolds.

The Persuasion

In the summer of 1806, Captain Frederick Wentworth, recently made commander, had some months leave in Somerset; and there he met and fell in love with Anne Elliot, second of three daughters of Sir Walter Elliot, Bart., of Kellynch Hall. Anne was the one surviving intelligent member of a family of fools: she had inherited her late mother's sense and charm – and the friendship and care of her mother's closest friend, Lady Russell. Lady Russell was a woman of sense, but neither quick-witted nor truly perceptive: the young sailor was impetuous, too lively by half, too little established, of a family inferior (in Lady Russell's eyes) to the Elliots. Anne was only 19: she was too young. Lady Russell, with the authority of a mother, opposed the match, and Anne's father and eldest sister – who cared nothing for Anne – looked coldly on it. With infinite reluctance and sorrow, Anne broke off the engagement.

Eight and a half years later the engagement was resumed, and they married.[2] He was now a rich, successful full Captain, she had been tried in the crucible of suffering; the two were linked by a love matured by years of separation and experience. The persuasion which gives the book its title had taken place long before the action of the book: Anne had accepted Lady Russell's advice, and suffered for it – and yet, in a curious way,

[2] From the summer of 1806 to February 1815 (see *P* pp. 280–2 – Appendix on chronology).

benefited from it too. Both partners were readier to appreciate each other's characters, more securely founded in the conviction of all that united them, than they could possibly have been eight years before.

Jane neither condones nor condemns the persuasion: rather, she presents it under all its aspects; the book is a running, imaginative discussion of the pros and cons of taking good and bad advice – or of following our instincts. She makes pretence (as elsewhere) that the book lacks a moral.[3]

> When any two young people take it into their heads to marry, they are pretty sure by perseverance to carry their point, be they ever so poor, or ever so imprudent, or ever so little likely to be necessary to each other's ultimate comfort. This may be bad morality to conclude with, but I believe it to be truth; and if such parties succeed, how should a Captain Wentworth and an Anne Elliot, with the advantage of maturity of mind, consciousness of right, and one independent fortune between them, fail of bearing down every opposition?[4]

But this moral, like the opposition, is entirely superficial. A page or two before, she has stated one of many much deeper morals which the book explores. Here is Anne talking to Wentworth on the very evening that their engagement was renewed.

> I have been thinking over the past, and trying impartially to judge of the right and wrong, I mean with regard to myself; and I must believe that I was right, much as I suffered from it, that I was perfectly right in being guided by the friend whom you will love better than you do now. To me, she was in the place of a parent. Do not mistake me, however. I am not saying that she did not err in her advice. It was, perhaps, one of those cases in which advice is good or bad only as the event decides; and for myself, I certainly never should, in any circum-stance of tolerable similarity, give such advice. But I mean that I was right in submitting to her, and that if I had done otherwise, I should have suffered more in continuing the engagement than I did even in giving it up, because I should have suffered in my conscience. I have now, as far as such a sentiment is allowable in human nature, nothing to reproach myself with; and if I mistake not, a strong sense of duty is no bad part of a woman's portion.

To this Wentworth, not unnaturally, makes no direct reply: he looks at Lady Russell, who is not far away, looks back at Anne, and replies, 'as if in cool deliberation –

' "Not yet, but there are hopes of her being forgiven in time." '[5]

[3] E.g. at the end of *Northanger Abbey*. See p. 192.
[4] *P* II, c. 12, p. 248.
[5] *P* II, c. 11, pp. 246–7.

But this was only a part of the lesson Anne had learned. Much earlier in the book, Anne's philosophy is revealed.

> How eloquent could Anne Elliot have been, – how eloquent at least, were her wishes on the side of early warm attachment, and a cheerful confidence in futurity, against that over-anxious caution which seems to insult exertion and distrust Providence! – She had been forced into prudence in her youth, she learned romance as she grew older – the natural sequel of an unnatural beginning.[6]

But we have ourselves to read such passages with caution; for every thoughtful reader of Jane Austen knows her habit of passing from the author's view to the heroine's without warning: where Jane ends and Anne begins in this passage cannot be entirely unravelled.

The Story

After eight years' separation, a curious chance has brought them together again. Her father is vain and extravagant, and deeply in debt – nor can he see any way in which the customary style of life at Kellynch Hall can be abbreviated. His agent, by clever manoeuvring, with the support of Lady Russell, convinces him that the right course is to move to lodgings in Bath – where he can live in style but within his income – and let Kellynch Hall; and the tenant he finds is Admiral Croft, whose wife is Wentworth's sister. Anne's own youngest sister Mary is married to the eldest son of a respectable landowner in Uppercross nearby; and when Sir Walter and his eldest daughter go to Bath, Anne settles at Uppercross for a while.

The Musgroves of Uppercross are a cheerful, lively, extrovert family with many children. When Captain Wentworth is staying with his sister and her husband at Kellynch, he comes visiting at Uppercross – and so meets Anne again. He has harboured over the years a warm resentment of her treatment of him, which he attributes to weakness and submissiveness – to lack of resolution and self-will. In the two eldest Musgrove daughters, Louisa and Henrietta, he finds outgoing, friendly young women; and in Louisa especially one who is not readily turned from her purposes – superficially, at least, firm and resolute. The Admiral expects his brother-in-law to marry one of them. He and his wife have given Anne a lift in their carriage, and so she hears the Admiral's musings.

> 'He certainly means to have one or other of those two girls, Sophy,' said the Admiral; – 'but there is no saying which. He has been running after them, too, long enough, one would think, to make up

---

[6] *P* I, c. 4, p. 30.

his mind. Ay, this comes of the peace. If it were war, now, he would have settled it long ago. – We sailors, Miss Elliot, cannot afford to make long courtships in time of war. How many days was it, my dear, between the first time of my seeing you, and our sitting down together in our lodgings at North Yarmouth?'

'We had better not talk about it, my dear,' replied Mrs Croft pleasantly; 'for if Miss Elliot were to hear how soon we came to an understanding, she would never be persuaded that we could be happy together. I had known you by character, however, long before.' [We observe in passing that Anne would need little *persuasion* to think the Admiral happy to have wedded Frederick's sister.]

'Well, and I had heard of you as a very pretty girl; and what were we to wait for besides? – I do not like having such things so long in hand. I wish Frederick would spread a little more canvas, and bring us home one of these young ladies to Kellynch . . . And very nice young ladies they both are; I hardly know one from the other.'

'Very good-humoured, unaffected girls, indeed,' said Mrs Croft, in a tone of calmer praise, such as made Anne suspect that her keener powers might not consider either of them as quite worthy of her brother; 'and a very respectable family. One could not be connected with better people. – My dear Admiral, that post! – we shall certainly take that post.'

But by coolly giving the reins a better direction herself, they happily passed the danger; and by once afterwards judiciously putting out her hand, they neither fell into a rut, nor ran foul of a dung-cart; and Anne, with some amusement at their style of driving, which she imagined no bad representation of the general guidance of their affairs, found herself safely deposited by them at [Uppercross] Cottage.[7]

With a few light strokes Jane has shown how superficial are the charms of Henrietta and Louisa – 'I hardly know one from the other' – has hinted that Wentworth is in no real hurry to pursue either – and sketched an immortal portrait of a marriage; there are few couples in any of her novels so happily united as Admiral and Mrs Croft.

But if Wentworth was not serious in pursuit of the Musgroves, he could still enjoy their company and stand aloof, in seemingly eternal resentment, from Anne's. Jane breaks the impasse in two ways: first, by the sheer passage of time. At first he thinks Anne greatly altered – her bloom has gone; but as he sees more of her, his earlier feelings slowly revive underneath the resentment and estrangement of the years. Next, his mind is cleared by one of the most brilliantly contrived of catastrophes.

[7] *P* I, c. 10, p. 92.

Lyme

Captain Wentworth visits Lyme Regis to see some friends of his settled there for the winter – Captain and Mrs Harville and their children, and Captain Benwick, formerly betrothed to Harville's sister who has recently died – and inconsolable. When Wentworth next visits Uppercross and describes his visit –

> The young people were all wild to see Lyme . . . Though November, the weather was by no means bad; and, in short, Louisa, who was the most eager of the eager, having formed the resolution to go, and besides the pleasure of doing as she liked, being now armed with the idea of merit in maintaining her own way [for Captain Wentworth has commended her for what he deems firmness of purpose], bore down all the wishes of her father and mother for putting it off till summer; and to Lyme they were to go – Charles [Louisa's eldest brother and Mary Elliot's husband], Mary, Anne, Henrietta, Louisa, and Captain Wentworth.[8]

At Lyme they enjoy a splendid seaside town in the quietest season of November; they meet the Harvilles and Captain Benwick; Louisa makes Wentworth jump her down the steps of the Cobb once too often – and she falls and suffers severe concussion. In this crisis Anne alone shows strong presence of mind: she instantly sends Captain Benwick in search of a surgeon, sustains and directs the others. Louisa is taken to the Harvilles' home to be nursed; and though the injury seems serious, the surgeon speaks hopefully of her recovering.

Also crucial to the story is a brief encounter between Anne and a stranger, first on 'the steps, leading upwards from the beach' in an early morning walk – before Louisa's fall; then in the inn. On the first occasion, 'it was evident that the gentleman, (completely a gentleman in manner) admired her exceedingly' – for 'her very regular, very pretty features, [had] the bloom and freshness of youth restored by the fine wind which had been blowing on her complexion . . . Captain Wentworth looked round at her instantly in a way which shewed his noticing of it.'[9] After his departure, they find that the man was Mr Elliot, her cousin and Sir Walter's heir. Anne's presence of mind in the crisis reveals to Captain Wentworth her superiority – for the deeper qualities of mind and personality she shows, for the maturity eight years have brought – over Louisa; Mr Elliot's admiration carries a similar message – at a deeper level Anne still has the power to excite his warmest admiration.

[8] *P* I, c. 11, p. 94.
[9] *P* I, c. 12, p. 104.

But if Lyme has opened Captain Wentworth's eyes, it does not make his course smooth or easy. Captain Harcourt – not alone – thinks he has been courting Louisa, and he finds himself entangled; and Mr Elliot goes on to Bath to become a rival to him for Anne's attention and perhaps for her hand. From these difficulties Wentworth is rescued by two of Jane Austen's minor shocks – the first similar to the marriage of Lucy and Robert Ferrars in *Sense and Sensibility*, but a happier event in itself. While Louisa lies sick at Lyme, the forlorn Captain Benwick finds solace: they fall in love and are betrothed; Captain Wentworth is free.

The Denouement

He is free, that is, to pursue Anne to Bath, whither she has now gone to join her family. But in Bath he finds her in the company of Mr Elliot, whom he believes to be a rival – not wholly without reason, for Lady Russell has set her heart on Anne's marrying Mr Elliot, and so ultimately succeeding to her mother's place as mistress of Kellynch Hall; and this vision even Anne finds alluring for a moment. She is saved from temptation by her insight into Mr Elliot's character. He is now outwardly everything he should be: gentlemanly, attentive to her father and all the family, lively, witty, sensible, good company. But a few years before he had been extremely disrespectful to her father; and Anne saw some signs that his character has not wholly changed. 'She saw that there had been bad habits; that Sunday-travelling had been a common thing'; and although 'he might now think very differently [from his former habit of mind], who could answer for the true sentiments of a clever, cautious man, grown old enough to appreciate a fair character? How could it ever be ascertained that his mind was truly cleansed?'[10] Anne could give no such answer – nor would Jane: he is reserved for her gallery of rakes, in the line of Willoughby and Wickham. Sunday travel may not seem so secure a sign of wickedness to us as it did to Jane; and some critics have supposed an Evangelical touch at this point. But the decent observance of Sunday was the central event of village life in a parson's home; there was nothing specifically evangelical in objection to Sunday travel.[11] His behaviour has indeed much improved. He had earlier married the rich heiress of a grazier and become rich himself; she had died, and he was now concerned (as he had not been in earlier days) to ensure his inheritance of the Baronetcy and the Hall. But both he and Anne suspect that a clever young widow – a friend of Anne's eldest sister who virtually lives with the family – called Mrs Clay has designs to marry Sir Walter; and Mr Elliot schemes to counter her plans by marrying Anne –

[10] *P* II, c. 5, p. 161.
[11] See pp. 132–6.

and by his proximity to Sir Walter, to foil Mrs Clay's plots. The second minor shock which clears the path for the denouement is the full revelation of Mr Elliot's character: Anne's doubts are resolved by a chance meeting with an old school friend – a widow whose husband in prosperous days had befriended Mr Elliot when he was poor; but had received nothing from him in return when the husband became financially embarrassed – still less would he help the widow in her poverty. With such young men, Jane is merciless, and nothing is left of his character; when he learns of Anne's betrothal, he solves the problem of Mrs Clay by making her his mistress – and it remains doubtful in the end whether he or she is the victor, whether 'he may not be wheedled and caressed at last into making her the wife of' Mr Elliot, the future Sir William.[12]

The final scenes are enacted in Bath, where Captain Wentworth's jealousy is finally overborne – first, by her friendly reception of him when they meet; secondly, by receiving new evidence that her heart is still with him. As mentioned above, *Persuasion* has two endings. The first survives in manuscript – presumably Cassandra kept it precisely because it provided a text otherwise totally lost.[13] The Admiral hears the rumour current in Bath that Anne and Mr Elliot are to marry, and wishes to ascertain if they would wish to live at Kellynch – for he realises that Mr Elliot could well afford to do so. The Admiral's idea of a delicate enquiry is to make Captain Wentworth ask Anne to her face if the rumour is true – and the cheerful firmness with which she denies it breaks down his reserve, and they are reconciled.[14] Jane herself evidently felt that this ending did too little justice to Anne's role in the book: that what was needed was for Anne to convince Captain Wentworth of the eternal nature of her love. In the revised version she falls into conversation with Captain Harville, while Wentworth is not far away – just near enough to pick out what Anne is saying. She and Harville develop a friendly argument as to whether a man's or a woman's love is more enduring – and he gives eloquent expression to the feelings a sailor has when separated from his family – and reunited to them.

> 'I believe you capable of every thing great and good in your married lives [Anne replies]. I believe you equal to every important exertion, and to every domestic forbearance, so long as – if I may be allowed the expression, so long as you have an object. I mean, while the woman you love lives, and lives for you. All the privilege I claim for my own sex (it is not a very enviable one: you need not covet it) is that of loving longest, when existence or when hope is gone.'[15]

---

[12] *P* II, c. 12, p. 250.
[13] See pp. 45, 111.
[14] *P*, pp. 253–63.
[15] *P* II, c. 11, p. 235.

Anne's eloquent claim to constancy forces Wentworth to try his fortune: he scribbles a note to her and finds an opportunity to lay it in her hands – and the denouement follows.

The plot of *Persuasion* is simpler than that of any other of Jane Austen's major novels: in its nature, it cannot fill all the echoing spaces of a three-volume novel. It is a *Novelle*, and a marvellously successful one. But no summary, however penetrating, can do justice to its riches. Thus, for example, Lady Russell, the benevolent, childless widow, who is responsible for the near-tragedy on which the story turns, is a character lightly sketched. But the touches are singularly effective.

After the catastrophe in Lyme, the Musgroves, Louisa's parents, move there for a time to be near her, and to give some help to Mrs Harville who is nursing Louisa and managing her own family at the same time. But as things improve, and the Christmas holidays approach, they 'came back to receive their happy boys and girls from school, bringing with them Mrs Harville's little children, to improve the noise of Uppercross, and lessen that of Lyme'.[16]

'Lady Russell and Anne paid their compliments to them once, when Anne could not but feel that Uppercross was already quite alive again' – Jane paints a delectable picture of childish noise, with one family of Harvilles, and two of Musgroves, 'the whole completed by a roaring Christmas fire, which seemed determined to be heard, in spite of all the noise of the others . . . It was a fine family piece . . .

> 'I hope I shall remember, in future,' said Lady Russell, as soon as they were reseated in the carriage, 'not to call at Uppercross in the Christmas holidays.'
>
> Everybody has their taste in noises as well as in other matters; and sounds are quite innoxious, or most distressing, by their sort rather than their quantity. When Lady Russell, not long afterwards, was entering Bath on a wet afternoon, and driving through the long course of streets from the Old Bridge to Camden-place, amidst the dash of other carriages, the heavy rumble of carts and drays, the bawling of newsmen, muffin-men and milk-men, and the ceaseless clink of pattens, she made no complaint. No, these were noises which belonged to the winter pleasures; her spirits rose under their influence; and, like Mrs Musgrove, she was feeling, though not saying, that after being long in the country, nothing could be so good for her as a little quiet cheerfulness.[17]

'Anne did not share these feelings': she had no love for Bath, and looked back with pleasure to Uppercross and Kellynch. But the irony is on her too: for she goes to Bath (however little she expects it) to find happiness and a joyful reunion with Captain Wentworth.

[16] *P* II, c. 2, p. 133.
[17] *P* II, c. 2, pp. 134–5.

13

Church and Clergy

The Church in the Eighteenth Century

The Anglican church of the eighteenth century has had a bad press. Until recently, most accounts of it made much of its 'fat slumbers', of pluralism, decadence, lack of spiritual vigour, and so forth. From this it was said to have been awakened, first by the Evangelical Revival, then by the Oxford Movement. More recent study has revealed much more variety, much more spirituality, much more vigour than this stereotype suggests; and a wider view of the history of the Church puts the corruption of the eighteenth century in a rather different perspective.[1] Thus a major purpose of this chapter is to show some of the ways in which the stereotype of the eighteenth-century church needs to be dismantled if we are to have a clear view of the religious background and assumptions of Jane Austen's novels. Recent study has done much to this end, but a more radical view is still needed if justice is to be done to the immense variety of both temporal and spiritual experience – creative and uncreative – of the age.

The stereotype was the product of reformers; and much conventional history has been based on the propaganda of reformers. The Evangelicals had a fervent belief in hell, and in the need for conversion; naturally they emphasised the sins and failings of those they hoped to snatch from its jaws. The Tractarians wished to instil a loftier view of the Church and its authority than they found in the Church of England of their day, and they naturally emphasised the inadequacy of eighteenth-century theology and spirituality. But the Evangelical movement is one of the most characteristic products of eighteenth-century England; and although the Oxford

---

[1] The theme of this chapter has been delightfully related to Jane Austen by Irene Collins in Collins 1993. The spiritual background is admirably expounded in Rupp 1986; recent studies of the structures and variety of the eighteenth-century church are admirably represented in Walsh, Taylor and Haydon 1993, to which I owe much; Taylor 1995; see also Virgin 1989. For the Evangelical tradition, see esp. Walsh 1966; for the Latitudinarian, esp. Hoadly (bishop of Winchester, 1734–61), see Rupp 1986, pp. 88–101. Some visitation records of the parishes in the see of Winchester have been edited, with penetrating commentary, by W.R. Ward, in Ward 1994–95. Beyond that, the recent literature is vast, and changing views of the eighteenth-century church bewilderingly varied.

Movement was not under way before the 1830s, its roots and origins illustrate the rich and creative variety of the eighteenth-century legacy.

The point can be made clearer by an analogy. The sixteenth-century English Reformers laid great stress on the study of the Scriptures; and among their supreme achievements was the translation of the English Bible, which in the versions of Tyndale, Coverdale, Geneva and James I represent a new awakening in the understanding of how to translate the Bible – or any great literature.[2] But when they gloried in their achievement, they greatly exaggerated the darkness that lay behind them. The Wycliffite Bible of the late fourteenth century – the supreme achievement of John Wyclif's disciples – survives in over 250 manuscript copies, in spite of being proscribed by the hierarchy of the Church since it had been composed by heretics.[3] But one may read most of its text without encountering tendentious passages; and many respectable Catholics as well as many Lollards valued it. It circulated very widely indeed – far more widely than Langland's *Piers Plowman* or Chaucer's *Canterbury Tales*. The same is true of the Bible in many European vernaculars, and the books themselves were but the tip of an iceberg of oral tradition whose history is very imperfectly known.[4] Doubtless many were ignorant of the Bible, then as now. But the crowds who attended their parish churches heard in the homilies presented to them by the clergy bible stories in a tongue they could understand – or listened as clergy and other guides expounded the stories framed about them in wood and stone and glass; the throngs who witnessed the miracle plays knew or learned the biblical stories on which they were based. Behind the Wycliffite translators lay a tradition of learning in the schools: biblical studies formed half the curriculum in medieval theological courses in the universities – and the reformers who settled in Emmanuel College in Cambridge when it was founded in the 1580s would have been amazed to learn that when its buildings had formed the core of the medieval Dominican house, and especially in the mid-fourteenth century, in the age of Robert Holcot, the biblical studies within their precinct had been famous throughout Europe.[5] The blinding effect of the reformers' genuine love of the Bible, and arrogant denunciation of their predecessors, so obscured these simple truths that they have only been painfully rediscovered in our own generation.

By the same token, the eighteenth century has been viewed through the

---

[2] See esp. Hammond 1982.

[3] On the Wycliffite Bible, see esp. Hudson 1988, pp. 228–47; for an example of a vernacular Bible in a Dominican Library (Cambridge, according to Leland), Humphreys 1990, p. 196.

[4] Lampe 1969, chap. 9. The influence of oral tradition, which is likely to have been very extensive, has been very inadequately explored.

[5] See Brooke in Bendall, Brooke and Collinson, *History of Emmanuel College* (Woodbridge, 1999), chap. 1.

eyes of the reformers of the nineteenth. But the truth is that in every age of the Church's history there have been at one and the same time fearful abuses and amazing spiritual vitality. The Church condoned slavery for over a thousand years, while deprecating the enslavement of Christians. It was precisely in the eighteenth century that it came to be seen by numbers of enlightened folk to be a scandal. It had ceased in England itself many centuries before, and that made it the easier to turn a blind eye to the plunder of African slaves, their sale into the Indies and America, and their use on plantations in British colonies there – for these events were distant and (for the majority) invisible. In Britain the spearhead of the movement to end the slave trade was formed by a group of Quakers in the 1780s; and their Society was quickly joined by folk of other persuasions, especially the Evangelical Anglicans Thomas Clarkson and William Wilberforce, who brought the issue into Parliament in the late 1780s. Although a bill to abolish the trade was not passed till 1807, it early won support from the leaders of all Christian communions, and a large number of the bishops voted steadily for abolition in the House of Lords.[6] Sir Thomas Bertram allowed Fanny to ask him questions about the slave trade in the 1810s, even though he presumably ran his Antiguan estates with the aid of slaves – and the abolition of the trade might have been one of the causes of the declining revenue from the Antiguan estate which had given him so much concern.[7]

The influence of the Quakers and Evangelicals represents another very striking feature of the eighteenth-century Church: the acceptance of much greater influence from the separated churches and communities of Christians. The Evangelical Movement itself indeed sprang from the heart of the Anglican establishment: John Wesley was fellow and tutor of Lincoln College, Oxford, and in origin his was the Oxford movement of the eighteenth century. But as soon as he and his followers took to charismatic field meetings they incurred the unpopularity with the clerical establishment that the friars had incurred in the thirteenth century. Wesley himself remained an Anglican in principle and much of his practice to the end of his days, but his movement was becoming a church – a group of churches indeed – of its own. This only serves to illustrate how deep the influences flowing from one Church to another had become.

The Anglican Church after the Restoration of 1660 had seemed to have inherited the medieval tradition that the Church was a persecuting Church – without the tortures and the flames of the Inquisition, but with much of its consequences in ostracism and disability, and exclusion from university and parliament. The Toleration Act of 1689 had checked the worst excesses of religious persecution; but many disabilities remained, and they were only slowly dismantled in the nineteenth century. Meanwhile two

---

[6] Anstey 1975, p. 393.
[7] *MP* II, c. 3, p. 198; cf. the reference in *Emma* II, c. 17, pp. 300–1.

winds blew through the Church of England in the eighteenth century: one maintained that it was still the Church of the English people, whose intimacy with the state gave guidance and moral and religious control to an otherwise secular and barbarous parliament. The other observed the varieties of religious thought and practice and experience, and sought to enlarge their acceptance and toleration. When Jane Austen's father was beneficed in the early 1760s, Benjamin Hoadly, the eminent Latitudinarian bishop of Winchester, had recently died; Joseph Butler of Durham, philosopher and high churchman – whose practices made him much revered by the Tractarians – had died in the previous decade; Thomas Secker, who openly defended some aspects of the Evangelical movement and of the Methodists, was archbishop of Canterbury.[8] There was a spirit of peace-making abroad, as well as of the sharp and acrimonious controversies which split the English Church and divided Christendom, sadly preserving one of the most ancient traditions of the Christian Church.

Church Music

To understand Jane Austen's religious background, two things above all are necessary: to forget the stereotype of eighteenth-century Anglicanism, and to appreciate the wide variety of the spiritual inheritance into which she and her family entered. A study of church music – and in particular the music of parish churches – is an exceptionally revealing example of the weaknesses of some conventional views. The century of Bach and Handel must reign supreme in the history of church music; and it was a dean of Canterbury in the late eighteenth century who declared that the *Messiah* 'furnished the best idea we shall ever obtain on earth of what is passing in heaven'.[9] It was first heard in Chester Cathedral, not very well performed, then in Dublin, then in many great churches and concert halls in England. Many cathedral choirs had an exquisite repertory of music; many great organs were built in the seventeenth and early eighteenth centuries. But in some cathedrals one hears of neglect and decline, of chapters paying little attention to the quality of the services or of the music.[10] Meanwhile the early eighteenth century was a great age of hymn-writing. The reformation had carried away the great medieval hymns, and replaced them only with paraphrases of psalms, a few distinguished, the majority mediocre. The seventeenth century had left a marvellous legacy of religious poetry, some

---

[8] See esp. Taylor 1995, p. 198. On Secker, see Gregory 1995.
[9] Collinson, Ramsay and Sparks 1995, p. 229 and n. 105 (J. Gregory quoting Dean Horne, 1784).
[10] On the history of organs see esp. Thistlethwaite 1990; on Lincoln Minster in the eighteenth century, Thistlethwaite 1994, esp. pp. 87–97, and on the organ, pp. 87–8, 93–7.

of which could be adapted as hymns – some of George Herbert, a little of Milton and Dryden remain among the finest hymns in the repertory; Thomas Ken provided a few which quickly won a place with the psalms as a respectable part of the services of the church. But the explosion came with Isaac Watts (1674–1748), who wrote 697 hymns on the latest count.[11] Watts was a Dissenter all his days; but his hymns spread about the land – his *Hymns and Songs* of 1707 went into sixteen editions in his lifetime. Even he had to yield in productivity to Charles Wesley, who wrote at least 7,300,[12] the best of which, with many others from former times and from the circle of the Wesleys, passed into the great *Collection of Hymns for the Use of the People called Methodists*, issued by John Wesley in 1780.[13] Many or most of the hymns of both Watts and the Wesleys have been justly forgotten; but many survive and are among the best loved, sung now by all communions.

Music in Parish Churches

It has often been thought – it was apparently said by some at the time – that there was little or no music in parish churches in the eighteenth century.[14] A variant of this is the notion which attributes the singing of hymns solely to Evangelical imitation of the Methodists – or else to the Tractarians, who made hymns within the liturgy respectable, changing the 'status of the hymn itself from an unauthorised addition to an integral part of the service of public worship'.[15] A further variant is the notion that urban churches, which could afford organs and choirs, might have music – sometimes as sophisticated as cathedral music – but that country parishes had to make do without any music at all.

Professor Nicholas Temperley, in his very thorough and learned study of *The Music of the English Parish Church*, lists 333 collections of psalms, anthems, hymns and other music – but mostly psalms – primarily for use in parish churches published before the end of 1800 – thereafter they become so numerous his list is only selective.[16] Of these, 14 are from the sixteenth century, 36 between 1601 and 1700, 283 between 1701 and 1800. When every qualification has been made for problems of definition, for the very

[11] Rupp 1986, p. 157; see ibid. pp. 152–61; Manning 1942, pp. 78–105; and for what follows Manning 1942; Rupp 1986, pp. 157, 407–16.
[12] Rupp 1986, p. 410, citing Rattenbury 1941, p. 20.
[13] See esp. Manning 1942, pp. 7–31.
[14] Collins 1993, pp. 181, 221 n. 5, citing Lowther Clarke 1944, p. 4, citing 'Mrs Trimmer'.
[15] Temperley 1979, p. 262. There was a view that hymns (as opposed to metrical psalms) were not an authorised part of the liturgy; some even wished them to be excluded from the course of normal services.
[16] Temperley 1979, pp. 366–81, numbered 1–326, but there are some additions numbered 'a'.

variable size of editions, for changing habits in printing music and chances of survival, for the extent to which music then (and always) has circulated in manuscript rather than print, these figures make it abundantly clear that there was a very rapid increase in the demand for music for parish churches in the eighteenth century. Much of this music relates to psalmody – and a very varied pattern of psalm-singing can be traced in different churches and different circles. They could be accompanied by instruments or groups of instruments – the old church bands familiar from Hardy's *Under the Greenwood Tree* – or by organs; for churches of modest resources, from the late eighteenth century anyway, barrel-organs were available, elaborate musical boxes which played a variety of hymn tunes.[17] To the modern taste there is a surprising lack of hymn-books, as we understand the term. But this was partly a matter of definition: the traditional hymns of Protestant England had been metrical psalms; and although a few seventeenth-century hymns – such as the morning and evening hymns of Bishop Ken – had entered the canon and were frequently reprinted, the majority of seventeenth-century hymns circulated in books of private devotion, or only later acquired tunes. Eighteenth-century hymns found fortune in the Methodist collections, and so were not necessarily intended for parochial use – though perhaps often used in parish churches under Evangelical influence – till later.[18] The most celebrated of the Anglican Evangelical collections, William Cowper and John Newton's *Olney Hymns* (1779) is not included in Temperley's list (presumably because it was printed without tunes), though it could be used in parish churches.[19]

Traditional methods of singing psalms and metrical psalms continued in favour, especially among high churchmen; and novel fashions grew and spread – accompanied by a flood of new hymns – among the Evangelicals. But it seems likely that the distinction between high and low church in this regard was superficial: much more depended on the musical tastes of vicars and congregations – and the labels 'high' and 'low' have been much too glibly attached to many churchmen.[20] It is still so today. A keen musician, even of modest capacity, may create a village choir or draw a group of churchgoers to sing. Yet in many a village church there is no organist – or the organ is in need of repair, and music languishes. Yet again, there are many to whom a quiet, meditative, said service is more devotional than noisy congregational hymns or the sophisticated anthems of a cathedral choir – there are others to whom one or other or both are of the essence of

[17] Temperley 1979, pp. 234–40.
[18] Confusion is easy: Charles Wesley was an Anglican divine all his days, and must have hoped at least that many of his hymns would be sung in parish churches.
[19] As it was by the so-called high churchman Reginald Heber very early in the nineteenth century (Temperley 1979, p. 262).
[20] This emerges from a careful reading of many passages in Temperley 1979.

true worship; in the wider world of Christendom a very wide variety of musical fashions may be encountered. Churchgoers are infinitely variable. Thus among the Cambridge colleges in the eighteenth century the endowed choirs of King's, Trinity and St John's maintained a musical tradition – doubtless with ups and downs, but never forgotten – while in most college chapels the services were said. It is no longer so: choirs flourish exceedingly in many other colleges. As a student I particularly relished the quiet, said service of the chapel; in my sixties and seventies I prefer the exquisite singing of the choir. This variety was always available. It may be right to assume that in a modest village church, such as those in which Jane Austen chiefly worshipped, music was modest or non-existent: there is nothing in her writings to prove the matter one way or the other – or to reveal her tastes in church music.[21] But the notion that there was no music in a late-eighteenth-century parish church is a myth.

To what extent the practice of hymn singing seeped into Anglican parish churches in the eighteenth century is very hard to determine: no doubt much less than into the chapels of the people called Methodists. But the distinction was for long very unclear: John Wesley expected to the end of his life that his followers would attend their parish churches and receive communion there, and it is highly probable that a majority of his early followers were by origin pious members of the Church of England.[22] One striking feature of the Methodist movement was its attempt to revive eucharistic worship – and in this Isaac Watts was its precursor. His most celebrated hymn 'When I survey the wondrous cross' was composed to be sung at the Lord's Table – at the eucharist – and unites the Body and Blood of Christ with the crucified Saviour – so that –

> Forbid it, Lord, that I should boast
> Save in the Cross of Christ my God

is a paraphrase of St Paul – Galatians 6:14 – and what follows is a commentary on Paul's vision of 'the Cross of our Lord Jesus Christ, by whom the world is crucified unto me, and I unto the World'.

> His dying crimson like a robe
> Hangs o'er his body on the tree,
> Then I am dead to all the globe,
> And all the globe is dead to me.[23]

It is difficult to determine when this great hymn was first commonly sung in Anglican churches; but it is abundantly clear that the dissenting,

---

[21] In Piggott 1979, a delightful study of Jane Austen's interest in music, church music plays little part.

[22] Rupp 1986, pp. 436–48.

[23] Quoted Rupp 1986, p. 160.

evangelical love of hymns spread far and wide as the eighteenth century advanced: it is most powerfully reflected in the *Olney Hymns in Three Books*, in which the poet William Cowper and the fire-eating Anglican Evangelical John Newton collaborated. Newton gathered in his capacious mind many of the impulses of the age. He died rector of St Mary Woolnoth in the City of London, and his tomb there calls him 'a Servant of Slaves in Africa' in daring (if perhaps unconscious) imitation of the papal title 'Slave of the slaves of God' (*servus servorum Dei*). He had been master of a slave-trading vessel; then a convert to a stern Calvinist creed; in his later years he gave crucial evidence of the cruelty of slavery; yet his hymns are full of the joy of divine grace in the best Evangelical tradition –

> How sweet the name of Jesus sounds
> In a believer's ear –

and

> Glorious things of thee are spoken,
> Sion, city of our God . . .

delectable hymns, if poignant companions to the slaves of Africa.[24]

All this is eloquent testimony to the variety of spiritual inspiration and outlook which is so characteristic of the eighteenth century – and yet lacking in some caricatures, and even in some mature portraits, of it – and to the conflict between the stereotype and the historical evidence.

Jane Austen and the Evangelicals

We may, therefore, be prepared to find a considerable distance between conventional accounts of Jane Austen's religious background and the evidence she provides, seen in perspective. A striking example lies in the question of whether Jane Austen was influenced by the Evangelical Movement, and what signs of such influence may be found in her novels. One element in this question can quickly be disposed of. It has sometimes been asserted that the evident moral chasm between the tolerance of Lydia's vice in *Pride and Prejudice* and the rigorism of *Mansfield Park* may be attributed to some kind of conversion that Jane Austen underwent about 1813. But the one book was finished and published and the other written at virtually the same time: there is assuredly no space for a conversion between, and the truth seems much more likely to be that the contrast is not between Jane unregenerate and Jane converted as between the views she has allotted to her characters in each book.[25]

[24] On Newton, see Rupp 1986, pp. 481–2; Martin 1950; Davie 1993, chap. 10.
[25] See p. 46.

On the other hand, it is most unlikely that she was in no way influenced by the Evangelicals. Some critics have written as if the Evangelical Movement was a new wave of the early nineteenth century, which might have come on Jane Austen in middle life. Undoubtedly much of its greatest influence came from the Clapham circle in the heyday of Wilberforce and the Venns, at the turn of the century – and much more was to spread from Cambridge in the later years of Charles Simeon in the opening decades of the nineteenth century. But its origins lay far back in the work of the Wesleys in Oxford in the 1720s and 30s – with its roots farther back still in many of the spiritual impulses of the seventeenth century. By the middle of the eighteenth century, wrote a leading authority thirty years ago, 'it was scarcely possible for an Anglican clergyman not to have heard something of Methodism [in origin a synonym for Evangelical fervour] and its doctrines'.[26] Jane Austen was brought up in a rectory in the late eighteenth century: some knowledge of Evangelical ideas and impulses is almost certain to have been part of her early education. Furthermore, one of her many clerical cousins was the Reverend Edward Cooper, rector of Hamstall Ridware in Staffordshire, an Evangelical of the second generation, for his father, another Edward Cooper, had preached Evangelical sermons before him. Jane found Mr Cooper pompous and tiresome, and that may have affected her view of his sermons; but she assails them precisely for their Evangelical doctrines. Thus, to her sister Cassandra, 9 September 1816 – incidentally, two years after the publication of *Mansfield Park*: 'We do not much like Mr Cooper's new sermons; – they are fuller of Regeneration and Conversion than ever – with the addition of his zeal in the cause of the Bible Society.'[27]

There is copious evidence that, among contemporary poets, she knew the works of William Cowper particularly well. In a letter of November 1798 she tells of the family acquiring some work of Cowper's, though in the following month she speaks of her father reading Cowper without excessive enthusiasm: 'I listen when I can.'[28] But his long discursive poem *The Task* impinges quite deeply on *Mansfield Park* and *Emma*. The quotations from Cowper in the novels are mainly from the passages in *The Task* reflecting his love of nature and country walks, or Emma's love of fancy – or about the homesick schoolboy in the *Tirocinium*.[29] Marianne's devotion

---

[26] Walsh 1966, p. 137.

[27] *Letters*, L no. 145, p. 322; C no. 134, p. 467 and Index 2; M, F-414. Cf. Collins 1993, pp. 186–7. The published *Sermons* of Edward Cooper were his father's: father and son were both Edward.

[28] *Letters*, L nos. 12, 14, pp. 22, 27; C, nos. 12, 14, pp. 33, 39; M, F-21; for a reminiscence of *The Task*, see *Letters*, L no. 50, p. 119, 386 n. 5; C no. 49, p. 178, and note; cf. Collins 1993, p. 80.

[29] See esp. *Emma* II, c. 4, p. 56 (cf. p. 542) from *The Task* (Cowper, p. 150); *MP* p. 431 (cf. p. 550) from *Tirocinium*.

to Cowper – and Thomson and Scott – in *Sense and Sensibility* provokes Edward Ferrars to mild satire on her love of twisted trees, appropriate to Cowper's *Yardley Oak*.[30] But Jane can hardly have read without reflection the religious passages in *The Task* – nor lived in ignorance of the *Olney Hymns*. What she read, indeed, may not have appeared peculiarly Evangelical to her.

> The dearest idol I have known,
>   Whate'er that idol be;
> Help me to tear it from thy throne,
>   And worship only thee.

> So shall my walk be close with God,
>   Calm and serene my frame;
> So purer light shall mark the road
>   That leads me to the Lamb.[31]

Cowper's frame was commonly far from serene: but when writing in this mould, he spoke of a deep piety not specific to any party in the Church.

This is perhaps the key to the divergent views of the Evangelicals reflected in Jane Austen's letters: her piety was that of her family, not of any party – the devout observance of the country parsonage, ready to absorb the influences of the diverse world of eighteenth-century religion – be it deriving from the high church books of devotion of Jeremy Taylor and William Law, or the Puritan and Methodist tradition of Watts and the Wesleys. Jane's comment on regeneration and conversion – written near the end of her life – makes clear that the theological emphases peculiar to the Evangelicals – and no doubt the Calvinist emphasis on predestination and hell[32] – were uncongenial to her. She took a broad view of divine compassion. '*May thy mercy be extended over all mankind*', she wrote in one of her prayers, 'bringing the ignorant to the knowledge of thy truth, awakening the impenitent, touching the hardened. Look with compassion upon the afflicted of every condition, assuage the pangs of disease, comfort the broken in spirit.' In 1798 Jane had greeted the news of the death of her father's half-brother with the words: 'The goodness which made him valuable on earth, will make him blessed in Heaven' – which might suggest

---

[30] For Marianne's delight in Cowper, see *SS* I c. 17, p. 92; cf. Cowper p. 306.

[31] *Olney Hymns* (1779), p. 4; Cowper, p. 242. On Cowper's religious verse, see Davie 1993, chap. 11.

[32] John Wesley himself was not a Calvinist; and as to those who were, we do well to heed Gordon Rupp's words: 'If in the eighteenth century the problems of predestination and reprobation were . . . the theme of acrimonious debate, it cannot be too often said that the Calvinists were in the main concerned not about these things, but about the free and sovereign grace of God' (Rupp 1986, p. 483).

he had earned the path to Heaven, a sentiment savouring of Pelagianism, the layman's heresy *par excellence*.[33]

Of dissent and dissenters there is little trace in her letters and none in the novels. There is no reason to suppose she had the strong prejudice against them which was affected by some leading Anglicans, such as the high Tory Richard Farmer, master of Emmanuel College, Cambridge.[34] They are never pilloried in her novels. There is no trace of the attitude caricatured by Mrs Gaskell in 1853: Mr Peter reminds one of the ladies of Cranford that 'he had been living for a long time among savages [actually, in the ancient civilisation of India] – all of whom were heathens – some of them, he was afraid, were downright Dissenters'.[35] The general drift of Jane Austen's mind and opinions prepares us for a certain sympathy with other viewpoints. One certainly cannot make any deduction from the favour shown to the Roman Catholic Church in *The History of England*, nor from a rare sidelong glance at it – but strictly, a comment on Alexander Pope – accepting with a smile a possible change of her and Cassandra's plans: ' "Whatever is, is best." – There has been one infallible Pope in the world.'[36]

In letters to Cassandra of January 1809 she indulges in a confession of plain prejudice. Cassandra had written about Hannah More's *Coelebs in Search of a Wife* – and Jane thinks Cassandra has improved the name Caleb into Coelebs: 'the diphthong I always saw, but knowing how fond you were of adding a vowel wherever you could, I attributed it to that alone'; and as for Caleb:

> You have by no means raised my curiosity after Caleb; – My disinclination for it before was affected, but now it is real; I do not like the Evangelicals. – Of course, I shall be delighted, when I read it, like other people, but till I do, I dislike it.[37]

One may suspect that she was chiefly expressing a prejudice against Hannah More.

That Jane Austen retained to the end of her days a preference for a traditional Anglican theology, free from Calvinist doctrines of predestination, election and conversion, seems strongly confirmed by her choice of sermons. Fordyce's *Sermons to Young Women* were chosen by Mr Collins to read to his female cousins, a circumstance which is comment enough in itself – Jane evidently for once approved of Lydia's reaction to serious

---

[33] For the prayer, *MW*, p. 456 (italics mine); for the letter of 1798, *Letters*, L no. 8, p. 13; C no. 8, p. 19; M, F-13.

[34] On Farmer, see Brooke in Bendall, Brooke and Collinson, *History of Emmanuel College*, chap. 13. For other evidence of hostility, especially from Farmer's friend, the Whig Samuel Parr, see Rupp 1986, p. 447.

[35] See Cranford (1853), c. 16. For the *History of England* (below), see *MW*, p. 147.

[36] *Letters*, L no. 94, p. 245; C no. 89, p. 362; M, F-285.

[37] *Letters*, L no. 67, p. 172; C no. 66, p. 259; L no. 66, pp. 169–70; C no. 65, p. 256.

instruction.[38] Miss Crawford reckoned a sensible preacher who could not compose his own sermons would use Blair's. Hugh Blair (1718–1800) was the author of highly popular discourses, of which the most favourable view is that 'they are the best examples of the sensible, if unimpassioned and rather affected, style of the moderate divines of the time'.[39] Jane's own choice was stated in a letter to her niece Anna of 28 September 1814, after the publication of *Mansfield Park* – 'I am very fond of Sherlock's Sermons, prefer them to almost any'.[40] In theory this could refer either to William Sherlock, dean of St Paul's, or to his son Thomas Sherlock (1678–1761), master of St Catharine's College, Cambridge, and successively bishop of Bangor, Salisbury and London – a Tory who none the less prospered in a Whig world, a convinced Anglican who was on good terms with some free churchmen. The son is the more likely, and a new edition of his works (as Chapman noted) was published at Oxford in 1812. It is not difficult to see why they appealed to Jane: they represent a plain, intelligible, clear-headed, reasonable, imaginative interpretation of the Christian gospel. There is a strong appeal to reason and to the moral teaching of the Church: 'the true end of religion is to make men better . . . God may favourably accept our endeavours.' The Gospel is presented as a rule of action; what we should call snobbery is roundly condemned. But Sherlock was not a latitudinarian in any advanced sense of the term: the strong lines of orthodox Christian doctrine are also sketched. Yet there is no Evangelical trace in them.

None the less there is no doubt that she had, or was coming to have, a more tolerant attitude to Evangelicals in her later years. There is a strange passage about a threat of renewal of war with the United States in 1814, addressed to her friend Martha Lloyd – if it were to Cassandra one might suspect more confidently that she had her tongue in her cheek – 'If we *are* to be ruined, it cannot be helped – but I place my hope of better things on a claim to the protection of Heaven, as a Religious Nation, a Nation in spite of much Evil *improving in religion*, which I cannot believe the Americans to possess.'[41] It could be that she felt the growing influence of the Evangelicals in the Church of England one of the signs of improvement, or supposed improvement. In any event, when faced in 1814 with a favourite niece being courted by an Evangelical, she showed her most sympathetic face to his point of view. Fanny Knight, eldest daughter of her brother Edward, was wooed by a Cambridge graduate, John Plumptre, a solemn and serious young man of Evangelical tendency. She turned to Jane for advice, which was given in two letters, models of the genre, in which with great

---

[38] *PP* I, c. 14, pp. 68–9.
[39] Leslie Stephen in *DNB*. Cf. *MP* I, c. 9, p. 92; Blair 1777–1801.
[40] *Letters*, L no. 108, pp. 278, 437; C no. 101, p. 406 and note to no. 101; M, F-338. See Sherlock 1812, esp. I, 37, 76, 109, 115–17, 132; and on him, Carpenter 1936.
[41] *Letters*, L no. 106, pp. 273–4; C no. 99.1, p. 508: M, F-329.

perceptiveness and affection she lays out the arguments on this side and that for accepting or rejecting him.

> And as to their being any objection from his *Goodness*, from the danger of his becoming even Evangelical, I cannot admit *that*. I am by no means convinced that we ought not all to be Evangelicals, and am at least persuaded that they who are so from Reason and Feeling, must be happiest and safest. Do not be frightened from the connection by your Brothers having most wit. Wisdom is better than wit, and in the long run will certainly have the laugh on her side; and don't be frightened by the idea of his acting more strictly up to the precepts of the New Testament than others.

Then she turned round and set out the arguments against:

> Anything is to be preferred or endured rather than marrying without Affection.[42]

In her next letter to Fanny she tantalises us. 'I cannot suppose we differ in our ideas of the Christian religion. You have given an excellent description of it. We only affix a different meaning to the Word *Evangelical*.'[43] We get a little more light on Fanny's view of the thing from the extracts from her diary which her son Lord Brabourne printed with these letters – and above all in his own comments. A little before these exchanges, in the autumn of 1814, Fanny noted: 'Plagued myself about Methodists all day' and 'had a nice conversation with Mr Sherer [the vicar of Godmersham] about Methodists'.[44] The use of the word Methodists – clearly here intended for Anglican Evangelicals as well as Dissenters, as was common use at the time – may be pejorative; and it seems likely that it was his austerity rather than his theology which alarmed her.

'The gentleman was of a very serious disposition', wrote Lord Brabourne, 'and eventually his religious views induced him to think dancing and other social amusements of the same sort things which ought to be eschewed and avoided by Christian people' – eventually, for Mr Plumptre is recorded to have danced once at least with Fanny, though only once, at a ball that August.

> My mother was of a different opinion. I do not suppose there ever was a woman more profoundly and really religious; throughout the whole of her life she attended assiduously to her religious duties, never a day passed that she did not devote some portion of it to the perusal of some

[42] *Letters*, L no. 109, p. 280; C no. 103, p. 410; M, F-341.

[43] *Letters*, L no. 114, p. 287; C no. 106, p. 420; M, F-351.

[44] Brabourne 1912, II, 312. Deirdre Le Faye has identified and used these diaries in her notes: see *Letters*, L, p. 474: they are now in the Centre for Kentish Studies, Maidstone, U951 F24/1-69.

pious author (which she called 'reading my goodness'), and no one ever strove more earnestly to do her duty and to follow the teaching of the Gospel. But she entertained a strong opinion that this might be done without a severance from the ordinary pursuits and amusements of other people; that a person might live 'in the world' without being 'of the world', and that to perform the duties which came before her in life, and set a practical example of a Christian life in her everyday existence, was as likely to be acceptable to God as the withdrawal from pursuits in which everybody else indulged . . .[45]

In the end Fanny rejected Mr Plumptre, and it was not until after Jane's death, in 1820, that she married Edward Knatchbull.

We may take it Jane saw the Evangelicals as serious Christians with a biblical and social conscience; Fanny saw them as puritans. Certainly Jane would have had no sympathy with any aversion to dancing: her letters are full of balls and rumours of balls. True, she shudders at Mr Collins' dancing, and makes Elizabeth Bennet surprised that he indulges in it – and deeply sorry she enquired, when he claims her for the first two dances in the ball at Netherfield; but that is because she had hopes of a better partner, and in the event Mr Collins 'gave her all the shame and misery which a disagreeable partner for a couple of dances can give'.[46]

Sunday Travelling

A pendant to Jane Austen's supposed conversion to Evangelical fervour has often been found in a passage in *Persuasion* in which Anne Elliot is apprised of her cousin Mr Elliot's worldly manner of life, first of all by evidence that 'Sunday-travelling had been a common thing.'[47] Critics who know little of the true history of Sunday observance have reckoned this marks a posting stage on the way to the Victorian Sunday. 'That Catherine Morland, or any of the early heroines, would have felt this way about travelling on Sunday is unthinkable', wrote one such.[48]

We can readily agree that the passage presupposes some of the attitudes we attach to the Victorian Sunday. But in a considerable measure the Victorians who laboured to keep holy the Sabbath Day – in accord with their interpretation of the Fourth Commandment – were simply trying to enforce (however unconsciously) the rules and ideals of the late-medieval

[45] Brabourne 1912, II, 311–12; for Mr John Plumptre dancing, see *Letters*, L, no. 105, p. 270; C no. 99, p. 397 (23–24 August 1814). The Reverend Edward Cooper danced in the 1790s: see *Letters*, C and L nos. 1–2.
[46] *PP* I, c. 17, pp. 87, 90.
[47] *P* II, c. 5, p. 161.
[48] Roberts 1979, p. 154.

Church, which had been observed by many and admired by more ever since. There is equally a sense in which *common* Sunday travelling must mean neglect of church going – and, more than that, the failure to set an example to those less well off by not attending the services of the church. Only the well-to-do could afford to travel extensively on Sunday, since there was apparently no public transport on that day; and in the country villages in which Jane Austen was brought up, and was living once again when *Persuasion* was written, this meant the neglect by the rich of one of their most fundamental duties – to be leaders in church going.

The issue is confused because it was indeed the case that Sabbath day observance – interpreted to mean avoidance of work and travel and unsuitable sports and pleasures on Sundays – had been a major theme with the Puritans and remained so with the Evangelicals. It is not my purpose to belittle the influence of the Evangelicals. But Sunday travel – save in one's own private carriage or on horseback – was forbidden by the law of England long before John Wesley was born; and devout Christians of all persuasions would have united to condemn *common* Sunday travelling, which interfered with church going. It is true that Jane and Elizabeth Bennet travelled on Sunday together – but only the three miles from Netherfield Park to Longbourn House, and only 'after morning service'.[49] In the same novel, Mr Gardiner travels from Longbourn to London on a Sunday; but speed was of the essence, for it was urgent that he find and help Mr Bennet in the search for Lydia.[50] Still, these passages are a reminder that occasional Sunday travel was not such a shocking event. Indeed, the reformers of the day who denounced unsuitable sports and entertainments seem much less concerned about travel – to a degree that suggests they did not regard it as a major problem.[51]

When Dr Kenneth Parker set out to sketch the history of Sunday observance in the sixteenth and early seventeenth centuries, he found to his surprise – and everyone else's – that the most rigorous taboos in the main simply reiterated the rules of the medieval Church.[52] No branch of the Church or churches disputed that Sunday was for religious observance and not for idleness and dissipation; it was only putting it into practice that seemed constantly to fail or falter. It is also true that Puritan insistence on Sunday observance inspired a measure of reaction from James I and his councillors; and the obsession of some Puritan polemicists with the issue brought a bold reaction from Laud and his supporters in the 1630s, suggesting that too strict a sabbatarian doctrine – and the prohibition of reasonable

[49] *PP* I, c. 12, p. 60 ('only three miles', *PP* I, c. 7, p. 32).
[50] *PP* III, c. 6, p. 295. One may suspect confusion in this passage, since he set off as soon as the post arrived (p. 294) – and one is surprised that it could arrive on a Sunday.
[51] See works cited in n. 52.
[52] Parker 1988, chap. 2; for the eighteenth century, see Whitaker 1940.

festivities – was unacceptable; and that religious observance should not be confined to Sunday.[53] Naturally, this caused some disarray among high churchmen; for neither Laud, nor his more genial allies, believed for a moment in relaxing the basic rules. It was indeed when Laud was first coming into the ascendant, early in the reign of Charles I, that the act of 1627 which laid the foundations for the next three centuries of the legal rules about Sunday observance came to pass. It is generally interpreted as a surprising concession by Charles I to Puritan sentiment, but it contained little or nothing offensive to high churchmen.[54] It was confirmed and enlarged by an equally high church regime – when Gilbert Sheldon was about to be succeeded by William Sancroft as archbishop of Canterbury – in 1676.[55] Under these draconian measures no Sunday trading was permitted until successive acts of the 1930s and the 1990s; and trading included the plying for hire of waggons and carriages of every description. So sweeping was this measure that it had soon to be modified lest it defeat its own purpose – for no one who depended on a hired vehicle to go to church could legally get there; and an amending act of 1693 allowed a limited number of hackney carriages to ply by turns each Sunday. Such was the law in Jane Austen's lifetime: only the rich could travel freely on Sundays, and they only in their own carriages. This is not to say that the law was enforced; that is more than we know. In the present state of knowledge, it is evident that many folk used their carriages for driving in the London parks and the like; that merchants sometimes used Sundays – when trading as such was impossible – to move from place to place.[56] But it is evident also that there was a basic assumption – doubtless of religious origin, doubtless fostered by Evangelical propaganda, but felt as a secular custom too in the eighteenth as in the twentieth century – that Sunday was for the quieter pleasures of home, the day of the family.

A pleasing coda from the next generation comes in the diary of Julia Lawrence. Sunday 18 April 1841 at Cirencester, recently linked via Kemble to the GWR:

> A steam-engine came up to the station from London for the first time about 9 o'clock. It occasioned so much confusion and bustle that papa

---

[53] Parker 1988, chaps. 6–7.

[54] For the act of 1627, see Parker 1988, esp. pp. 175–6.

[55] Gibson 1713, pp. 269–72, recited the authorities, the acts of 3 Charles I, c. 1 (1627), 29 Charles II, c. 7 (1676: this restrains waggoners etc. from Sunday journeys); 5, 6 William and Mary, c. 22 (1693), allowing *some* hackney coaches to ply for hire on Sundays.

[56] There seems little evidence about the timing of stage coaches in the late eighteenth century; the fullest account I have seen of the early nineteenth century is in Bates 1969, a comprehensive collection for 1836. Where the days of the week are specified, Sunday services are very rare and usually much reduced. But as many are not given specific days, or 'daily' is implicit or explicit, caution is necessary. For Sunday services see e.g., pp. 89–91, 120–1, 124–5, 145, 147.

[a leading local solicitor much involved in railway business] ordered it to be sent back again to Kemble . . . It was very extraordinary and wrong to send it up on Sunday. Mr Powell [the rector], in a short and interesting address before his sermon, mentioned the efforts which had been successfully made to stop such a profanation of the Sabbath, and entreated all his hearers to remember the Sabbath day to keep it holy.[57]

In Julia Lawrence many influences met and mingled – Quaker grand-parents, a traditional Anglican family, contemporary high, middle and low church – in the mind of a forceful, intelligent and well-educated young woman born three years or so after Jane Austen died. But her favourite reading was in the hymn book of the Oxford Movement, Keble's *Christian Year*.

There is a myth abroad that the Victorian Sunday was preceded by a per-missive eighteenth century. The truth is that there was much variety of practice and attitude in both eras: it could indeed be argued that the shrill-ness of Victorian propaganda for sabbath day observance is an indication of how little it was often heeded; that the quieter voice of eighteenth-century churchmen reflects a world in which a certain measure at least of Sunday observance was simply taken for granted. This probably exaggerates the error of popular legend. For the eighteenth-century churchmen were not so quiet on the subject; and in the 1780s Beilby Porteus, bishop of London, could rouse Parliament to legislate for the better observance of Sunday. But, significantly, the Act of 1781 says nothing specifically about travel: on this theme it had nothing to add to that of 1676.[58] Porteus was not himself an Evangelical in doctrine; but like many men of good will of that age he had great sympathy with Evangelical views on many themes; it surprises a modern audience to learn that his own views on the Sabbath could command a majority in both Houses of Parliament. It would be absurd to deny Evangelical influence in this success – and equally false to attribute it wholly to the Evangelicals. There is no hint or indication in *Persuasion* of anything remarkable or partisan in the religious views of Anne Elliot, who was presumably a conventional, churchgoing, squire's daughter – excep-tional only in intelligence and perceptiveness. If we wish to understand the assumption underlying the text of *Persuasion* that any reader might think common Sunday travelling a sign of frivolity and lack of serious thinking, we need look no further than the country parsonage – of whatever religious colouring it might be. It was the business of Jane's father and brothers to urge their flock to proper religious observance every Sunday – such as we

[57] Cripps 1914, p. 30. Her copy of *The Christian Year* (1839 edn), much annotated, is in my possession: Julia Lawrence, later Mrs Cripps, was my great-grandmother.
[58] Whitaker 1940, pp. 155-8.

have every reason to suppose Jane herself adhered to. Few more vexatious impediments to this purpose could be imagined than habitual Sunday travelling by the well-to-do. For travelling in this sense meant going a long journey – on the road all day, preventing attendance at even one service. Jane and Elizabeth Bennet went to the morning service; perhaps Mr Gardiner went to evensong. But even if he did not, his Sunday travelling was not habitual; and none is recorded in the other novels.[59]

Jane Austen's Religion

The brief and moving biographical notice attached to *Persuasion* and written by her recently ordained brother Henry late in 1817 is occasionally at variance with her letters: thus – 'She never uttered either a hasty, a silly, or a severe expression' – he is talking of her comments on others, and what he says is incredible.[60] We can believe that she curbed her tongue in his presence – the full flavour of her cattiness was reserved for Cassandra. Yet the Letters also show her capacity to be charitable in unlikely quarters; and we need not doubt Henry's sincerity. Nor need we be unduly sceptical of his final statement:

'She was thoroughly religious and devout; fearful of giving offence to God, and incapable of feeling it towards any fellow creature. On serious subjects she was well-instructed, both by reading and meditation, and her opinions accorded strictly with those of our Established Church.'[61] In fact, her views seem likely to have been very similar to Fanny Knight's, as described by her son. She was perhaps more open than Fanny to influences from other circles than those in which she had been brought up; but her comments and her prayers suggest a middle-of-the-road Anglicanism – rather high than low church.

Her observation of people – her appreciation of evil as well as good – were much too sharp for Henry's portrait of her bland, charitable kindness to be convincing. It has often puzzled her readers to understand how a single woman living a relatively secluded, static life in rural England – even allowing for her years in Bath and Southampton – could have acquired such a store of shrewd insight into the vagaries and varieties of human nature. I have sometimes wondered if Agatha Christie had Jane Austen in mind in forming the character of Miss Marple, who could solve every vile crime by its likeness to something she witnessed in the village of St Mary Mead. Furthermore, 'there is a quickness of perception in some, a nicety in the discernment of character, a natural penetration, in short, which no

---

[59] Even Mr Crawford does not leave Portsmouth until Monday: *MP*, pp. 410, 415, 555.
[60] *Biographical Notice* attached to *NA and P*, p. 6. See p. 4.
[61] Ibid. p. 8.

experience in others can equal', as Jane herself observed in *Persuasion*.[62] But I think in truth that Jane Austen's knowledge of human nature tells us something rather profound about the eighteenth-century church – or about the life and experience of clergy and their families in many ages.

I vividly recall the impression of a first reading of the passage in G.K. Chesterton's *The Innocence of Father Brown* in which it is revealed that the humble priest knows more of crime than the world-class criminal – owing to his experience of the confessional. 'Has it never struck you that a man who does next to nothing but hear men's real sins is not likely to be wholly unaware of human evil?'[63] George Austen and his daughter presumably knew nothing about the confessional (though that cannot be quite certain); but to be a parson's daughter in an eighteenth-century village – if the parson was conscientious and resident, and the daughter more than commonly observant – opened a similar window into human nature. The chief message of Jane's novels for the student of Anglican clergy is the light it sheds on what they might know of the vagaries of human nature and their human flock.

The Clergy in the Novels

The professions of the day were unevenly represented in Jane Austen's novels. There are a few soldiers scattered about, both good and bad; a few lawyers; far more – and more important – sailors, at least in *Mansfield Park* and *Persuasion*; yet more clergymen. The proportions are hardly surprising: she sprang from a long line of divines, on both sides of her family; her father and eldest brother James were clergymen, her brother Henry, after a spell in the militia and as a banker, was ordained towards the end of her life: two more brothers, Frank and Charles, were sailors.[64] She knew more of these professions, and made more of them. One might indulge a fancy that her family responded with such alarm to her portrayal of Mr Collins in *Pride and Prejudice* that she determined on a more serious clergyman in her next book – hence Edmund Bertram in *Mansfield Park*. If so, there was backsliding in *Emma*: Mr Elton is one of her least attractive clergy, anyway after his marriage. One might also suggest that the portrait of Admiral Crawford in *Mansfield Park* – who buried his wife and brought his mistress into his house, thus exiling Mary Crawford to Mansfield and setting part of the plot of the book in motion – even granted that he is balanced by Lieutenant William Price – led to a similar reaction in the highly congenial sailors of *Persuasion*. But this is pure speculation, and it is likely that Jane enjoyed

[62] *P* II, c. 12, p. 249.
[63] 1st edn, London, 1911, p. 31.
[64] See pp. 17–18.

pulling her brothers' legs in the portrayal of their professions while in the same breath showing respect for them.[65]

It is of more relevance to observe that the opinions she collected from her brothers on *Mansfield Park* and *Emma* – with backward glances to *Sense and Sensibility* and *Pride and Prejudice* – show no inclination at all to comment on the clergy or the sailors. Mr Collins was a favourite character with her mother; Mr Sherer, the vicar of Godmersham, where her brother Edward lived and which she and Cassandra often visited, apropos of *Emma*, was 'displeased with my picture of clergymen'.[66] Ben Lefroy, a clergyman to be, thought 'Mr and Mrs Elton admirable'; but Mrs Wroughton, whoever she may have been, 'thought the authoress wrong, in such times as these, to draw such clergymen as Mr Collins and Mr Elton'; the Reverend Samuel Cooke, as she noted in a letter of June 1814, thought *Mansfield Park* ' "the most sensible novel he ever read" – and the manner in which I treat the clergy, delights them very much'.[67] Yet the clergy brothers made no comment on her clergy – though it is true that James and his wife were also delighted with *Mansfield Park* and less so with *Emma*; nor did the future admirals, Frank and Charles, comment on the portrait of Admiral Crawford. There was every variety of opinion recorded in Jane Austen's notes, but no sign of professional concern or disapproval from her brothers. This is negative evidence; but it strongly suggests that they took most of her clergy to be natural and reasonable – or anyway entertaining – portraits, however tiresome and absurd some of them might be.

It has often been observed that her clergy do not seem very clerical. But that is partly because the novels were written before the apotheosis of the professions in the nineteenth and twentieth centuries, and before the days of clergy schools or theological colleges in the Church of England.[68] Henry Tilney, Edward Ferrars and Edmund Bertram at least had been to Oxford, and Mr Collins either to Oxford or Cambridge. It was a striking feature of the ancient English universities in this period that they were regarded as seminaries for Anglican clergy, and taught them everything except theology – or rather, provided most of them with its bare rudiments, and only offered the path to real theological learning to the very few. As late as the 1850s Fenton Hort, who was to be one of Cambridge's most eminent theologians, wrote a pamphlet defending the kind of training classics and mathematics and the life of Cambridge offered for would-be pastors.[69] Jane's attitude to Oxford was evidently ambivalent: it had by implication

---

[65] See pp. 17–18.
[66] *MW*, pp. 436–7.
[67] *MW*, pp. 438–9; *Letters*, L no. 101, p. 263; C no. 96, p. 389.
[68] On the apotheosis of the professions, see Perkin 1989; cf. my comments in Brooke 1993, pp. 242–3.
[69] Brooke 1993, pp. 9–14, esp. p. 10 and n. 42.

fostered the good manners and good learning of Mr Tilney and helped to make a sound and gentlemanly clergyman of Edmund Bertram. But as well as Henry Tilney, and the shadowy James Morland, Oxford had been the home of the rattle John Thorpe, who made a tenuous claim to have been dissipated there. Edward Ferrars himself averred that at 18 'I was . . . entered at Oxford and have been properly idle ever since' – a sentence doubtless aimed a little at Jane's brothers;[70] and Mr Collins profited little or nothing from keeping the necessary terms at 'one of the universities'.[71] But Jane herself came from the Oxford establishment: her great uncle had been master of Balliol for much of the eighteenth century – 1726/7–1785 – and her father and eldest brother had both been students and fellows of St John's – which may also be Edmund's college, which Fanny can pass as the coach enters Oxford.[72] Jane was evidently very much aware of Oxford as the training ground of the clergy, with many family links. She was a little aware of Cambridge too, from which Samuel Blackall had come to visit and perhaps to woo her in 1798, and John Plumptre to woo Fanny Knight in 1814.[73] But in her novels she reserved it for two of her rakes – George Wickham and Henry Crawford.[74] If Wickham was there, perhaps Mr Darcy himself might have been a gentleman commoner at Trinity or Emmanuel: but there is no hint that he was, and the difference in age from Mr Bingley seems to make it clear that their friendship was not formed at university.[75] As she watched the coaches pass Chawton Cottage in July 1816 carrying the young Wykehamists to their holidays, she described them to her nephew Edward, who was one of those who had just left Winchester, as 'full of future heroes, legislators, fools and vilains' – a remarkable analysis of those about to fill the universities.[76] In spite of her ambivalent view of Oxford, there seems some hint of loyalty to it in the way she reserves her villains for Cambridge – though the Oxford of John

[70] For Henry Tilney at Oxford, see *NA* I, c. 14, p. 107; for John Thorpe and James Morland at Oxford, *NA* I, c. 9, p. 64; for Edward Ferrars at Oxford, *SS* I, c. 19, p. 103.

[71] *PP* I, c. 15, p. 70.

[72] *MP* III, c. 7, p. 376. Theophilus Leigh died 3 Jan. 1785 (Horn and Sherwin Bailey 1979, p. 97).

[73] See pp. 29–32, 130–2.

[74] See p. 68.

[75] Mr Bingley 'had not been of age two years' when he took Netherfield (*PP* I, c. 4, p. 16); when, approximately a year later, Darcy and Elizabeth become engaged, Darcy is 'eight and twenty' (*PP* III, c. 16, p. 369; for chronology, cf. pp. 402–6). Maybe there was not more than four years between them; but the implication of *PP* I, c. 4 is that London was their meeting place – and this is perhaps confirmed by his often seeing Bingley in love before he met Jane Bennet (p. 197), since female society was more readily available in London than Cambridge – and if Jane Austen had wanted them to go to university, she might well have said so.

[76] *Letters*, L no. 142, p. 316; C no. 130, p. 458.

Thorpe had its share of fools. Crawford and Thorpe apart, all the characters specifically assigned to universities were planning to be clergymen.

The unprofessional aspect of her clergy also reflects the rural world in which she sets the greater part of most of her novels. The beneficed rector or vicar is a central figure in the village community. He is second only to the squire or squires in status, helping the squires and other magistrates to preserve social harmony, or – to use what Miss Austen might have called the fashionable cant – as an instrument of social control. Mr Knightley and Mr Elton, squire-magistrate and parson, are the central characters in the parish meetings in *Emma*.[77] Mr Elton – not one of her more amiable clergymen – is shown much involved in the business of the parish, and his wife asserts that his day was frequently punctuated by calls for advice and help.[78] By the same token, the country parson was more deeply involved in the agricultural work of his community than his modern successor. He often had glebe land to cultivate: the Reverend Edward Ferrars and Elinor his wife, once settled in their parsonage at Delaford, had 'nothing to wish for, but the marriage of Colonel Brandon and Marianne, and rather better pasturage for their cows'.[79] More modestly, Mrs Collins found charms in 'her home and her housekeeping, her parish and her poultry, and all their dependent concerns'.[80] From Jane Austen's letters one might gain the impression that her father's hobby was pig-keeping.[81]

The duties of a clergyman were laid out in proper order by Mr Collins at Mr Bingley's ball at Netherfield.

> I consider music as a very innocent diversion, and perfectly compatible with the profession of a clergyman. – I do not mean, however, to assert that we can be justified in devoting too much of our time to music, for there are certainly other things to be attended to. The rector of a parish has much to do. – In the first place, he must make such an agreement for tythes as may be beneficial to himself and not offensive to his patron. He must write his own sermons; and the time that remains will not be too much for his parish duties, and the care and improvement of his dwelling, which he cannot be excused from making as comfortable as possible. And I do not think of light importance that he should have attentive and conciliatory manners towards

---

[77] *E* III, c. 16, p. 456.

[78] *E* III, c. 16, pp. 455–6.

[79] *SS* III, c. 14, pp. 374–5.

[80] *PP* II, c. 15, p. 216.

[81] *Letters*, L nos. 12–13, pp. 22, 25; C nos. 12–13, pp. 32, 36. One wonders if Lord Bolton (L, p. 25) who 'is particularly curious in *his* pigs, has had pigstyes of a most elegant construction built for them, and visits them every morning as soon as he rises' was the model for P.G. Wodehouse's Lord Emsworth. After Jane's father's death, her mother received her share of the pork of Steventon, much like Mrs and Miss Bates: *Letters*, L no. 78, p. 200; C no. 75, p. 296 (1813).

every body, especially towards those to whom he owes his preferment. I cannot acquit him of that duty . . .

– and he duly bows to Mr Darcy, as the nephew of his patron, Lady
Catherine de Bourgh.[82] We note the order – tithes first, but obeisance to
the patron the climax; that the maintenance of his house is dwelt on, the
chancel of his church not mentioned.[83] Yet the parish duties are there, even
if buried under the sermons – and we can presume him to include among
his duties the services of the church, the welfare of his flock and visiting the
poor. Most of these duties did not differentiate him from the better-off
members of his flock: Emma and Anne Elliot visit the poor as much as any
of the clergy in the novels. Many householders kept poultry: it was Mrs
Weston's turkeys whose theft frightened Mr Woodhouse into accepting
the protection of a son-in-law in his own house, and so to speeding
Emma's marriage.[84] But that is only another way of saying that the clergy
were deeply integrated into the life of the community – sharing its interests,
its gossip and its good works.

The medieval church had been richly endowed in lands and tithes and
other dues. In the course of the centuries, greedy monarchs, especially
Henry VIII, abetted by equally rapacious courtiers, had considerably
eroded the landed endowment. It still sufficed to support a few bishops in
the princely style of their predecessors, and all the bishops and cathedral
chapters in some measure. But the vast majority of the clergy owed their
income to tithes.

Tithes were a welfare tax of ancient origin, which had become by the
eleventh century a compulsory levy of a tenth of all income of every kind,
from land, trade, craftsmanship, what-have-you. As the canon law crystal-
lised in the twelfth century it became established that tithes were a form of
spiritual property – that is, they could only be levied by the Church and
administered by the Church. Their prime purpose had been to help the
poor; but poverty was widely interpreted, and from a very early date a proportion of them was allowed for the support of the clergy, who had no
other – or very little other – means of support. In course of time they came
primarily to be reckoned as income for the clergy; but it was never
accepted that the whole of the tithes of a parish should necessarily go to
support one clergyman. Nor was it possible in practice to prevent rapacious
laymen getting their hands on some of them. Tithes were always in theory
and largely in practice handed over to a variety of clergy to administer and
enjoy, not all of them as poor as one might wish. It became a common

---

[82] *PP* I, c. 18, p. 101.

[83] On the history of tithes, see esp. Constable 1964; for tithes in the early nineteenth
century, Cripps 1850, bk. 2, chap. 2. For the effects of the Reformation, see esp. Hill
1956.

[84] *E* III, c. 19, pp. 483–4. For what follows, see esp. Best 1964.

practice to divide tithes into two unequal proportions – approximately two thirds to the rector who might be an absentee, doing the necessary work of Church or state elsewhere, or a monastery or a college; one third to a vicar who served the parish on the rector's behalf. After the dissolution of the monasteries in the 1530s vast quantities of tithes came on the market, so to speak, and it was exceedingly difficult for the Church to reclaim them. None the less, a great part of the tithe which was collected went still, down to the early twentieth century, to support the clergy of the Church of England. The tithes of different parishes were extremely unequal, depending on the quality of the land, the energy of the farmers, and the extent to which the rector 'improved' them – that is, extracted his due.[85] The allocation to the clergy who did the work of the parish was even more unequal. Many Victorians viewed the levying of tithe with great suspicion, or contempt, because all taxes are unpopular, and there were two particular reasons for disprising tithes. First of all, they were exacted from the believer and the unbeliever alike, from Anglican, Catholic, Free Churchman, Jew and agnostic – yet those which had not been appropriated or misappropriated went solely for the support of the Anglican clergy. The levying of a tax for the Church became increasingly anomalous as the Church became less and less identifiable with the nation. Even more unpopular was the church rate, levied as a tax on all for the maintenance of the nave of the parish church and the support of its services.[86] Furthermore, though tithes had originally been a welfare tax levied on every kind of income, they had by custom and attrition long, long before the days of Jane Austen become attached to agricultural produce alone. In country districts, this could mean a reasonable proportion between the income of the leading parishioners and the support of the rector or vicar. Doubtless all manner of friction and difficulty could arise – but not necessarily so. It was an accepted part of the custom of the community; it gave rector and local landlords and farmers a common interest in the prosperity of the land; in a curious ironical fashion, it brought them closer together. In a similar way the fabric of the church was a joint responsibility: the parishioners had to care for the nave, the rector for the chancel. The splendour of many church naves reflects the pride the community could take in their church; and even if few new naves were built in the eighteenth century, many were repaired and restored. On the other hand, the striking difference in date and style which often persists between nave and chancel also shows how often rector and parishioners each went their own way: it would be as foolish to romanticise the relationship of rector and parish as to denigrate it.

But all this relates to country parishes alone. After the Industrial Revolution the balance of population shifted – and the shift grew steadily more

---

[85] On improving tithes, cf. *SS* III, c. 3, p. 283.
[86] On church rates, see Cripps 1850, pp. 442–74.

conspicuous as the nineteenth century advanced. Most tithes were col-lected from the countryside: how were new parishes in the rapidly expand-ing towns to be supported? The Victorians found an answer to this problem, of a kind: they built new churches and schools in new centres of population with a lavish hand, though a great part of the population were still relatively remote from them. From the 1830s on, they increasingly centralised the resources of the Church in the hands of the Church Com-missioners – a process completed in the twentieth century, when tithes have been finally commuted. Cathedral chapters retained a shadow of their landed endowment; Oxbridge colleges retained their share of tithes to the end, and still maintain many chancels in parishes of which they were once rectors (they are still quaintly called 'lay rectors'). But the endowments of the Church have shrivelled: the Church Commissioners can barely pay pensions for the clergy today; the bulk of the income for the working clergy comes from parish quotas, collected by the faithful. All this is more just and equal, no doubt; but the evil of pluralism has returned and will stay with us. The effect of shifting population and a changing religious ethos is that many country villages cannot now support a resident clergyman: three, five or even ten parishes are united, sometimes with a team, sometimes with a single clergyman. The ordination of women has enormously increased the potential pool of ordinands, but the Church cannot pay even the lowly stipends of the late twentieth century, or adequately staff its country parishes. The Victorians poured scorn on the customary arrange-ments of the eighteenth-century church. A modern Anglican can look back with envy.

Pluralism is an ancient abuse. Clergy have not always been less prone to the pursuit of mammon than laity: where rich tithes were to be garnered, pluralism flourished already in the twelfth and thirteenth centuries, and doubtless long before. The efforts of the late medieval Church, led by the fourteenth-century popes, to curb it had a considerable measure of success. Yet an extraordinary ambivalence ran through the practice of the late medieval and early modern church, and the Reformation was but a ripple on this particular pool. The popes put down pluralism with an iron hand, but made an exception for the cardinals – some of them friars vowed to holy poverty. Among the favourite clergy of King Henry VII (1485–1509) were Christopher Urswick, who held five archdeaconries, and John Fisher, the austere saintly bishop of Rochester, who as bishop was a model of devotion, and whose early pluralism had been of the most modest charac-ter.[87] In the eighteenth century Urswick's record was never approached; but a man might be Master of Trinity and archdeacon of Ely, as was the

---

[87] On Urswick and Fisher see Brooke 1989b, pp. 55–6, 64–5, nn. 42, 44. Fisher combined a fat rectory in Yorkshire with his academic offices in Cambridge – not technically pluralism according to contemporary rules.

great classical scholar Richard Bentley, or Master of Caius, canon of two cathedrals and later, successively bishop of three, as was Sir Thomas Gooch, Bart.[88] More to the point, the modest accumulation of country livings was common: Jane's eldest brother, James Austen, was absentee vicar of Sherborne St John and of Cubbington as well as rector of Steventon in his later years: he resided at Steventon and for a modest sum his other livings could be served by curates. By this means young clergy were given modest stipends till better times came, and the Reverend James put together a reasonable income for a married man with a growing family.[89]

Jane Austen's novels have many references to tithes and to the temporal affairs of a parson's life. They play too conspicuous a role in Mr Collins's catalogue of his duties; but she was doubtless enjoying a joke at the expense of all her clerical friends and relations – a joke relished by her mother, who especially enjoyed Mr Collins among the clergy and Mrs Norris among their wives.[90] But tithes played an equally conspicuous part in Edward Ferrars' preparation for orders in *Sense and Sensibility*. Colonel Brandon says of Delaford: 'it is a rectory, but a small one; the late incumbent, I believe, did not make more than 200*l.* per annum, and though it is certainly capable of improvement, I fear, not to such an amount as to afford him a very comfortable income'.[91]

The novels have a little to say of the basic duties of the parson – of weekly services, of marriage and baptism – and more of their relation to their patrons. Of services, indeed, there is very little said, though much assumed. When Edmund Bertram is recently ordained, and Henry Crawford is trying to impress Fanny Price, Crawford himself embarks on a discussion of the liturgy: it is curious that Miss Austen should have given such opportunities for the serious discussion of a clergyman's duties to Mr Collins and Mr Crawford.

> Edmund had already gone through the service once since his ordination; and upon this being understood, he had a variety of questions from Crawford as to his feelings and success; questions which being made – though with the vivacity of friendly interest and quick taste . . . he had true pleasure in satisfying; and when Crawford proceeded to ask his opinion and give his own as to the properest manner in which particular passages in the service should be delivered, shewing it to be a subject on which he had thought before, and thought with judgment, Edmund was still more and more pleased. This would be the way to Fanny's heart. . . .

[88] Bentley was archdeacon of Ely 1701–42 (Horn 1992, p. 14); on Gooch see Brooke, Horn and Ramsay 1988.
[89] Collins 1993, Index, p. 232; *Letters*, L p. 486.
[90] *MW*, pp. 432, 436.
[91] *SS* III, c. 3, pp. 282–3; cf. p. 368.

'Our liturgy', observed Crawford, 'has beauties, which not even a careless, slovenly style of reading can destroy; but it has also redundancies and repetitions, which require good reading not to be felt. . . . A sermon, well delivered, is more uncommon even than prayers well read. A sermon, good in itself, is no rare thing. It is more difficult to speak well than to compose well; that is, the rules and trick of composition are oftener an object of study. A thoroughly good sermon, thoroughly well delivered, is a capital gratification. I can never hear such a one without the greatest admiration and respect, and more than half a mind to take orders and preach myself. There is something in the eloquence of the pulpit, when it is really eloquence, which is entitled to the highest praise and honour. The preacher can touch and affect such an heterogeneous mass of hearers, on subjects limited, and long worn thread-bare in all common hands; who can say any thing new or striking, any thing that rouses the attention, without offending the taste, or wearing out the feelings of his hearers, is a man whom one could not (in his public capacity) honour enough. I should like to be such a man.'

Edmund laughed [and Crawford proceeds].

'I should indeed. I never listened to a distinguished preacher in my life, without a sort of envy. But then, I must have a London audience. I could not preach, but to the educated; to those who were capable of estimating my composition. And, I do not know that I should be fond of preaching often; now and then, perhaps, once or twice in the spring, after being anxiously expected for half a dozen Sundays together; but not for a constancy; it would not do for a constancy.'

And Fanny thinks the last words all too characteristic, and shakes her head – diverting Crawford from his theme.[92]

Although there are hints from time to time that Jane Austen assumed her characters were regular churchgoers – thus on a Sunday at Northanger spare time comprised the space between morning and afternoon service[93] – she rarely takes us to church save to a wedding – or to have a first view of Mrs Elton.[94] Theology and the sacraments were too solemn things, it seems, to introduce into the frivolous context of a novel. She presupposes a reasonable standard of piety, as unobtrusive, undemonstrative, as her own appears to have been. But a decline in family prayers – not in her own home, doubtless, but as the fashion in great houses – does seem to be admitted. When Mrs Rushworth shows her visitors the neglected chapel at Sotherton, and explains that family prayers were read in it 'within the

[92] *MP* III, c. 3, pp. 340–1.
[93] *NA* II, c. 9, p. 190.
[94] *E* II, c. 14, p. 270.

memory of many. But the late Mr Rushworth left it off' – Mary Crawford observes that 'Every generation has its improvements' – and Fanny retorts 'It is a pity . . . that the custom should have been discontinued. It was a valuable part of former times. . . .' An apostrophe from Miss Crawford on the profane thoughts of former occupants of the chapel closes the debate.[95]

If there is little on services in the church, there is less on its structure. Dr Grant acquires a prebendal stall in Westminster Abbey; but in general the country parish, with its church and parson, is the centre of religion in the novels. In marked contrast to Trollope, who fills his Barchester Novels with bishops and archdeacons, as well as with lesser clergy, Jane Austen never mentions an archdeacon and only twice (so far as I know) a bishop and once an archbishop. When the secret engagement of Edward Ferrars and Lucy Steele has come to light, and his prospects seem blighted, Lucy's sister tells Elinor that he will soon be ordained. 'Edward have got some business at Oxford, he says; so he must go there for a time; and after *that*, as soon as he can light upon a Bishop, he will be ordained. I wonder what curacy he will get!' There is a hope for Charles Hayter in *Persuasion* 'of getting something [a benefice] from the Bishop'. Mr Collins, an incumbent of the diocese of Canterbury – when he danced – 'was very far from dreading a rebuke either from the Archbishop or Lady Catherine de Bourgh'.[96] We have no evidence, within the novels or in the letters, of contact with any bishop: they failed to attract either her reverence or her laughter; she can be very caustic about lords temporal, but spared the lords spiritual.

The working of patronage in Jane Austen's day and her circles has been very fully described by Irene Collins.[97] Patronage in the church was part of a large structure, fundamental to the workings of lay and clerical society – of all the professions, and of the whole world of politics as well. The duke of Newcastle had made a profession of manipulating the workings of patronage in parliament; in his later years, as chancellor of the University of Cambridge, he played the game in Cambridge as a hobby. The distinction should not be too sharply drawn. In the eyes of the rising clergy in Oxford and Cambridge, the leading politicians were the source of major preferment; and when Newcastle had departed, the next generation of Cambridge dons gathered round the young Mr Pitt, who was both MP for the University and Prime Minister – with all the bishoprics, and much else, at his disposal. But for most rising clergy the prospect lay either with a curacy under a benevolent clerical friend, or – if they were so fortunate – with a living provided by a private patron. Patronage, like tithes, had been a fundamental part of the structure of the medieval church; unlike tithes, it is

[95] *MP* I, c. 9, pp. 86–7.
[96] *SS* III, c. 2, p. 275; *P* I, c. 9, p. 76; *PP* I, c. 17, p. 87.
[97] See esp. Collins 1993, chap. 2.

with us still – but in a very much modified form. Where it still exists in the Church of England, it has nowadays to be exercised in collaboration with the parish and the bishop: both have the right to veto any candidate the patron may propose. In the middle ages, and still in the eighteenth and nineteenth centuries, the ordinary folk of the parish had no say at all. The bishop had a theoretical veto: he alone could ordain – and he could refuse an unworthy candidate. This right does not seem to have been very frequently exercised; nor was the process of preparation an elaborate one. Edmund Bertram sets off for Peterborough on 23 December, expecting to return a week later – thus missing Christmas at home.[98]

Even allowing for Jane's ruthless simplification of the process, this probably does not much misrepresent what would have happened – a few days for examination and the service itself were all that was reckoned necessary. It was assumed that the candidate had acquired the necessary education at Oxford or Cambridge – even though there was little formal teaching of theology in either university.[99] That apart, the patron was free to choose; his patronage had for many centuries been seen as a valuable piece of property. Colonel Brandon used the living of Delaford to reward the loyalty of Edward Ferrars – first to Lucy then to Elinor – when his mother cut him off. This gave him a favourable view of Edward's character, and he knew that he had studied at Oxford. But he knew little else.[100]

John Dashwood's reaction to Brandon's generosity prepares us for the more subtle proprietary attitude of Sir Thomas Bertram. Dashwood finds it hard to believe that the Colonel could really have presented Edward.

> 'Really! – Well, this is very astonishing! – no relationship! – no connection between them! – and now that livings fetch such a price! – what was the value of this?'
>
> 'About two hundred a-year' [replies Elinor].
>
> 'Very well – and for the next presentation to a living of that value – supposing the late incumbent to have been old and sickly, and likely to vacate it soon – he might have got I dare say – fourteen hundred pounds.'

---

[98] *MP* II, cc. 8, 11, pp. 255, 282, 286. He stayed longer than a week, not on account of the bishop – but to avoid Miss Crawford (as he wrongly expected to do): c. 3, p. 334. For the chronology, cf. pp. 554–5. Christmas figures more substantially as a family festival in *Emma* (esp. p. 79); and in *Pride and Prejudice* all the Gardiners are to join the Darcys at Christmas (p. 383) – though oddly they seem to have joined the Bennets the previous Christmas without their children: at least the children are not mentioned, as they are on a later visit (cf. *PP* II, c. 2, esp. p. 139, with II, c. 19, p. 239).

[99] But there was much else conducive – or not so conducive – to preparation for a clerical career. See Searby 1997; and cf. n. 69.

[100] *SS* III, c. 3, pp. 282–3, describes the favourable view he had obtained of Edward's character, and his readiness to make him rector of Delaford, even before he had any idea of his attachment to Elinor, or hers to him.

And John is amazed that the Colonel should have been so imprudent not to arrange matters so before the old incumbent died: 'I am convinced that there is a vast deal of inconsistency in almost every human character.' – And so is the reader, who the more appreciates the difference between John Dashwood's purely commercial view of patronage and the more humane – if not deeply religious – considerations of Colonel Brandon.[101]

Sir Thomas Bertram is given an altogether more admirable character than John Dashwood: he has high principles, and is very firm in living up to his duties and his notions of right. But he is also a man of very limited vision – as is most amply revealed in his failure to make any real contact with his daughters: for this he is punished by Maria's disgrace in the end, and he punishes her even more harshly.[102] We can expect a certain ambivalence in his treatment of his patronage; and we find it indeed a piquant mixture of high principle, family obligation and financial need; but in the reverse order.

The living of Mansfield had been held by Sir Thomas's friend and brother-in-law Mr Norris; and when he died it

> was hereafter for Edmund, and had his uncle died a few years sooner, it would have been duly given to some friend to hold till he was old enough for orders. But [the eldest son] Tom's extravagance had, previous to that event, been so great, as to render a different disposal of the next presentation *necessary*, and the younger brother must help to pay for the pleasures of the elder.[103] There was another family-living actually held for Edmund [Thornton Lacey, of which we hear much later on in *Mansfield Park*]; but though this circumstance had made the arrangement somewhat easier to Sir Thomas's conscience, he could not but feel it to be an act of injustice, and he earnestly tried to impress his eldest son with the same conviction, in the hope of its producing a better effect than any thing he had yet been able to say or do.
>
> 'I blush for you, Tom,' said he, in his most dignified manner; 'I blush for the expedient which I am driven on, and trust I may pity your feelings as a brother on the occasion. You have robbed Edmund for ten, twenty, thirty years, perhaps for life, of more than half the income which ought to be his . . .'[104]

An ardent churchman might have objected that Sir Thomas was selling a church office for cash, thus committing simony, the sin of Simon Magus;

---

[101] *SS* III, c. 3, pp. 294–5.
[102] See p. 23.
[103] Italics mine: we are hearing the voice of Sir Thomas, rather than that of Miss Austen – or perhaps, rather, Miss Austen's in irony.
[104] *MP* I, c. 3, p. 23.

and in other respects Sir Thomas took a lofty view, for example, of a patron's and a parson's duty: it was not only paternal affection which made him settle the young couple at Thornton Lacey 'with every kind attention'.[105] But the presentation was his property, and family duty came before everything else. Providence, however, in the person of Jane Austen, was kind. The living of Mansfield had to be sold to Dr Grant; but she presently provided him to a stall in Westminster Abbey which enabled him to live in London – leaving Mansfield to a curate; then she carried him off in such a peremptory manner as only a parson's daughter could have conceived – by sending him to 'three great institutionary dinners in one week', leading to apoplexy and death.[106] By now Edmund and Fanny were married and living in Thornton Lacey; and on Dr Grant's death,

> they removed to Mansfield, and the parsonage there, which under each of its two former owners, Fanny had never been able to approach but with some painful sensation of restraint or alarm, soon grew as dear to her heart, and as thoroughly perfect in her eyes, as everything else, within the view and patronage of Mansfield Park, had long been.[107]

Edmund Bertram is the subtlest of Jane's clerical portraits: intelligent, thoughtful, a little prosaic perhaps – but conscientious and warm-hearted – redeemed above all by the kindness to Fanny which comes to mould both their characters. His vocation to be a clergyman may have been partly stimulated by the patronage at his father's command; but it is a real vocation, from which he cannot be diverted by Mary Crawford's charms and whims.[108] Some of Jane Austen's other clergy are more slightly sketched. Even the other heroes – the lively, witty, patronising but warm and kindly Henry Tilney and the diffident, shy, gauche, humorous, likeable Edward Ferrars – though they have life and breath – have not received anything like so many strokes of her brush as Edmund. The others are less kindly portrayed. Mr Collins is an immortal caricature and wholly absurd, his relations with Lady Catherine a parody of the more ridiculous features of patronage. Dr Grant 'is most kind and obliging to me', says his sister-in-law, Mary Crawford,

> and though he is really a gentleman, and I dare say a good scholar and clever, and often preaches good sermons, and is very respectable, *I* see him to be an indolent selfish bon vivant, who must have his palate consulted in every thing, who will not stir a finger for the convenience of any one, and who, moreover, if the cook makes a

[105] *MP* III, c. 17, p. 472.
[106] *MP* III, c. 17, p. 469.
[107] *MP* III, c. 17, p. 473.
[108] *MP* I, c. 11, pp. 108–9.

blunder, is out of humour with his excellent wife. To own the truth [we] were partly driven out this very evening, by a disappointment about a green goose, which he could not get the better of . . .[109]

Mary Crawford – and Jane Austen – for different reasons, were merciless to indolent clergymen, and Edmund does not defend them. In *Emma*, Mr Elton is a weak man easily led – whether it be by Emma into tasteless fantasy, or by Mrs Elton into mere vulgarity. In *Persuasion*, Charles Hayter becomes engaged to Henrietta Musgrave: thereafter he is just a young man awaiting his first benefice and his wife; and Dr Shirley is an aging parson whose function is to retire and make the young Hayter his curate. This is not quite the whole caste – there are some off-stage clergy like the talented curate at Mansfield who could sufficiently win Lady Bertram's attention that she later cried herself to sleep – but it represents the remarkable range of her characters. The clergy are not a group apart: Mr Collins is no more absurd than Mrs Bennet, nor Edmund Bertram more admirable than Mr Knightley. They are a cross-section of the community. But they have a clear and vital function, which Mary Crawford in the end fails to undermine.

[109] *MP* I, c. 11, p. 111.

14

Rank and Status

Rank and status are the themes of an immensely rich and complex learned literature. Their role in Jane Austen's life and novels has been used to justify the idea that she was traditional and hierarchical – or alternatively, liberal and revolutionary – in her views. In particular, especially since the publication of W. Roberts's *Jane Austen and the French Revolution* in 1979, there has been much debate on the effect of the French Revolution on the society in which she lived and on Jane Austen herself. I do not doubt that she was influenced by the French Revolution. It came on her when she was about the same age that I was when we learned about the Holocaust, which deeply affected me and coloured my attitudes on many things – though I have no Jewish relations, whereas Jane's cousin-in-law was guillotined. But discussions of such influences, though interesting, are purely speculative. My purpose is to look, quite simply, at the texts, and ask what they reveal of the range of attitudes in Jane Austen's world which she chose to illustrate in her novels – and which are revealed by her letters, and those of her circle.

Emma's Snobbery

One of the most striking features of *Emma* is the contrast between the heroine's snobbery and Mr Knightley's readiness to mingle with all about him on relatively equal terms. He is the squire of Highbury, though the word is never used of him: 'the landed property of Hartfield', the seat of Mr Woodhouse, 'certainly was inconsiderable, being but a sort of notch in the Donwell Abbey estate [Mr Knightley's], to which all the rest of Highbury belonged'.[1] The Woodhouses were 'the younger branch of a very ancient family'; they 'had been settled for several generations at Hartfield'; they were wealthy – but clearly their main wealth lay elsewhere – where, is not specified.[2] While Mr Knightley remains a bachelor, Emma sets herself up as the first lady of Highbury: 'the Woodhouses were first in consequence there'. There is perhaps a little confusion here – more probably a deliberate

---

[1] *E* I, c. 16, p. 136.
[2] Ibid.

ambiguity: Mr Knightley is clearly the squire and leader in the parish, yet Donwell Abbey is technically in a neighbouring parish.[3] In any event, Mr Knightley never puts on lordly airs – save that his candid nature makes it natural for him to lay down the law to Emma and his friends; but he always talks as one who is first among equals. Emma, at the start of the book, is a fearful snob – though not in all respects: both she and Mr Knightley treat Mrs Weston, her former governess, as an equal. Some of the best dialogue early in the book (chapter 5) is between Mr Knightley and Mrs Weston on her role as governess and their relations with Emma. Emma is happily at ease with her equals, patronises whom she will – and visits the poor. But when Harriet Smith reveals that Robert Martin, Mr Knightley's favourite tenant farmer, has proposed to her, and reluctantly agrees to reject him, Emma observes that Harriet's marriage to him would have cut them off from one another: 'I could not have visited Mrs Robert Martin, of Abbey-Mill Farm.'[4] In the denouement, when Harriet finally does become engaged to Robert Martin, Emma looks forward to meeting him; but meanwhile, the contrast of her and Mr Knightley's social attitudes forms a major theme in the book.

Emma's snobbery impinges again and again in the first half of *Emma*. Frank Churchill proposes a ball: but to collect sufficient dancers will mean collecting families with whom Emma would not normally associate.

> He seemed to have all the life and spirit, cheerful feelings, and social inclinations of his father, and nothing of the pride or reserve of [the Churchills of] Enscombe. Of pride, indeed, there was, perhaps, scarcely enough; his indifference to a confusion of rank, bordered too much on inelegance of mind. He could be no judge, however, of the evil he was holding cheap. It was but an effusion of lively spirits.

Or so she thought, little knowing he was engaged to Jane Fairfax, whose aunt and grandmother were among her lowlier acquaintances.[5] Soon after, Emma was contemplating the possibility of accepting an invitation to dine with the Coles, who 'had been settled some years in Highbury, and were very good sort of people – friendly, liberal, and unpretending; but, on the other hand, they were of low origin, in trade, and only moderately genteel'. After a while they had become more prosperous and with it very sociable, and Emma was determined not to let them think they could entertain Miss Woodhouse. But when they did plan a large dinner party – and invited Mr Knightley and the Westons, and so also Frank Churchill, but not herself – she began to regret it. 'Her being left in solitary grandeur, even supposing the omission to be intended as a compliment, was but poor

---

[3] *E* I, c. 1, pp. 5, 7; I, c. 3, p. 20; c. 7, p. 207; cf. III, c. 16, pp. 455–8.
[4] *E* I, c. 7, p. 53.
[5] *E* II, c. 6, p. 198.

comfort.' In the end the invitation came, and Emma went, very conscious of the favour she bestowed.[6]

One significant effect of harping on Emma's snobbery is to set in relief her romantic notions of Harriet's origin and destiny. The only thing known at the outset about Harriet's birth is that she was illegitimate; and this seemed to Mr Knightley to make it the more commendable in Robert Martin to be so keen to marry her. He regarded Emma's notion that she must be a gentleman's daughter (which indeed proves false in the end) as unlikely to be true and certainly not relevant.[7] What is interesting – and left for the readers to interpret as they will – is that Emma regards Harriet's birth as of little, or almost no, consequence: having brought her forward as her own intimate companion, she marries her off in imagination to Mr Elton, Mr Churchill and (in anguish) to Mr Knightley – to a clergyman, to the heir of a great estate, to the squire. This seems highly commendable to a modern reader: what is noteworthy is that it seemed reasonable to a highly intelligent young woman of strict principles in the 1810s. It may show Emma dwelling in a world of fantasy; or it may not.

In the end, Emma finds through her love of Mr Knightley that much of her snobbery is false and superficial. We see the layers of it peeling off, especially when she learns that Harriet is – after all – engaged to Robert Martin. What she had dismissed earlier as degradation – as separating Harriet from herself for ever – she greets now with nothing but delight and relief, to such a degree that she has to disguise her 'most unreasonable degree of happiness' from Mr Knightley. She has come to realise to the full how her romantic attempts to marry Harriet to this man and that have done nothing but harm; that she has bred in Harriet such fantasies as to imagine Mr Knightley in love with her; that the ideas of social hierarchy which Emma had fostered are fantasy. Emma sees at last through Mr Knightley's eyes, perceives Robert Martin's virtues, and all his eligibility for Harriet. 'Now there would be pleasure in [Harriet's] returning. – Every thing would be a pleasure. It would be a great pleasure to know Robert Martin.'[8]

Equality and Hierarchy

Without imputing the opinions of either Mr or Mrs Knightley to their creator, it is sufficiently clear that Jane Austen is puncturing any too rigid views of social hierarchy. Some critics have seen her as a social revolutionary: but it is hard to find much connection between the tiny, peaceful social world of Highbury and the storming of the Bastille. Others have seen her as

[6] *E* II, c. 7, pp. 207–8.
[7] *E* I, c. 8, p. 62.
[8] *E* III, c. 18, pp. 472, 475.

a subtle defender of the status quo. In any literal sense, that is equally improbable: her remorseless satire on human folly and wickedness – her social categories, however humorously devised, of the bright young Wykehamists, as 'future heroes, legislators, fools, and vilains'[9] – run counter to mere passive acceptance. Her portrait even of Mr Knightley is not uncritical. But she makes clear that it is as much his sense of responsibility, his good nature, his gentlemanly behaviour as his birth and inheritance which make him first – with Emma – in Highbury society.

Social historians love to discover evidence of change and novelty in the fields they cultivate: it is a natural temptation in too specialised research. There are many honourable exceptions, but many too who see in the very modest tendency towards egalitarianism in the novels a feature of a society grown more liberal.[10] That view would not have appealed to her niece Fanny Knight – daughter of her brother Edward who became a rich country gentleman by being adopted as the heir of Mr Knight, whose name he later took.

'They were not rich' wrote Fanny to one of her sisters about her aunts,

> and the people around with whom they chiefly mixed, were not at all high bred, or in short anything more than *mediocre* and they of course tho' superior in *mental powers* and *cultivation* were on the same level as far as *refinement* goes – but I think in later life their intercourse with Mrs Knight [Mr Knight's widow] (who was very fond of and kind to them) improved them both and Aunt Jane was too clever not to put aside all possible signs of 'common-ness' (if such an expression is allowable) and teach herself to be more refined, at least in intercourse with people in general.[11]

We can sense from this a little of what the poor relation had to put up with, even among close relations who loved and admired her.

The truth is that the issue of hierarchy versus equality is as old as the recorded social history of the human race. To take it no further back, St Paul had declared to the Galatians: 'There is neither Jew nor Greek, there is neither bond nor free, there is neither male nor female: for ye are all one in Christ Jesus'[12] – an utterance which has found echoes in all parts of Christendom in every age, and been sadly at variance with the facts of life. And not only with the facts: for that great theologian, the pseudo-Denis, a Syrian Greek of about 500 A.D. whose work was deeply influential among most of the theologians of the late Middle Ages, propounded a notion of hierarchy as of the very nature of heaven and of God's world. This

---

[9] See p. 139.

[10] Or influenced by the French Revolution: see above, p. 151.

[11] Collins 1993, pp. ix–x, quoting 'Aunt Jane', *Cornhill Magazine* 163 (1947–49), 72–3.

[12] Galatians 3:28.

remained a commonplace, eloquently and cynically expounded by Ulysses in pagan language in Shakespeare's *Troilus and Cressida*:

> Take but degree away, untune that string,
> And, hark! what discord follows.[13]

Hierarchy, like all concepts of social order, is profoundly ambiguous. In human terms, it may reflect a social order based on birth – with kings, nobles, gentlemen and commoners arranged in order. But in the medieval church – and in the eighteenth-century church too – the peerage, the House of Lords, comprised lords spiritual as well as lords temporal, who came there not by inheritance but by attaining office. In the English Church – both medieval and modern – the proportion of noblemen-bishops has always been small: an aristocratic clergyman doubtless had an advantage in the pursuit of higher offices, but it was rarely decisive – or there were too few of them to hinder men from other walks of life from climbing the ladder.

> 'But why are you to be a clergyman? [asked Miss Crawford of Edmund Bertram] I thought *that* was always the lot of the youngest, where there were many to choose before him.'
> 'Do you think the church itself never chosen then?'
> '*Never* is a black word. But yes, in the *never* of conversation which means *not very often*, I do think it. For what is to be done in the church? Men love to distinguish themselves, and in either of the other lines [as lawyer, or soldier, or sailor], distinction may be gained, but not in the church. A clergyman is nothing.'[14]

No peasant is known to have become archbishop of Canterbury; but only women were wholly excluded. No doubt politics played its part, as it always has in every arrangement and rearrangement of social hierarchy – but even politics were never alone decisive in determining the promotion of the English clergy, even in the eighteenth century. True, the bishop of Winchester through most of Jane Austen's life was Brownlow North, son of an earl and brother of a prime minister; but a bishop of more characteristic origin had held sway earlier in the century, Benjamin Hoadly, son of a schoolmaster.[15]

Yet perhaps the greatest of all qualifications to notions of hierarchy at any time – save for the uncertain play of human affection, which must be reserved for the chapter on marriage – has been the acquisition of wealth. A duke who fell into poverty in the fifteenth century was demoted; impecunious lords in the eighteenth century might find secret service funds (in

---

[13] *Troilus and Cressida* 1, 3, 109–10.
[14] *MP*, p. 92. 'Either' in Jane Austen's usage can mean one of three or more.
[15] See p. 16. On the two bishops, see *DNB*.

other words the royal privy purse) placed at their disposal.[16] But broadly speaking the nobility had to be and stay rich; and wealth was the key to social and political influence. For that very reason, a hierarchical society has commonly voiced a deep prejudice against *mere* wealth, not accompanied by noble ancestry and gracious manners – while many highly born have scrambled to acquire it, especially by marrying their sons and daughters to heiresses and heirs of wealth. There are frequent references in Jane Austen's novels to the respectable, and not-so-respectable, ways of acquiring wealth. Land, inheritance, marriage in one's own sphere, an honourable profession – army, navy, law and church – all were respectable. Jane's references to money-making are full of irony; and many which cannot be shown to be ironical may be so. But there can be no mistaking her approval of the way sailors made money, by winning prizes in war – however difficult it may be for us to distinguish this from piracy. On the other hand the country attorney, such as Mr Phillips, Mrs Bennet's brother-in-law, or Mr Shepherd, in *Persuasion*, was of a lower order; and Mr Elliot's first wife is described by Anne Elliot as 'a very low woman' – a phrase her friend Mrs Smith agrees to. 'Her father was a grazier, her grandfather had been a butcher' – but all Mr Elliot wanted at that time was money. 'She was a fine woman, had had a decent education' – yet these attributes, in Mrs Smith's eyes, cannot compensate for her origin.[17] We may doubt that Jane herself would have accepted the notion of Mrs Elliot as a 'very low woman' – even though Anne Elliot is as little a snob in other ways as Mr Knightley. But Mr Gardiner in *Pride and Prejudice* lives hard by his warehouses in Gracechurch Street, and though he prospered in 'a respectable line of trade', the City was not a part of London the fashionable of the west end much cared to visit. Yet he and his wife are deemed by the end of the book those among Elizabeth's relations most worthy to visit Pemberley.[18] The point in *Persuasion* is not to denigrate Mrs Elliot, who is a cipher, but to underline Mr Elliot's love of mammon. There are many such ambiguities in the novels; and Jane rarely makes the rich as vulgar as the highly born. The nobility in her books are unfailingly vulgar or dull.

The issue whether poor and rich, and those of different status, can marry one another is a major theme in *Sense and Sensibility*, *Pride and Prejudice* and *Mansfield Park*, and a minor issue in *Emma* and *Persuasion*. Jane took sardonic pleasure in detailing the dowries of her characters, only too aware of her own poverty. Behind the marriage of partners rich and poor lay a very long literary tradition which more or less faithfully reflects some of the eternal facts of social history. Marriage, indeed, is central to all the novels,

---

[16] As happened to the duke of Bedford in 1478 (*Complete Peerage*, II, 72) – and to several peers in the reign of George III (Namier 1928, pp. 221–5).

[17] *P* II, c. 9, p. 202.

[18] See p. 84. For Mr Gardiner's 'line of trade', see *PP*, p. 28.

and the theme of another chapter. But it cannot be wholly separated from social hierarchy, even, or especially, in imaginative literature.

The two issues are marvellously combined in Shakespeare's *All's Well that Ends Well*, which reveals these problems in a discussion of immense power two hundred years or so before Jane Austen's time, and bears a curious resemblance to *Pride and Prejudice*, which is not at all likely to have occurred to her. The resemblance lies solely in its themes, for the play has a story as far removed from Jane's domestic scenes as one could imagine; and seduction is a crucial element in it, in a form perhaps more allied to *Mansfield Park* than to *Pride and Prejudice*. A king has long suffered from a fearful illness; he is cured by Helena, a young woman whom he rewards by offering her a husband of her choice from his court. She chooses Count Bertram, with whom she has long been secretly in love – she had been given lodging and patronage by his mother, and so knew him well – though as she is a woman of inferior status and no wealth (even if a gentle-woman by birth) he has never given her a thought. She is not low enough to be fair game for his lust, nor high enough to tempt him to marriage. Helena chooses him in the court and the king commands him to marry her. Under protest, he submits to a church wedding, but swears he will never consummate the marriage. Disguised as a pilgrim Helena makes a plot with a woman of similarly gentle origin but in very humble circumstances, Diana, whom Bertram plans to seduce. Helena takes Diana's place when Bertram visits her, and their marriage is consummated. Then all is revealed before the king, and Bertram takes Helena to wife: the audience is left to take its choice of Helena's 'All's well that ends well yet' and the king's 'All yet *seems* to be well.'[19]

What converts the play from its superficially absurd plot to one of Shakespeare's most haunting achievements is the plainness of the exposition in contrast to the folktale romance of the plot. In my understanding of the play I am much indebted to the late N.S. Brooke, who calls the quality naturalism, with full awareness of the ambiguity of the term. But what he describes is language unadorned – not ordinary, since Shakespeare was its author – and plain human sentiments.[20] The point is made very early in the extraordinary scene in which Helena and Parolles discuss virginity: this is no heroine of romance, but a witty, earthy, intelligent woman such as abound in Shakespeare's comedies. Bertram is too much of a snob to see her as such: he is a mere man, and as such, predatory. But Helena manages to catch him engaged in seduction, and turn his folly against himself. She wins him after a fashion in the end; but the conclusion is brilliantly managed to be at once moving and unconvincing. We are moved, with the

---

[19] *All's Well that Ends Well*, esp. 5, 1, 25; 5, 3, 322.
[20] N.S. Brooke 1977.

old lord Lafew, to tears, but we are inclined to agree with the king's perplexity – all *seems* to be well.

Equality *in* Pride and Prejudice

There are no such doubts in *Pride and Prejudice*. Darcy's first instinct is to look at Elizabeth as Bertram looks at Helena, with scant attention: she is beneath him. But as Darcy sees more of Elizabeth he becomes infatuated, and being a decent and honest man (unlike many men in the novels) he sees no alternative but to marry her – and proceeds to expound his perplexities in making his first proposal to her at Hunsford. He has to learn, painfully and slowly, that his marriage cannot be an unequal partnership. Elizabeth herself believes that because her father is a gentleman they are really equals; however that may be, it is Elizabeth's combination of personality and intelligence with beauty which makes Darcy realise that rank and status form no barrier between them; he has to accept that in some senses and qualities, she is his superior. This is difficult: he has grown up with many male chauvinist assumptions. Her quality is all the more remarkable, since in some folks' eyes, women, like tradesmen, were inferior anyway. This was not the case with Mr and Mrs Darcy, though in other marriages Jane Austen allows the ambivalences of human experience freer play.[21]

Money: Northanger Abbey *and* Sense and Sensibility

It is striking that in both *Northanger Abbey* and *Sense and Sensibility* the main barrier to the heroines' marriage is money. General Tilney comes of an old Gloucestershire family and lives in an ancient house, however much provided with modern amenities. But his idea of marriage is entirely unromantic and mercenary: he delights to bring Catherine Morland and his second son Henry together, and invites her to Northanger, because he thinks she comes of prosperous family and is an heiress. When John Thorpe contradicts his first estimate of her wealth – enlarges on the throng of her brothers and sisters and sinks her chances of Mr Allen's estate – the General is seized with panic, banishes Catherine from his house, and tries to banish her from Henry's thoughts. It may well be that he would look for family as well as dowry in his eldest son's marriage; and he is himself exceedingly rich, and under no necessity to plan mercenary alliances. But money plays a large role in all his plans.

It is much the same with Mrs Ferrars in *Sense and Sensiblity*. She is a very stupid as well as disagreeable woman, and so prefers her second son Robert,

[21] See e.g. below, p. 162.

a conceited coxcomb, to the subtler, deeper, superficially duller Edward; she is fair game for the wiles of Lucy Steele. Jane Austen distributed folly and stupidity among her characters with a lavish hand, but in *Sense and Sensibility* these qualities are particularly to be found among the rich and highly born – as Mrs Ferrars and Sir John Middleton bear witness. Mrs Ferrars determines that if Edward will not go into Parliament or join some grand profession, the only hope for him is to marry Miss Morton, who is to be sure the daughter of the late Lord Morton, and so from the ranks of the aristocracy, but whose chief attraction seems to be her £30,000. For a different reason, Marianne's affair with Willoughby is terminated by the purse. Willoughby is deeply in debt and needs to marry a rich wife to mend his fortunes. So he repudiates one of Jane's most enchanting heroines, and marries Miss Gray, for the sake of her wealth. It is only too clear that money is the key to Elinor's and Marianne's troubles, for they are by ancestry and birth fully the equals of the men who woo them. Mr Ferrars had died very rich:[22] how he came by his money is not clear, though some of it had evidently been invested in land. But there is no suggestion that he or his wife came of ancient families; and the Dashwoods were an old family of country gentlefolk.

Pride and Prejudice *and the Equality of Gentlemen*

The concept of a gentleman has always been ambiguous: it has been used, time out of mind, both to denote a certain measure or kind of courtesy – both 'gentle' and 'courteous' were words with a long history in the courtly, romantic world of medieval literature, a world no less inspiring and absurd than the fantasies of Emma – and a certain kind of social inheritance. Both meanings are fundamental in *Pride and Prejudice*. Elizabeth rebukes Darcy for his ungentlemanly conduct when he first proposes to her: her concept of courtesy thus begins to alter his.[23] He is driven to discourtesy by the conflict between his love for her and the sense of social difference between them – and his snobbery puts an edge on her reaction, for she is exceedingly sensitive to any imputation on her family's standing. Near the end of the book, in a scene of high melodrama, Lady Catherine de Bourgh outbids his discourtesy – one might almost say, parodies his ungentlemanly conduct – by calling Elizabeth an upstart.

'What is to divide [Darcy and her daughter, whom she hopes he will marry]? The upstart pretensions of a young woman without

---

[22] *SS*, p. 15. For landed investment, note that Robert was given £1,000 per annum from the Norfolk estate (*SS*, pp. 266, 269).
[23] See *PP*, pp. 192, 367.

family, connections, or fortune . . . If you were sensible of your own good, you would not wish to quit the sphere, in which you have been brought up.'

'In marrying your nephew, I should not consider myself as quitting that sphere. He is a gentleman; I am a gentleman's daughter; *so far we are equal.*'[24]

Elizabeth here pronounces the classic statement of a powerful doctrine: all gentlemen were equal. It is to her a crucial fact in her debate with Lady Catherine – and in her much longer and deeper debate with Darcy – that her father and his were alike in social standing. She does not disguise that in other respects they were very different: Darcy was far richer, his other connections were with the aristocracy, hers with trade and the lower professions. But all this is turned upside down by the fact that she avoids the manifest vulgarity of Lady Catherine's conduct and Darcy's snobbery. Jane Austen does not portray a world of equals, but one of paradoxes.[25]

Mansfield Park, Emma *and Women*

It was possible for women of fortune in Jane Austen's time to hold positions of wealth and independence, and two of them appear in her novels. Mrs Ferrars in *Sense and Sensibility* had free use of a large fortune – save for the inconvenience of annuities to a few old retainers – and abused her position as only the stupid and arrogant can do; and Emma is so much superior to her father in intelligence and initiative that she can do pretty much what she likes. 'The real evils indeed of Emma's situation were the power of having rather too much her own way, and a disposition to think a little too well of herself.'[26] Jane Austen herself had only too clear a view of the disabilities of women in her age; but that did not lead her to present independent women in altogether too favourable a light. Far from it: it was the salvation of Emma that she fell in love with Mr Knightley. Jane's most forceful women are the heroines who are fully the equals of strong husbands – Emma and Elizabeth.

Allowing that her characters – or those who play any serious part in the novels – are all genteel or gentlefolk, it is noteworthy that three of her mature novels turn on women in circumstances of particular disadvantage, and a fourth on the lot of a poor relation. Fanny Price is at once downtrodden and happy, frightened of and devoted to all that pertains to Mansfield Park: hers is an immortal portrait of one poor relation composed by

---

[24] *PP* III, c. 14, p. 356: see p. 77. I have italicised '*so far we are equal*'.
[25] See also p. 165.
[26] *E* I, c. 1, p. 2.

another.[27] In *Pride and Prejudice* Mr Bennet's estate is entailed to heirs male, and his five daughters must shift for themselves when he is dead: the estate goes to his cousin Mr Collins. In *Persuasion* Kellynch Hall and the baronetcy must go to Mr Elliot, cousin of Sir Walter Elliot, since he has only daughters – and their predicament is all the worse because their father is feckless: instead of putting by reserves for their dowries he accumulates only debts. In *Sense and Sensibility* the old Mr Dashwood leaves his estate and his wealth to his nephew – but only for his lifetime; thereafter it becomes wholly the property of the nephew's son by a first marriage and *his* son; the second wife and her three daughters are left very modestly provided for. In this case, Jane attributes such extraordinary injustice to a preference on the old man's part for his great-nephew, who

> had so far gained on [his] affections . . . by such attractions as are by no means unusual in children of two or three years old: an imperfect articulation, an earnest desire of having his own way, many cunning tricks, and a great deal of noise.[28]

In *Mansfield Park*, Sir Thomas's estates will one day fall wholly to the unworthy Tom.[29]

But this kind of disposition would commonly have been inspired, in part at least, by the desire of a landowner to keep together a notable estate. It is to us the strangest of ambitions: the natural course of human affection looks to provide for all children equally – or as near equally as circumstances allow; where there is too little to divide, the weakest, often the youngest, have commonly been favoured.[30] But the notion that an estate, like a title, should pass from father to *eldest* son, or to the eldest *male* relative – the rule of primogeniture – was one of the absurd legacies of medieval society; and many aspects of contemporary life in Jane Austen's time served to perpetuate it. Norland Park and Mansfield Park were great houses, immensely expensive to preserve or rebuild or refurnish; they were supported by great estates, but these in their turn needed to remain large if the traditional status and privileges and obligations of their owners were to be preserved – or so most of the owners thought.

---

[27] See pp. 85–8.

[28] *SS* I, c. 4, p. 4.

[29] The even more unworthy Mr Rushworth may have inherited Sotherton from a relation none too close. *MP*, pp. 38–9, 76–7, 85–6 may seem to suggest this: see Chapman's note, p. 543. But they do not enforce it; and 'the late Mr Rushworth left [prayers] off' (*MP*, p. 86), though not free from ambiguity, points the other way. If the relationship had not been close, it is strange that Jane Austen does not make this explicit on p. 39. Nor is there any indication that he might have by-passed women heirs. For his £12,000 per annum, see *MP*, p. 40.

[30] As anthropologists have noted in a number of different regions and cultures; for ultimogeniture in medieval England, see Pollock and Maitland 1895, II, 279–80.

Jane knew about estates and wills. Her brother Edward was a rich country gentleman; but he had eleven children, and so little to spare for his impecunious mother and sisters – though he did settle them comfortably in Chawton. Her aunt and uncle Leigh Perrott were rich; but their will gave no direct benefit to their poorest relations – a discovery which Jane, now terminally ill, received with undisguised bitterness. 'A few days ago', she wrote to her brother Charles,

> my complaint appeared removed, but I am ashamed to say that the shock of my uncle's will brought on a relapse, and I was so ill on Friday and thought myself so likely to be worse that I could not but press for Cassandra's returning . . .[31]

Thus in book after book Jane Austen shows us the woman's predicament: marriage or permanent dependence. Even the relatively prosperous *Mansfield Park* offers little freedom to the women. Tom will inherit the estate and Edmund enjoy the livings under its patronage. Maria marries Mr Rushworth to win her freedom and enjoy the delights of a large income in the hands of a man she can manage. Julia marries Mr Yates as the only way to escape insupportable tutelage after Maria's elopement and disgrace. The absence of opportunity for women – only too obvious to the unmarried daughter of a relatively poor parson – was all too palpable, and is driven remorselessly home – not by rhetoric, of which there is none, but by plain exposition.

It is hardly surprising that Jane Austen had an exceptionally wide and incisive view of the role of women in her world – of their opportunities and restrictions. Here are two texts from *Mansfield Park*.

> About thirty years ago, Miss Maria Ward of Huntingdon, with only seven thousand pounds, had the good luck to captivate Sir Thomas Bertram, of Mansfield Park, in the county of Northampton, and to be thereby raised to the rank of a baronet's lady, with all the comforts and consequences of an handsome house and large income. All Huntingdon exclaimed on the greatness of the match, and her uncle, the lawyer, himself, allowed her to be at least three thousand pounds short of any equitable claim to it.

Some thought her two sisters as handsome as she, and 'did not scruple to predict their marrying with almost equal advantage. But there certainly are not so many men of large fortune in the world, as there are pretty women to deserve them' – so the eldest had to be content to marry a parson, and the third ran away with a Lieutenant of Marines.[32]

The second text describes Mrs Maria Rushworth's fate, after she has

---

[31] *Letters*, L no. 157, p. 338; C no. 144, p. 491; and notes; M, F-445.
[32] *MP* I, c. 1, p. 1.

eloped and lived for a while with a man not her husband. Her father was determined that 'she should be protected by him, and secured in every comfort [in some meanings of the word], and supported by every encouragement to do right, which their relative situations admitted' – but he would not afford 'his sanction to vice, or . . . lessen its disgrace' by admitting her back home or 'be anywise accessary to introducing such misery in another man's family, as he had known himself'.[33] So she was incarcerated in a distant county in the company of Mrs Norris – a fearful punishment.

In the view of Sir Thomas, it was a woman's business to marry and live in fidelity to her husband: no profession, no alternative abode could take her from her home save to her husband's or to that of a respectable friend. Jane Austen herself spent all her early life with her parents – all her later life with her mother and sister: she had many friends, and visited them so far as difficulties of travel and her limited resources allowed. She was indeed the supreme professional writer of her age: yet it was not in contemporary eyes a profession. Brother Henry might tour the land proudly revealing his sister's achievement.[34] But a woman's place was with her family or her husband – though an educated woman without endowment, like Jane Fairfax, could be a governess; and there were many professions open to women artisans, none of them accessible to Miss Fairfax or Miss Austen.

Maria broke the rules, and received a harsh sentence – far more severe than Henry Crawford's.

> That punishment, the public punishment of disgrace, should in a just measure attend *his* share of the offence, is, we know, not one of the barriers, which society gives to virtue. In this world, the penalty is less equal than could be wished

– a thunderous understatement which gives the sentence infinitely more weight than if she had indulged in rhetoric –

> but without presuming to look forward to a juster appointment hereafter, we may fairly consider a man of sense like Henry Crawford, to be providing for himself no small portion of vexation and regret – vexation that must rise sometimes to self-reproach, and regret to wretchedness – in having so requited hospitality, so injured family peace, so forfeited his best, most estimable and endeared acquaintance [with Fanny Price], and so lost the woman whom he had rationally, as well as passionately loved.[35]

To be made to live secluded with Mrs Norris was Jane's version of hell.

---

[33] *MP* III, c. 17, p. 465.

[34] Jane Austen to her brother Frank, 25 Sept. 1813: *Letters*, L no. 90, p. 231; C no. 85, p. 340. Frank had kept the secret; Henry had revealed it on a visit to Scotland.

[35] *MP* III, c. 17, pp. 468–9. Cf. Willoughby's fate, p. 171.

The comparison we have made elsewhere with Mr Bennet's treatment of Lydia in *Pride and Prejudice* underlines the point.[36] Even allowing that Lydia had broken no marriage vows – that Maria's sin was adultery – the difference is striking. The morality of Sir Thomas Bertram and his circle was stricter than that of the Bennets. They are indeed both examples of the remarkably wide variety of standards which obtained in Regency England. It was notoriously a time when what Sir Thomas would have regarded as exceedingly loose morals flourished in high society, and were widely condoned.[37] In the wide spectrum of differing views on sexual morality, we need not doubt that Jane Austen's own opinions were tolerably strict; but it would be a false assumption to presume she agreed wholeheartedly with Sir Thomas. It would be equally false to attribute her views or his to a specific religious affiliation: both were orthodox Christians according to their lights; neither was – in any strict sense – Evangelical.[38] Sexual morals were not necessarily a party matter at all; and if Jane was strict on Christian principle, Sir Thomas was stricter – as he is presented to us – because of the standards of his family and social order.

Rank and Status in Persuasion

Social comment in *Persuasion* offers a kind of summary, of characteristic subtlety, of the problems and attitudes expounded in the earlier novels.

> 'Good company requires only birth, education, and manners, and with regard to education is not very nice. Birth and good manners are essential; but a little learning is by no means a dangerous thing in good company, on the contrary, it will do very well.'

Thus Mr Elliot to his cousin Anne, who demurs. Mr Elliot tries again:

> 'My dear cousin, . . . you have a better right to be fastidious than almost any other woman I know; but will it answer? Will it make you happy? Will it not be wiser to accept the society of these good ladies in Laura-place [the Dowager Viscountess Dalrymple and her daughter, the Elliots' cousins], and enjoy all the advantages of the connexion as far as possible? You may depend upon it, that they will move in the first set in Bath this winter, and as rank is rank, your being known to be related to them will have its use in fixing your family (our family, let me say) in that degree of consideration which we must all wish for.'[39]

[36] See p. 126.
[37] See p. 199; *Letters*, L no. 82, p. 208; C no. 78, p. 504; M F-245-6.
[38] See pp. 126–32.
[39] *P* II, c. 4, p. 150.

Even the devil can quote scripture, and it could on occasion serve Jane Austen's ironic turn to put good sense into the minds of her evil characters – and Mr Elliot is wicked, not foolish. But in all the many arguments in *Persuasion*, spoken and assumed, between snobbery and reasonable human feeling, the fools and knaves are for snobbery, Anne Elliot and the sailors against. The snobbery of Anne's sister Mary is of a special quality: it snubs even her admirable mother-in-law to whom she claims precedence as a baronet's daughter. Lady Russell bridges the gap between the enlightened and the fools. She is intelligent, well educated, had been a very close friend of Anne's mother – and sees with total clarity that Anne is the brightest and the most admirable of the family. She is a sensible, matter-of-fact person who tries to judge fairly by all. But she is more for rank and status than Anne, and judges too readily by a man's manner what he is worth – to the extent that she has been blinded to the virtues of Captain Wentworth and to the vices of Mr Elliot: so she condemned Captain Wentworth when she first encountered him – and was very quickly won by Mr Elliot's good manners even to think of him as Anne's future husband. Critics have made much ado of the delay in Anne telling Lady Russell the truth about Mr Elliot, as if it represents a change or weakness in Jane's plan – and we all know that she had much difficulty with the conclusion of *Persuasion*.[40] But the truth seems to be that Lady Russell's conversion was always intended to be a total conversion – an acceptance 'that she had been pretty completely wrong, and [a readiness] to take up a new set of opinions and of hopes'; this part of the conclusion was never altered.[41] Anne's objection to Lady Dalrymple is that this tedious old lady is subjected to obsequious behaviour by her father the Baronet – she whimsically laments his lack of pride. The sailors, all in some measure self made, act with far greater dignity than the Baronet. Anne admittedly has the ease of being a baronet's daughter, and does not have to struggle for status – but she is shown very clearly able to talk without condescension to every rank she encounters, including the poor of Kellynch.

Persuasion is not radical or subversive; it does not make a baron marry a chambermaid as did the original of *Lovers' Vows*; or the servants humiliate their masters, as in the *Marriage of Figaro*. The author had condescended to dedicate *Emma* to the Prince Regent, with every appearance of feeling he did her an honour in agreeing to it.[42] But *Persuasion* was not designed to bolster the fabric of society, if that might be supposed to depend in any degree on respect for rank. Does that mean that Jane Austen was a gentle revolutionary? In a very limited sense it does. But more truly it illustrates

---

[40] See p. 45.
[41] *P* II, c. 12, p. 249.
[42] *Letters*, L nos. 125, 130–2, 138, pp. 296–7, 304–7, 311–12; C, nos. 113, 120–2, 126, pp. 429–30, 442–7, 452–3.

the ambiguity in social structure which we have pursued through the other novels. Her last novel gives no encouragement to the gentry or the aristocracy to believe that birth gives them any true superiority. What after all had birth given her? – She was a poor relation all her days – and it was not birth, but the happy accidents of human relations, which had made her brother Edward the squire of Godmersham and Chawton. And it is her talents alone which have set her in a place of honour above all the lords and ladies and right reverends and wrong reverends – above the Prince Regent himself – as the first citizen of Regency England.

15

Marriage in the Novels

No theme in social history has been more popular than the history of marriage, and our knowledge of it has been enormously enriched in recent years. It has not all been gain. The eminent social historian Lawrence Stone started a new debate with his *The Family, Sex and Marriage in England, 1500–1800* (1977), which has been very fruitful in many ways. But one of his central doctrines, 'the growth of affective individualism' – freedom of choice and marriage for love – especially in the seventeenth and eighteenth centuries, has never found favour among those of us whose primary experience of the literature on marriage and the family lay in the Middle Ages. Once again, there is a danger that the great variety of human relations and attitudes of the past will be arranged in some sort of chronological order, rather than seen as natural variations observable in many different historical periods. Thus I myself wrote in my *Medieval Idea of Marriage* (1989): 'the dialectic between this arranged marriage and free consent is active in almost every chapter of this present book', that is, from the twelfth century to the sixteenth.[1] There is copious evidence of marriage for love in the world of Heloise and of Condwiramurs; granted the nature of human affection, it would be astonishing if it were not so. Under these circumstances it seems especially helpful to inspect the variety of ideas and attitudes and experiences of marriage reflected in Jane Austen's novels as they appear in the source – not weighed down, in the first instance, with the great load of gloss and interpretation which too easily accompanies them in the wake of the debate on 'affective individualism'.

Jane Austen's own personal experience of wooing and being wooed has made a short appearance in an early chapter. It tells us little or nothing of her formed opinions. The *Letters* have a little more to say – especially her letters of advice of 1814 to her niece Fanny. Otherwise they only provide ironical advice inspired by the second marriage of the dismal Mary-Elizabeth Milles, Lady Sondes. She was a daughter of a gentry family near Canterbury – evidently known to Jane and her sister from their visits to Godmersham Park and Canterbury. She first married Lord Sondes and had

---

[1] Brooke 1989a, p. 20.

six children, then (in 1808) General Sir Henry Tucker Montresor, also of
Kentish gentry stock.

> Lady Sondes' match surprises, but does not offend me; – had her
> first marriage been of affection, or had there been a grown-up single
> daughter, I should not have forgiven her – but I consider everybody
> as having a right to marry *once* in their lives for love, if they can – and
> provided she will now leave off having bad head-aches and being
> pathetic, I can allow her, I can *wish* her, to be happy.

Next day she returned to the theme.

> I have laid Lady Sondes' case before Martha [Lloyd, later Francis
> Austen's second wife] – who does not make the least objection to it,
> and is particularly pleased with the name of Montresor. I do not agree
> with her there, but I like his rank very much – and always affix the
> ideas of strong sense, and highly elegant manners, to a general.[2]

We do not have to be reminded that the only general to appear in her
novels was General Tilney (in *Northanger Abbey*, finished in 1803) to know
how little we can depend on the fantastical humour of this passage. The
novels have more to tell us.

Marriage in esse

It has often been alleged that Jane Austen's novels are about the entry to
marriage – about falling in love and becoming engaged – but that she
always stopped short at the threshold of marriage. It is evidently the case
that entry to marriage is a central theme in all her novels, and that once she
has brought her heroes and heroines to church, she is content: glimpses into
their married future are rare. But these are not the only marriages which
interested her; and her books are full of marriages *in esse*, observed with as
shrewd an eye as the processes by which marriages were formed.

She can summarise a marriage – for good or ill – in a sentence or a para-
graph. Of this her two admirals are excellent examples. Admiral and Mrs
Crawford were at loggerheads, and although we never meet them face to
face, Mary Crawford's account of 'my poor aunt' leaves no doubt that they
had little in common except devotion to their nephew and niece and a
hearty dislike of one another. The admiral meanwhile consoled himself
with a mistress, whom he introduced into his own house when Mrs
Crawford died – forcing Mary to find a more respectable home. This
unhappy marriage plays an essential role in *Mansfield Park* because it takes
Miss Crawford to Mansfield and helps to form the views of the young

[2] *Letters*, L no. 63, pp. 159, 161 (cf. 551); C no. 62, pp. 240, 243.

Crawfords on marriage and morals. 'My poor aunt always felt affected, if within ten miles of the sea, which the Admiral of course never believed, but I know it was so.'[3] In his turn 'the Admiral hated marriage, and thought it never pardonable in a young man of independent fortune'.[4]

In contrast, Admiral and Mrs Croft in *Persuasion* are never willingly separated. She only felt ill if he were at sea without her; she sailed everywhere with him. A childless marriage made this a possibility and gave Jane Austen the chance to expound – in her most economical vein – an exceptionally successful marriage.

' "My dear admiral, that post! – we shall certainly take that post." ' – Thus Mrs Croft, as she and her husband are giving Anne Elliot a lift home in their gig.

> But by coolly giving the reins a better direction herself, they happily passed the danger; and by once afterwards judiciously putting out her hand, they neither fell into a rut, nor ran foul of a dung-cart; and Anne, with some amusement at their style of driving, which she imagined no bad representation of the general guidance of their affairs, found herself safely deposited by them at the cottage.[5]

She particularly delights in sketching marriages of opposites. Some of these unions seem to have mainly or solely the function of explaining highly contrasting characters and abilities within a family – which helps her to make the Bennets or the Elliots a microcosm of humanity as she portrays it: most of them stupid, selfish and ignorant, a few intelligent and sympathetic. Sir Walter Elliot and two of his daughters are vain and absurd; Anne is highly intelligent – and this is because she took after her mother.

> Lady Elliot had been an excellent woman, sensible and amiable; whose judgment and conduct, if they might be pardoned the youthful infatuation which made her Lady Elliot, had never required indulgence afterwards. – She had humoured, or softened, or concealed [her husband's] failings, and promoted his real respectability for seventeen years; and though not the very happiest being in the world herself, had found enough in her duties, her friends, and her children, to attach her to life, and make it no matter of indifference to her when she was called on to quit them.[6]

Mary, the first of the young Elliots to marry, fared better than her mother. She is a valetudinarian of Woodhousian proportions, selfish, stupid and a frightful snob; unlike many of Jane Austen's wives, she has done nothing to

---

[3] *MP* I, c. 4, 5, pp. 40–1, 46; *MP* III, c. 12, p. 416.
[4] *MP* II, c. 12, p. 292. Contrast Sir Thomas Bertram's view, n. 33 below.
[5] *P* I, c. 10, p. 92.
[6] *P* I, c. 1, p. 4.

improve her husband, who is a fairly idle country squire in the making, fond of country sports – but in his own way fond of his wife and children too. Mary is too stupid to feel the discontents her mother had felt: she has plenty of her own – but they are all quite trivial.

The differences in Emma's family are more subtly shaded. The reader is very early confronted with a baffling contrast: Emma is highly intelligent, lively, witty, cheerful, always in the best of health; her father is slow-witted, literal minded, easily depressed, almost as devoted to his apothecary as he is to his daughters. Mr Knightley, in conversation with Mrs Weston – Emma's former governess and companion – candidly observes why Emma has been spoilt.

> 'She was always quick and assured: Isabella [her elder sister] slow and diffident. And ever since she was twelve, Emma has been mistress of the house and of you all. In her mother she lost the only person able to cope with her. She inherits her mother's talents, and must have been under subjection to her.'[7]

We are vouchsafed no further account of Mr Woodhouse as a husband; but the unequal – yet successful – marriage carries on into the next generation. When Mr Knightley and Mrs Weston have agreed to differ, he concludes:

> 'Christmas brings John and Isabella. John [Mr Knightley's younger brother] loves Emma with a reasonable and therefore not a blind affection, and Isabella always thinks as he does; except when he is not quite frightened enough about the children. I am sure of having their opinions with me.'[8]

When John and Isabella arrive, we encounter a couple utterly devoted to one another, yet wholly divergent in abilities and temperament. John is a self-confident, fast-thinking man, inclined to be impatient with Mr Wood-house, and even at times with Isabella. She shares her father's slow wits and devotion to her apothecary. John is a busy lawyer, and in spite of these differences Isabella provides him with an idyllic home and numerous lively children – five so far.[9] Later, much later, when Mr Knightley escaped from his home to avoid seeing any more flirtations between Emma and Frank Churchill, he rides to London to stay with his brother.

> He had gone to learn to be indifferent. – But he had gone to a wrong place. There was too much domestic happiness in his brother's house; woman wore too amiable a form in it; Isabella was too much like Emma – differing only in those striking inferiorities, which always

---

[7] *E* I, c. 5, p. 37.
[8] *E* I, c. 5 p. 40.
[9] *E* I, cc. 11, 13, pp. 91, 108.

brought the other in brilliancy before him, for much to have been done, even had his time been longer. . . .[10]

In *Sense and Sensibility* Jane Austen had expounded unlikely partnerships with a lavish hand. Sir John Middleton, noisy, extrovert, warm, very much the country squire, is married to a woman as coolly elegant as he is boisterous; and Lady Middleton's sister Charlotte, exceptionally foolish even by Miss Austen's generous standards of folly – but cheerful, chattering, and wholly amiable – is married to a man of some intelligence and occasional good feelings, who finds it necessary to be forever superior to those about him, forever showing up his wife's stupidity; yet both these marriages are, within their very narrow limits, stable and affectionate. Mr Willoughby, the villain, marries Miss Gray wholly for her money – as she well knows – but even that marriage turns out not too badly – in spite of Willoughby's regrets for the loss of Marianne Dashwood, a much more vivid and attractive character than his wife. But Mrs Willoughby 'was not always out of humour, nor his home always uncomfortable; and in his breed of horses and dogs, and in sporting of every kind, he found no inconsiderable degree of domestic felicity'.[11] This tale of unlikely marriages in *Sense and Sensibility* could be extended; but they all serve to set in high relief two marriages in which the partners have very much in common and learn to have more. John Dashwood

> was not an ill-disposed young man, unless to be rather cold hearted, and rather selfish, is to be ill-disposed: but he was, in general, well respected; for he conducted himself with propriety in the discharge of his ordinary duties. Had he married a more amiable woman, he might have been made still more respectable than he was: – he might even have been made amiable himself; for he was very young when he married, and very fond of his wife. But Mrs John Dashwood [Fanny Ferrars] was a strong caricature of himself; – more narrow-minded and selfish.[12]

We are soon treated to the immortal training session in which Fanny Dashwood reduces the support of his impoverished half-sisters – promised to his and their father on his deathbed – from three thousand pounds to 'such kind of neighbourly acts' – helping them to move house, sending presents of fish and game 'and so forth, whenever they are in season' – 'as his own wife pointed out'.[13]

The other true partnership is of a very different quality: the tastes and

---

[10] *E* III, c. 13, pp. 432–3.
[11] *SS* III, c. 14, p. 379.
[12] *SS* I, c. 1, p. 5.
[13] *SS* I, c. 2, pp. 12–13.

interests of Elinor Dashwood and Edward Ferrars are much closer than in other marriages in the book. They are sketched lightly and subtly through many passages, and summarised at the end. Mrs Jennings

> was able to visit Edward and his wife in their Parsonage by Michaelmas, and she found in Elinor and her husband, as she really believed, one of the happiest couples in the world. They had in fact nothing to wish for, but the marriage of Colonel Brandon and Marianne, and rather better pasturage for their cows.[14]

Marianne's marriage has hardly taken place when the book closes: we have hitherto been shown Colonel Brandon as an experienced, kindly, diffident, depressed gentleman; it is very difficult to deduce how he will appear after a year or two of marriage to the still very young, impressionable, intense, impulsive Marianne. But there are hints of a more impulsive Colonel Brandon, who twice falls in love with very young, very attractive, romantic women – and fights a duel with Willoughby when he learns he has seduced his ward. We are not allowed to know more of his and Marianne's future.

One of the most unequal marriages in the novels is that of Mr and Mrs Bennet. This is what we are told at the outset.

> Mr Bennet was so odd a mixture of quick parts, sarcastic humour, reserve, and caprice, that the experience of three and twenty years had been insufficient to make his wife understand his character. *Her* mind was less difficult to develope. She was a woman of mean understanding, little information, and uncertain temper. When she was discontented she fancied herself nervous. The business of her life was to get her daughters married

– all the more as the estate which supported the family was entailed to a male cousin, Mr Collins, no less – 'its solace was visiting and news'.[15]

Much later, when we have been exposed to Mr Bennet's caprices and Mrs Bennet's hysteria to a considerable extent, we are given Elizabeth's view of her parents' marriage.

> Had Elizabeth's opinion been all drawn from her own family, she could not have formed a very pleasing picture of conjugal felicity or domestic comfort. Her father captivated by youth and beauty, and that appearance of good humour, which youth and beauty generally give, had married a woman whose weak understanding and illiberal mind, had very early in their marriage put an end to all real affection for her. Respect, esteem, and confidence, had vanished for ever; and

---

[14] *SS* III, c. 14, pp. 374–5.
[15] *PP* I, c. 1, p. 5.

all his views of domestic happiness were overthrown. But Mr Bennet was not of a disposition to seek comfort for the disappointment which his own imprudence had brought on, in any of those pleasures which too often console the unfortunate for their folly or their vice. He was fond of the country and of books; and from these tastes had arisen his principal enjoyments. To his wife he was very little otherwise indebted, than as her ignorance and folly had contributed to his amusement. This is not the sort of happiness which a man would in general wish to owe to his wife; but where other powers of entertainment are wanting, the true philosopher will derive benefit from such as are given.

Elizabeth, however, had never been blind to the impropriety of her father's behaviour as a husband. She had always seen it with pain; but respecting his abilities, and grateful for his affectionate treatment of herself, she endeavoured to forget what she could not overlook, and to banish from her thoughts that continual breach of conjugal obligation and decorum which, in exposing his wife to the contempt of her own children, was so highly reprehensible. But she had never felt so strongly as now, the disadvantages which must attend the children of so unsuitable a marriage

– for Mr Bingley had been separated from Jane by his sisters and Mr Darcy on account of the vulgarity of her family, and her two youngest sisters thought of nothing but flirting with the officers.[16]

Thus far the astonishing range of marriages observed in the novels. To probe deeper, we need first to look more closely at three very different theories of marriage – those of Marianne Dashwood, Elizabeth Bennet and Sir Thomas Bertram.

A Romantic View of Marriage: Marianne Dashwood and Elizabeth Bennet

Marianne Dashwood, at 16 and 17, holds it for dogma that true love – the only sound basis for a real, deep, devoted marriage – only comes once. ' "Your sister, I understand" ', says Colonel Brandon observing Marianne's intense love for Willoughby, ' "does not approve of second attachments".'

> 'No,' replied Elinor, 'her opinions are all romantic.'
> 'Or rather, as I believe, she considers them impossible to exist.'
> 'I believe she does. But how she contrives it without reflecting on the character of her own father, who had himself two wives, I know not. A few years however will settle her opinions on the reasonable basis of common sense and observation; and then they may be more

16 *PP* II, c. 19, pp. 236–7.

easy to define and to justify than they now are, by any body but herself.'

'This will probably be the case,' he replied; 'and yet there is something so amiable in the prejudices of a young mind, that one is sorry to see them give way to the reception of general opinions.'

Elinor demurs: ' "her systems have all the unfortunate tendency of setting propriety at nought; and a better acquaintance with the world is what I look forward to as her greatest possible advantage." '[17] When Marianne is deserted by Willoughby the reader is invited to agree with her sister's strictures. Yet that is not the end of the story.

Much later in the book Colonel Brandon reveals to Elinor that he himself when very young had been passionately in love with a girl of 17. Her affection 'for me, was, I believe, fervent as the attachment of your sister to Mr Willoughby . . .' – and had a like though even more unhappy outcome. The young woman was forcibly married to another and came to a tragic end – leaving a child of like disposition who has been seduced by Willoughby.[18] But the Colonel has lost none of his devotion to very young, ardent, beautiful women; and the likeness between Marianne and his first love has inspired him to fall in love again. In the end even Marianne has to set aside her devotion for Willoughby.

> Marianne Dashwood was born to an extraordinary fate. She was born to discover the falsehood of her own opinions, and to counteract, by her conduct, her most favourite maxims. She was born to overcome an affection formed so late in life as at seventeen, and with no sentiment superior to strong esteem and lively friendship, voluntarily to give her hand to another!

and to one who has also suffered an earlier attachment and whom she had previously thought too old to marry at all.[19] But the rather crude satire of this passage disguises a remarkably sympathetic picture of romantic attachments, which when shorn of their more grotesque features reveal the lasting impression and depth that they can comprise and impart.

Elizabeth Bennet's early views of marriage are implied rather than expounded – and often revealed in disagreement with others, especially with Charlotte Lucas, whose function it is in part to set off Elizabeth's views by contradicting them. Common interests, mutual understanding and real affection – all the things Elizabeth's parents lacked – she takes for granted as of the essence. Charlotte later shocks Elizabeth by marrying Mr

[17] *SS* I, c. 11, pp. 55–6.
[18] *SS* II, c. 9, pp. 205–11.
[19] *SS* III, c. 14, p. 378.

Collins, a union of sense and nonsense hardly to be endured. Yet as Charlotte points out:

> I am not romantic, you know. I never was. I ask only a comfortable home; and considering Mr Collins's character, connections, and situation in life, I am convinced that my chance of happiness with him is as fair, as most people can boast on entering the married state.

'Miss Lucas . . . accepted him solely from the pure and disinterested desire of an establishment.'[20] A good while before, Charlotte's advice for Jane in what she supposed to be her pursuit of Mr Bingley was to ' "make the most of every half hour in which she can command his attention. When she is secure of him, there will be leisure for falling in love as much as she chuses." '

To which Elizabeth retorted:

> 'Your plan is a good one . . . where nothing is in question but the desire of being well married; and if I were determined to get a rich husband, or any husband, I dare say I should adopt it. But these are not Jane's feelings; she is not acting by design. As yet, she cannot even be certain of the degree of her own regard, nor of its reasonableness.'

She has hardly seen enough of him to 'understand his character'. Charlotte thinks differently.

> 'I wish Jane success with all my heart; and if she were married to him tomorrow, I should think she had as good a chance of happiness, as if she were to be studying his character for a twelvemonth. Happiness in marriage is entirely a matter of chance. If the dispositions of the parties are ever so well known to each other, or ever so similar before-hand, it does not advance their felicity in the least. They always continue to grow sufficiently unlike afterwards to have their share of vexation; and it is better to know as little as possible of the defects of the person with whom you are to pass your life.'
>
> 'You make me laugh, Charlotte; but it is not sound. You know it is not sound, and that you would never act in this way yourself.'[21]

This passage is full of ironies, above all in its conclusion, for Charlotte does act in exactly that way. More than that, her suggestion that married couples grow more unlike as time passes is the reverse of the experience reflected in many marriages, and very well known to Jane Austen: yet not wholly false, as Mr and Mrs Bennet bear witness. But perhaps the deepest problem she brings to light is the difficulty engaged couples must encounter in having more than a very superficial knowledge of one another. As she was completing *Pride and Prejudice* Jane Austen was planning *Mansfield Park*,

---

[20] *PP* I, c. 22, pp. 125, 122.
[21] *PP* I, c. 6, pp. 22–3.

in which hero and heroine have known each other intimately from child-hood; so too Mr Knightley and Emma; and long and deep knowledge between Anne Elliot and Captain Wentworth also lies at the heart of *Persuasion*. It was an aspect of entry to marriage on which Jane Austen meditated profoundly.

With her aunt Mrs Gardiner, Elizabeth had more common ground than with Charlotte Lucas. Mrs Gardiner had married, evidently for affection, Mrs Bennet's sensible, respectable brother: she was 'several years younger than Mrs Bennet', had a family of very small children and was especially close to Jane and Elizabeth.[22] When she comes for Christmas, she finds Elizabeth a good deal taken up with Mr Wickham, and is anxious on this account, since neither Wickham nor Elizabeth has any fortune. A few months later Wickham is evidently courting one Miss King.

> 'What sort of girl is Miss King? I should be sorry to think our friend [Wickham] mercenary.'
> 'Pray, my dear aunt, what is the difference in matrimonial affairs, between the mercenary and the prudent motive? Where does dis-cretion end, and avarice begin? Last Christmas you were afraid of his marrying me, because it would be imprudent; and now, because he is trying to get a girl with only ten thousand pounds, you want to find out that he is mercenary.'[23]

The argument continues for some time in similar pleasantries; but the essential point is made. The line between the prudent and the mercenary is not easy to draw.

A while later, after Darcy's first proposal and very decided rejection, and after Elizabeth's visit to Pemberley – which completes the revolution in her view of him – they part in the inn at Lambton, and Elizabeth fears that the disgrace which has fallen on the family through Lydia's elopement will bring an end to Darcy's regard for her.

> As she threw a retrospective glance over the whole of their acquaintance, so full of contradictions and varieties, [she] sighed at the perverseness of those feelings which would now have promoted its continuance, and would formerly have rejoiced in its termination.
> If gratitude and esteem are good foundations of affection, Eliza-beth's change of sentiment will be neither improbable nor faulty. But if otherwise, if the regard springing from such sources is unreasonable or unnatural, in comparison of what is so often described as arising on a first interview with its object, and even before two words have been

---

[22] *PP* II, c. 2, p. 139. Mrs Gardiner was considerably younger than she appeared in the *PP* Video.
[23] *PP* II, c. 4, p. 153.

exchanged, nothing can be said in her defence, except that she had given somewhat of a trial to the latter method, in her partiality for Wickham, and that its ill-success might perhaps authorise her to seek the other less interesting mode of attachment. Be that as it may, she saw him go with regret . . .[24]

Love at first sight is a parody of the romantic view of marriage, and it is evident that Jane Austen has left out a middle term in this comparison – and that once again Elizabeth's own view is implied rather than revealed. Her feeling for Darcy has been altered by the slow revelation – starting with his letter, enhanced by his housekeeper's testimony and his own behaviour at Pemberley – that his character may be very different from the one she had deduced from her earlier acquaintance with him; and stimulated by gratitude for the love and affection he has shown, which could even survive her angry rejection of his first proposal – and is soon to be enhanced by his generous treatment of Lydia and Wickham. But the process was much more subtle and complex than this passage reveals or admits. After she has accepted Darcy, she answers Jane's question ' "Will you tell me how long you have loved him?" ' – with a jest – ' "It has been coming on so gradually, that I hardly know when it began. But I believe I must date it from my first seeing his beautiful grounds at Pemberley".'[25] – This was at once absurd and true: for the visit to Pemberley in all its aspects, including the sad parting at Lambton, was the catalyst which determined and revealed Elizabeth's affection for Darcy. If at the end of the novel she had been allowed to explain her philosophy of marriage as candidly as Charlotte had presented hers at the outset, it might have gone something like this. True affection alone could justify a woman in accepting a proposal of marriage – but many, many elements went into its forming: gratitude, esteem, common principles – even prudence; if adequately compensated by the madness of love.

But she did not talk to her aunt of prudence then. When Mrs Gardiner had written to her about Darcy's role in the marriage of Lydia, and conjectured something of the relations of Darcy and Elizabeth,

> you supposed more than really existed. But *now* suppose as much as you chuse; give a loose to your fancy, indulge your imagination in every possible flight which the subject will afford, and unless you believe me actually married, you cannot greatly err . . . I am the happiest creature in the world . . . I am happier even than Jane; she only smiles, I laugh. Mr Darcy sends you all the love in the world, that he can spare from me . . .[26]

[24] *PP* III, c. 4, p. 279.
[25] *PP* III, c. 17, p. 373. See pp. 76, 81.
[26] *PP* III, c. 18, pp. 382–3.

Marriage in Principle: Sir Thomas Bertram's View

Within a single capacious mind, Sir Thomas enshrined as wide a range of incompatible views about the entry to marriage as any of Jane Austen's major characters. *Mansfield Park* opens with his own: 'Miss Maria Ward of Huntingdon, with only seven thousand pounds, had the good luck to captivate Sir Thomas Bertram, of Mansfield Park.'[27] He could not be ignorant of the claims of love and beauty. Yet as his daughters grew up, 'while they retained the name of Bertram, [they] must be giving it new grace, and in quitting it he trusted would extend its respectable alliances'.[28] This Maria, the elder daughter, proceeds to do by becoming engaged to Mr Rushworth of Sotherton Park, who has inherited an income larger than her father's. The connection has every possible advantage – he is even of the right interest in politics, surprising as it seems that Mr Rushworth has any political understanding at all.[29] But when Sir Thomas returns from Antigua and meets the young man, it dawns on him that he is 'an inferior young man, as ignorant in business as in books, with opinions in general unfixed, and without seeming much aware of it himself'; and Sir Thomas offers to help Maria break the engagement.[30] But Maria is desperate for independence – and to show Mr Crawford that his trifling with her, his attentions and obvious indifference, have not ruined her prospects. Sir Thomas was too easily satisfied: against his better judgment he hopes that Rushworth will improve; he reckons that she is not a person of acute feelings – quite falsely, for he has no notion of her feeling for Henry Crawford; and he finds various excuses and even advantages in a cool alliance which may bring her oftener to Mansfield from Sotherton. So she is allowed to go forward into the marriage.

> In all the important preparations of the mind she was complete; being prepared for matrimony by an hatred of home, restraint, and tranquillity; by the misery of disappointed affection, and contempt of the man she was to marry. The rest might wait. The preparations of new carriages and furniture might wait for London and spring, when her own taste could have fairer play.[31]

As for Mrs Norris, who had planned the marriage and strained every nerve to promote it, 'no one would have supposed, from her confident triumph, that she had ever heard of conjugal infelicity in her life, or could have the

---

[27] *MP* I, c. 1, p. 1.
[28] *MP* I, c. 2, p. 20.
[29] *MP* I, c. 4, p. 40: 'in the same county, and the same interest'.
[30] *MP* II, c. 3, pp. 200–1.
[31] *MP* II, c. 3, p. 202.

smallest insight into the disposition of the niece who had been brought up under her eye'.[32]

When Mr Crawford falls in love with Fanny and makes definite proposals for her to Sir Thomas, he sees no possible excuse for her not accepting him. Once again, the marvellous convenience of Fanny marrying Mr Crawford blinds his judgment – nor has he been a witness of Crawford trifling with his own daughters: she is a niece and deserves a good home: but she is portionless, a poor relation, and cannot hope for anyone approaching Crawford in affluence – his charm and good services to her brother make it altogether imperative that Fanny accept him. At first, indeed, Sir Thomas simply takes it for granted that she will. When she shows signs of opposition, he is furious.

> There is something in this which my comprehension does not reach. Here is a young man wishing to pay his addresses to you, with every thing to recommend him; not merely situation in life, fortune, and character, but with more than common agreeableness, with address and conversation pleasing to every body.[33]

Having satisfied himself (again, quite falsely) that she was not in love with either of his sons, he decides that she is simply being unreasonable.

> I had thought you peculiarly free from wilfulness of temper, self-conceit, and every tendency to that independence of spirit, which prevails so much in modern days, even in young women, and which in young women is offensive and disgusting beyond all common offence.[34]

These were the words of an angry man; and Sir Thomas, in moments of quieter reflection, sees how unjust they are to Fanny. None the less, the assumption remains: a dependent young woman offered the chance of a highly prosperous marriage will be deeply ungrateful to those who provide for her and protect her if she does not accept her suitor. As for Fanny, with equal confidence and under an opposite illusion, she hoped 'that her uncle's displeasure was abating, and would abate farther as he considered the matter with more impartiality, and felt, as a good man must feel, how wretched, and how unpardonable, how hopeless and how wicked it was, to marry without affection'.[35] Sir Thomas in his present mood would have thought that romantic nonsense; yet he was indeed too good a man to think well of

---

[32] *MP* II, c. 3, p. 203.

[33] *MP* III, c. 1, pp. 315–16. Sir Thomas 'would have every young man, with a sufficient income, settle as soon after four and twenty as he can' (*MP*, p. 317). Similarly Miss Crawford: 'every body should marry as soon as they can do it to advantage' (see below n. 39).

[34] *MP* III, c. 1, p. 318.

[35] *MP* III, c. 1, p. 324.

marriage without respect and affection; and in the end he comes to rejoice in her marriage to Edmund – admittedly in good measure for the selfish reasons that it keeps Fanny near him, and unites the two best loved of his family – but also because he sees true affection and likeness of outlook and principle, a deep community of principle and feeling, between her and Edmund. When she was first adopted at Mansfield, he had had some anxieties about 'cousins in love'.

> The joyful consent which met Edmund's application, the high sense of having realised a great acquisition in the promise of Fanny for a daughter, formed just such a contrast with his early opinion on the subject when the poor little girl's coming had been first agitated, as time is for ever producing between the plans and decisions of mortals, for their own instruction, and their neighbours' entertainment.[36]

Lady Bertram's View of Marriage

When Maria elopes Lady Bertram is almost as shocked as her husband – as nearly as her much cooler and more transient feelings allow. Otherwise her philosophy of marriage was much simpler and more superficial.

> She had been a beauty, and a prosperous beauty, all her life; and beauty and wealth were all that excited her respect. ['She felt all the injuries of beauty in Mrs Grant's being so well settled in life without being handsome.'] To know Fanny to be sought in marriage by a man of fortune, raised her, therefore, very much in her opinion . . . 'Well, Fanny,' she said . . . – and she really had known something like impatience, to be alone with her, and her countenance, as she spoke, had extraordinary animation – 'Well, Fanny, I have had a very agreeable surprise . . . I give you joy, my dear niece.' – And looking at her complacently, she added, 'Humph – We certainly are a handsome family.'

When Fanny points out how much her aunt would miss her if she accepted Mr Crawford, Lady Bertram replies.

> 'No, my dear, I should not think of missing you, when such an offer as this comes in your way . . . You must be aware, Fanny, that it is every young woman's duty to accept such a very unexceptionable offer as this.' This was almost the only rule of conduct, the only piece of advice, which Fanny had ever received from her aunt in the course of eight years and a half . . . Lady Bertram was quite talkative.

---

[36] *MP* III, c. 17, pp. 471–2. For 'cousins in love' see I, c. 1, p. 6.

She harks back to the recent ball at Mansfield when Crawford had evidently much admired Fanny – an admiration Lady Bertram in large part attributes to the help she imagines her maid had given in dressing her. ' "I am very glad I sent Chapman to you . . ." ' And as a crowning mark of favour, she promises Fanny a puppy 'the next time pug has a litter'.[37]

Miss Crawford's Views on Marriage

Like Sir Thomas, Mary Crawford could not be wholly opposed to the delights of falling in love as a prelude to marriage. She comes near to marrying Edmund Bertram, for all that he is a younger son and a clergyman, for no better reason than that she loves him; and when her brother falls in love with Fanny Price, she is delighted by his infatuation, and reckons Henry's ardent love, and Fanny's good character, ideal basis for a happy marriage – even though she has no fortune.[38] Yet she has other views, much at variance with her affection for Edmund. 'I would have every body marry if they can do it properly; I do not like to have people throw themselves away; but every body should marry as soon as they can do it to advantage.'[39] What this means is spelt out when she is contemplating her London friends, Janet and Flora Ross, now Mrs Fraser and Lady Stornaway.

> I look upon the Frasers to be about as unhappy as most other married people. And yet it was a most desirable match for Janet at the time. We were all delighted. She could not do otherwise than accept him, for he was rich, and she had nothing; but he turns out ill-tempered, and *exigeant*; and wants a young woman, a beautiful young woman of five-and-twenty, to be as steady as himself. And my friend does not manage him well; she does not seem to know how to make the best of it. There is a spirit of irritation, which, to say nothing worse, is certainly very ill-bred. In their house I shall call to mind the conjugal manners of Mansfield Parsonage with respect. [She has spoken before with contempt of Dr Grant's behaviour to his wife; yet allows he has respect and affection for her.] Even Dr Grant does shew a thorough confidence in my sister, and a certain consideration for her judgment, which makes one feel there *is* attachment; but of that, I shall see nothing with the Frasers. I shall be at Mansfield for ever, Fanny. My own sister as a wife, Sir Thomas Bertram as a husband, are my standards of perfection. Poor Janet has been sadly taken in; and yet there

[37] *MP* III, c. 2, pp. 332–3. [The passage in brackets is from *MP* I, c. 3, p. 32.]
[38] *MP* II, c. 12, pp. 292–3.
[39] *MP* I, c. 4, p. 43.

was nothing improper on her side; she did not run into the match inconsiderately, there was no want of foresight. She took three days to consider of his proposals; and during those three days asked the advice of every body connected with her, whose opinion was worth having; and especially applied to my late dear aunt [the most unhappily married wife in the book], whose knowledge of the world made her judgment very generally and deservedly looked up to by all the young people of her acquaintance; and she was decidedly in favour of Mr Fraser. This seems as if nothing were a security for matrimonial comfort! I have not so much to say for my friend Flora [Mrs Fraser's sister], who jilted a very nice young man in the Blues, for the sake of that horrid Lord Stornaway, who has about as much sense, Fanny, as Mr Rushworth, but much worse looking, and with a blackguard character. I *had* my doubts at the time about her being right, for he has not even the air of a gentleman, and now, I am sure, she was wrong.[40]

It is very instructive to explore the grounds on which marriage seemed impossible to Fanny, Mary and Edmund. Fanny hoped it was sufficient that she could feel no affection for Mr Crawford – she had it firmly in mind that marriage without affection was wrong; yet her hope of escaping from him was underpinned by two deeper convictions which could not be revealed to Sir Thomas – that she believed Henry Crawford disreputable owing to his behaviour towards her cousins, and that she was in love with Edmund. Mary was in love with Edmund, and yet felt his profession and his role as an impecunious younger son a barrier to matrimony: her mind is constantly divided. She has a deep prejudice against the clergy, never fully explained – but she clearly regarded Edmund's as the one unrespectable profession. 'It was a foolish precipitation last Christmas, but the evil of a few days may be blotted out in part. Varnish and gilding hide many stains' – as she wrote to Fanny hoping to hear that Tom was dying and that Edmund would succeed to the baronetcy and the estates.[41] Poverty was doubtless an even greater bar than ordination. Yet she admitted many claims in Edmund's favour, even or especially her recognition that the world of different values in which he lived, the high principles of Mansfield, had their attractions. For Edmund it was in the end impossible to marry the sister of the man who had seduced his own sister: that was the crunch, the compulsion that broke the threads that bound him to Mary. But he was also deeply stirred by her attitude: that she had no sense of wrong or guilt or sin in elopement and adultery. All three were moved by affection and love; but in the end Mary's views were

---

[40] *MP* III, c. 5, p. 361. Lord Stornaway's character improves on acquaintance (p. 416) – but that is a symbol of Mary Crawford's deeper involvement in the worldly pleasures of her London friends.
[41] *MP* III, c. 14, p. 434.

deeply cynical, Edmund's and Fanny's – with every qualification made – deeply principled.

Mr and Mrs George Knightley

At the end of most of Jane Austen's novels there is a light crack of the whip – a gentle flash of irony or satire – to put the romantic ending in perspective. In *Emma* it is singularly lacking. She has no doubt of 'the perfect happiness of the union'.[42] The grounds of this are complex; but the central point is that husband and wife had known each other intimately for many years – for all of Emma's and most of Mr Knightley's life. This is not all gain: for most of the book it leads Mr Knightley to regard her – and sometimes to treat her – as a spoilt child; and till near the end she thinks she regards him as a friendly quasi-uncle turned brother-in-law. Their engagement comes as a total surprise to all those closest to them – not only to Mr Woodhouse, who never foresees a wedding if he can possibly help it, but to Emma's closest friend Mrs Weston and to Mr Knightley's brother. But at least they cannot be victims of Charlotte Lucas's cynical view – that married couples can only learn each other's true character in the disillusionment of married life.

In all her three last novels Jane Austen explored partnerships formed by couples who had known each other for at least eight years – and under circumstances (anyway for part of the time) of special intimacy. Fanny Price owed her happiness at Mansfield to the kindness of Edmund; and her gratitude and affection mature rapidly into fervent love. Until close on the denouement Edmund sees this as a cousin's love – or if closer than that, as 'my only sister – my only comfort now'; but it draws them close together none the less for that: he is portrayed as 'loving, guiding, protecting her, as he had been doing ever since her being ten years old,' – and as for Fanny – 'her mind in so great a degree formed by his care, and her comfort depending on his kindness, an object to him of such close and peculiar interest, dearer by all his own importance with her than any one else at Mansfield' – thus his creator prepares for Edmund to 'learn to prefer soft light eyes to sparkling dark ones'.[43] Her mind had been formed by his – and she in her turn had revealed to him as in a mirror the principles in which he most deeply believed, the tastes he most enjoyed: all that he had been most concerned to teach her. If we ask the question: were her principles instilled by conviction of their truth, by a natural high-mindedness, or out of her love for Edmund who imparted them? – One answer must be that Jane Austen emphasises again and again that her love for Edmund was an overwhelming

---

[42] *E* III, c. 19, p. 484.
[43] *MP* III, c. 15, p. 444; c. 17, p. 470.

motive in her life. But that is not quite the whole truth: for his teaching fell on fertile soil; and though Fanny's insight into his errors and weaknesses when infatuated by Mary Crawford were partly the fruit of jealousy – they were also the product of an understanding naturally good, improved by Edmund in better times. Yet in truth every attempt to analyse – to bring to the surface – the deeper nature of this relationship disguises some of the subtlety of Jane Austen's insight and exposition. Nor will it escape observation that Fanny is a sister – as Emma a sister-in-law – turned wife; there is a deep and subtle ambivalence in the conversion or transformation in both cases.

It is not to the same degree true that Emma's mind was formed by Mr Knightley's as Fanny's by Edmund Bertram. She was attached to him all her life; but she was also wayward and self-willed, impatient of criticism. He made no secret at any time of his view that she should be under firmer discipline, more persevering in her reading, her painting and her music – in all of which she had talent spoilt by lack of persistent concentration – and that she should be less self-indulgent in her feelings and attitudes. None the less, she could not avoid being deeply influenced by him: the long passage of time was of the essence of their relationship. This is emphasised by the striking contrast of the sub-plot – the engagement and marriage of Jane Fairfax and Frank Churchill. Theirs is a marriage of very different characters: Jane is the more serious, the more deeply principled, the more elegant, the more accomplished; Frank has many good qualities, but he is the spoiled favourite of rich relations, light-hearted for ill as well as good – lively in a way which Jane found wholly bewitching on brief acquaintance by the sea at Weymouth. It was a flying romance – love at first sight – which survived and matured because there were deeper qualities in both, especially in Jane. But it is in any case utterly different from the entry to marriage of Emma and her betrothed – save only in one very curious resemblance: in both cases their love is a secret from all around them; in the case of Emma and Mr Knightley a secret from the partners themselves till the end is near.

The relation of Emma and Mr Knightley is the exact reverse of Charlotte Lucas's notion of how couples come together. It was precisely growing knowledge and self-awareness that led them to discover the depth of their attachment to one another. We have explored the hints which Jane Austen throws out of the strength of their feeling for one another – of which they and their friends were yet long unaware. It has often been thought – it has often been the case – that lovers create an image and fall in love with it, discovering in time the difference between the image and the beloved. That is something they have to come to terms with, if they can. But though Emma was full of illusions – they take up most of the book – she is not deceived about Mr Knightley's character and opinions. Likewise Mr Knightley is as candid about her faults after falling in love – or anyway recognising that he has fallen in love – as before.

When Mrs Weston's little girl is born, Emma observes that the mother will be able to educate the daughter with the

'advantage, you know, of practising on me . . . We shall now see her own little [Anna] educated on a more perfect plan.' 'That is,' replied Mr Knightley, 'she will indulge her even more than she did you, and believe that she does not indulge her at all. It will be the only difference.'

'Poor child!' cried Emma; 'at that rate, what will become of her?'

'Nothing very bad. – The fate of thousands. She will be disagreeable in infancy, and correct herself as she grows older. I am losing all my bitterness against spoilt children, my dearest Emma. I, who am owing all my happiness to *you*, would not it be horrible ingratitude in me to be severe on them?'

Emma laughed, and replied: 'But I had the assistance of all your endeavours to counteract the indulgence of other people. I doubt whether my own sense would have corrected me without it.'

'Do you? I have no doubt. Nature gave you understanding: – Miss Taylor gave you principles. You must have done well. My interference was quite as likely to do harm as good . . . The good was all to myself, by making you an object of the tenderest affection to me. I could not think about you so much without doating on you, faults and all; and by dint of fancying so many errors, have been in love with you ever since you were thirteen at least.'

'I am sure you were of use to me,' cried Emma. 'I was very often influenced rightly by you – oftener than I would own at the time. I am very sure you did me good. And if poor little Anna Weston is to be spoiled, it will be the greatest humanity in you to do as much for her as you have done for me, except falling in love with her when she is thirteen.'[44]

The observant reader knows that it is neither wholly true – nor to be sure wholly untrue – that he fell in love with her when she was 13. An alternative view has been offered the reader in the scene in which the pair reveal their affections to each other.

On his side, there had been a long-standing jealousy, old as the arrival, or even the expectation, of Frank Churchill. – He had been in love with Emma, and jealous of Frank Churchill, from about the same period, one sentiment having probably enlightened him as to the other.[45]

A modern novelist would explore in sensual detail the shift in both partners from friendship to sexual love. That is not Miss Austen's concern; she not

[44] *E* III, c. 17, pp. 461–2.
[45] *E* III, c. 13, p. 432.

only deliberately avoids it, she undercuts it. She has given many hints of early attachment between them: the shift from the love of older and younger intimate family friends, between brother and sister – if that is how we should define their earlier relationship – is revealed with extraordinary insight and subtlety, so that for all the ambiguities as to when Mr Knightley fell in love with Emma, the foundation is all the more clearly laid: the deep knowledge each had of the other, the influence each had exerted on the other, are the essential roots of their married love – roots surer far than the seaside idyll of Frank Churchill and Jane Fairfax. Or at least, so we may suppose: for there is no dogma in the exposition. Jane Austen reveals a variety of different elements in the married love of her characters; there is a place in the world for them all.

Persuasion

In *Emma* hero and heroine had known each other for all her 21 years: on his more romantic calculation, he had been in love with her for eight of them. In *Mansfield Park* the time between Fanny's arrival at Mansfield and Edmund's proposal is approximately eight or nine years – allowing for the author's deliberate refusal to calculate the exact time needed for 'the cure of unconquerable passions, and the transfer of unchanging attachments'.[46] In *Persuasion*, again, eight and a half years separate the first and the second engagement of Anne Elliot and Frederick Wentworth.[47] In 1806 the young and ardent Captain, 'with a great deal of intelligence, spirit and brilliancy', had been without fortune or family, and altogether too sanguine and headstrong for the prudent mind of Lady Russell, Anne's closest friend and adviser. Although they were deeply in love, and enjoyed a brief period 'of exquisite felicity', the cool reception her father and sister gave to her suitor – and, much more, the determined opposition of Lady Russell – overbore Anne's devotion to her lover. 'Anne Elliot, with all her claims of birth, beauty, and mind, [was not to be allowed] to throw herself away at nineteen.'[48] Anne broke off the

---

[46] *MP* III, c. 17, p. 470. Emma was nearly 21 at the outset of the book (I, c. 1, p. 1) – and so presumably fully 21 or even 22 when she married just a year later. Fanny was 'just ten' when she arrived at *Mansfield Park*, 18 when Mr Crawford proposed to her, and had been 'eight and a half' or 'eight or more' years at Mansfield – and so 19 at least when Edmund married her (*MP* I, c. 2, p. 12; II, c. 9, p. 270; III, c. 1, p. 319; c. 2, pp. 331, 333; III, c. 6, p. 369; for chronology see *MP*, pp. 554–7).

[47] The first engagement is more than seven, almost eight years past at the start, eight and a half at the end of the book: *P* I, c. 4, p. 28; c. 7, p. 60; II, c. 11, p. 237. There are various other indications, all more or less consistent with these calculations: see dates in *P*, p. 302: 1806–1814.

[48] *P* I, c. 4, p. 26.

engagement; but it left deep scars and powerful memories with both of them.

As in *Emma*, there is a contrast between two couples – but in this case it is between Anne and Captain Wentworth on the one hand, and Anne and her other suitor, Mr Elliot, on the other. Superficially, Mr Elliot seems to have much in common with Anne: he is intelligent, witty, elegant; he is the heir of Kellynch to which she still has a strong devotion – she is bewitched by the prospect Lady Russell sets before her of playing the role her mother had played many years before.[49] The difference is twofold. Mr Elliot's virtues are skin deep. We are treated to some melodramatic revelations of his heartlessness from Anne's school friend Mrs Smith – Jane Austen has no doubts as to the depth of male wickedness, and Anne and the reader have to be convinced – and are very thoroughly convinced – that Mr Elliot will not do. Even more significant, her knowledge of him is limited. Although there has been some contact between him and Sir Walter and Elizabeth in London, Anne was never included in the London trips and first meets him (without knowing it) in Lyme, and is properly introduced in Bath when the plot of the book is well advanced. His evident charm and the intimacy he claims and establishes with the family in Bath earn him Captain Wentworth's fierce jealousy.

> 'To see you,' cried he, 'in the midst of those who could not be my well-wishers, to see your cousin close by you, conversing and smiling, and feel all the horrible eligibilities and proprieties of the match! To consider it as the certain wish of every being who could hope to influence you! Even if your own feelings were reluctant or indifferent, to consider what powerful supports would be his! Was it not enough to make the fool of me which I appeared? How could I look on without agony? Was not the very sight of the friend who sat behind you [Lady Russell], was not the recollection of what had been, the knowledge of her influence, the indelible, immoveable impression of what persuasion had once done – was it not all against me?'
>
> 'You should have distinguished,' replied Anne. 'You should not have suspected me now; the case so different, and my age so different. If I was wrong in yielding to persuasion once, remember that it was to persuasion exerted on the side of safety, not of risk. When I yielded, I thought it was to duty; but no duty could be called in aid here. In marrying a man indifferent to me, all risk would have been incurred, and all duty violated.'[50]

Persuasion is brief and its story lightly sketched – though with the author's most mature skill and a depth of feeling equal at least to that of all her

[49] *P* II, c. 5, p. 160.
[50] *P* II, c. 11, p. 244.

novels. But it reveals in a series of vignettes how the pieces of Anne's character are revealed in a new light to Captain Wentworth. Both of them have spent much time in the years since their first engagement in deep reflection on love and marriage. In her case, this is made clear in many passages of the book; in his, in at least one: when he discusses matrimonial plans with his sister and brother-in-law, he concludes: 'If I am a fool, I shall be a fool indeed, for I have thought on the subject more than most men.'[51]

Little by little, after they have met again, his feeling for her is rekindled. After their first meeting he decides to stay longer in the neighbourhood than he had intended.[52] Anne thinks it is to flirt with the Musgrove girls; but it is clear in the end that he had himself harboured no serious thoughts of either of them – and whether consciously or unconsciously it may really be on Anne's account that he postpones his departure. Little by little he is made to believe once again in her uncommon force of character and sense, especially by her presence of mind and ready assumption of command at the disaster in Lyme – in marked contrast to the failure of command in the fearless naval captain. He is reminded by Mr Elliot's admiration of the beauty which had once bewitched him. It cannot be said that even at the end they had spent much time together; yet the two periods of courting, over eight years apart, lent depth and perspective to their knowledge of each other – just as it lent maturity to both. We are kept long in suspense – one supposes – because if his feelings for her were visibly returning too early, the plot of the book would dissolve. There has to be delay; and the device by which it is sustained is that the book is written – more than any other novel except *Emma*, and for a similar reason – almost wholly from the heroine's viewpoint. We are told plainly about the early progress of Darcy's feelings for Elizabeth; there is only a little suspense during the early part of her stay at Hunsford Parsonage, illuminated for the observant reader by Darcy's listless behaviour. But in that case the author had to prevent his proposal coming, for the reader, out of so clear a sky as it does for Elizabeth. Her problem in *Persuasion* is the reverse: the reader must know as little of Captain Wentworth's true feelings as Anne does.

When all is revealed, Anne can reflect that – though she regrets most bitterly all the suffering the long parting has meant for both of them – they come together again: 'more exquisitely happy, perhaps, in their reunion, than when it had been first projected; more tender, more tried, more fixed in a knowledge of each other's character, truth, and attachment . . .'[53] There is a very obvious sense in which *Persuasion* is a debate – or an invitation to the reader to debate – on the merits of early, romantic attachment compared with those of a union based on longer knowledge and

[51] *P* I, c. 7, p. 62.
[52] *P* I, c. 9, p. 73.
[53] *P* II, c. 11, pp. 240–1.

experience; and the author makes it impossible for the sensitive reader to determine the answer to the debate.

The Wooing of Fanny Knight

By a fortunate chance we have Jane Austen's own reflections on the place of affection in entry to marriage in her marvellous letters to her niece Fanny of November 1814 – written when a second edition of *Mansfield Park* was being considered, and *Emma* well advanced in the writing.[54] Her letters, like the novels, are evidence – not transcripts of her opinions. These were written very carefully and thoughtfully *ad personam*. She is trying to clear Fanny's mind by gentle shock tactics – but is herself very anxious not to give a wrong lead or bad advice, and not to be responsible in the end for an unhappy marriage. Fanny has been wooed by John Plumptre, a rather solemn but eligible young man; she has been falling in and out of love with him for a while, and has listed to her aunt the objections she has.

> Oh! dear Fanny, your mistake has been one that thousands of women fall into. He was the *first* young man who attached himself to you. That was the charm, and most powerful it is. – Among the multitudes however that make the same mistake with yourself, there can be few indeed who have so little reason to regret it; – *his* character and *his* attachment leave you nothing to be ashamed of.

She then offers numerous points in his favour, from the degree of encouragement Fanny has given him, to

> his situation in life, family, friends, and above all his character – his uncommonly amiable mind, strict principles, just notions, good habits – *all* that *you* know so well how to value, *all* that is really of the first importance – everything of this nature pleads his cause most strongly . . . – and is not it a fine character, of which modesty is the only defect? – I have no doubt that he will get more lively and more like yourselves as he is more with you; – he will catch your ways if he belongs to you . . . [And she defends him from the charge of being too good or becoming Evangelical –[55] then turns round and confronts her niece.]
>
> And now, my dear Fanny, having written so much on one side of the question, I shall turn round and entreat you not to commit yourself farther, and not to think of accepting him unless you really do like him. Anything is to be preferred or endured rather than

[54] The letters quoted below are in *Letters*, L nos. 109, 114, pp. 279–81, 285–6; cf. p. 491; C nos. 103, 106, pp. 409–11, 417–18; M-F 340–1, 349. The advice given to Anne in *Persuasion* was fundamentally different; yet there is a link.

[55] See p. 131.

marrying without affection; and if his deficiencies of manner etc. etc. strike you more than all his good qualities, if you continue to think strongly of them, give him up at once . . .

She must make up her mind, and not worry too much if the young man suffers from being rejected. 'It is no creed of mine, as you must be well aware, that such sort of disappointments kill anybody.' Fanny evidently replied that she set great store by her aunt's advice – for in Jane's next letter she expresses fright at the thought; but she goes steadily on discouraging Fanny.

When I consider how few young men you have yet seen much of – how capable you are (yes, I do still think you *very* capable) of being really in love – and how full of temptation the next 6 or 7 years of your life will probably be – (it is the very period of life for the *strongest* attachments to be formed) – I cannot wish you with your present very cool feelings to devote yourself in honour to him. It is very true that you never may attach another man, his equal altogether, but if that other man has the power of attaching you *more*, he will be in your eyes the most perfect.

Fanny sent her lover packing, and just under six years later – long after her aunt's death – became the devoted second wife of Sir Edward Knatchbull, and in due course the mother of nine children.

What must strike the historian of marriage is the extraordinary variety of sentiment and attitude which Jane Austen crammed into the relatively brief compass of her novels. Therein, for the historian's perception, lies the value of the evidence we have been studying. We observe that between hero and heroine in the end there is always real and deep affection – never the whim of idle fancy. Between a romantic approach and marriage for convenience, social advancement or prudence alone the scales in her books are heavily weighted against convenience. By mere convenience, 'all risk' is incurred, 'all duty violated': the words are Anne Elliot's; but Jane Austen's treatment of the Rushworths and Mr Elliot's first marriage – and her advice to her niece – shows clearly enough that she in essence agreed. The historian can point to such a marriage as that of the young Prince Edward, the future Edward I – who was sent to Castile in 1254 to marry the young princess Eleanor whom he had never met, who was little more than a child at the time. It was entirely a marriage of convenience, as was common among royalty – and in high society – from the Middle Ages until the nineteenth century. Nor was Edward I in other ways a sensitive or attractive character. But when she died he set up an exquisite monument to her at every resting place of the bier on its passage to Westminster, and there is no effigy among the medieval kings and queens in Westminster Abbey more beautiful than hers. No one who has contemplated his reaction to her death can doubt

190

that theirs was a deep and lasting love, that the monuments record a profoundly happy marriage. The reader of Jane Austen's novels will look in
vain for an arranged marriage, a marriage of convenience with such a happy
ending. Some marriages turn out better, some worse, than might have been
expected; but she shows little respect for any which are not founded in
affection from the first. Romantic attachments not supported by mutual
understanding and common principles can be fairly disastrous – like the
marriage of Fanny Price's parents. The marriage of Lydia Bennet and Mr
Wickham may be romantic in origin, but it was forced on him by Darcy,
and for all its unromantic destiny, turns out better than the spiteful old
ladies of Meryton had hoped. Differences of rank and wealth can also raise
problems: Mr Weston's first wife, though fond of her husband, never
forgot she was a Miss Churchill of Enscombe.[56] Jane Austen's range is wide,
but not infinitely wide. None the less our insight into human relations in
her age is greatly enriched by the reflections which her gallery of love and
marriage inspires.

If at the end of the day we ask: is her portrayal of marriage a faithful
mirror of her age? – We can never hope to give a sure and confident reply.
Historians tend to put the past in blinkers – to restrict beyond reason the
horizons of former generations; to construct imaginary *mentalités*, which
reflect how much more narrow-minded our ancestors were than we. If
they encounter real variety, they prefer to explain it chronologically: they
are much more inclined to seek variety in time – change from generation to
generation – than to observe the enormous variety of human nature, never
so profusely revealed as in its loves and hates. I have tried myself in a study
of marriage in the Middle Ages to show how the narrow horizons of conventional historical sources can be immensely widened by the use of imaginative literature – and in the sixteenth century the plays of Shakespeare are
a guide to what folk of his age could not possibly have imagined or thought
– or so one might suppose.[57] Some social historians have found in writers of
the seventeenth and eighteenth centuries – not least in Jane herself –
evidence of an increased, more widespread, deeper 'affect' – affection,
demonstration of human emotion – between married couples and their
children – than in earlier centuries.[58] Few serious medievalists now believe
this to be true: there is far too much evidence – from every century from
the twelfth (when the literature of love and marriage becomes copious) to
the twentieth – of an immensely wide range of personal relations between
married folk and lovers – between parents and children – for such generali-
sations to carry an atom of conviction.

[56] *PP* III, c. 8, p. 309; *E* I, c. 2, p. 16.
[57] See Brooke 1989a (on Shakespeare, chap. 9).
[58] For notions of chronological change in affect among married couples, Stone 1977; cf.
Brooke 1989a, p. 20; for parents and children, Wood 1994, esp. pp. 81–2 (Janet Nelson).

16

Convictions and the Moral Code

At the end of *Northanger Abbey* General Tilney reluctantly agrees to the marriage of his second son, the Reverend Henry, with Catherine Morland.

> To begin perfect happiness at the respective ages of twenty-six and eighteen, is to do pretty well; and professing myself moreover convinced, that the General's unjust interference, so far from being really injurious to their felicity, was perhaps rather conducive to it, by improving their knowledge of each other, and adding strength to their attachment, I leave it to be settled by whomsoever it may concern, whether the tendency of this work be altogether to recommend parental tyranny, or reward filial disobedience.[1]

The moral crusade continues in *Sense and Sensibility*, though confined to relatively minor characters, the scheming Lucy Steele and the vain fop Robert Ferrars, Edward's younger brother. Lucy succeeds in wheedling Robert into marrying her and his rich, stupid mother, Mrs Ferrars, into making a favourite of her.

> The whole of Lucy's behaviour in the affair, and the prosperity which crowned it, therefore, may be held forth as a most encouraging instance of what an earnest, an unceasing attention to self-interest, however its progress may be apparently obstructed, will do in securing every advantage of fortune, with no other sacrifice than that of time and conscience.[2]

On a similar note, in *Persuasion*, early in the final chapter, a moral is drawn.

> When any two young people take it into their heads to marry, they are pretty sure by perseverance to carry their point, be they ever so poor, or ever so imprudent, or ever so little likely to be necessary to each other's ultimate comfort. This may be bad morality to conclude with, but I believe it to be truth . . .[3]

[1] *NA* II, c. 16, p. 252.
[2] *SS* III, c. 14, p. 376.
[3] *P* II, c. 12 p. 248.

The supposed moral of *Northanger Abbey* grows out of the plot of the book; the reader is shocked – or amused – into seeing that in a sense it really is the moral of the book. The moral at the end of *Persuasion* is a throwaway line, of little relevance to the marriage of Anne Elliot and Captain Wentworth. Yet in both cases, the author is rejecting, or pretends to reject, the idea that she is a moralist in any deep or earnest sense.

Yet how can this be? Have we not been told, times out of number, that Jane Austen was first and foremost a moralist – one of the great moral teachers in our literature? Surely these passages are not seriously meant: they are ironical, shocking the reader into seeing more clearly the true moral – whatever that may be.

The tradition of Jane the moralist has been fed most effectively by *Mansfield Park*, and no one can avoid the high moral tone which seems to pervade it. Yet all is not plain sailing. Here is a rare use of the phrase 'moral obligation'.

> Being now in her twenty-first year, Maria Bertram was beginning to think matrimony a duty; and as a marriage with Mr Rushworth would give her the enjoyment of a larger income than her father's, as well as ensure her the house in town, which was now a prime object, it became, by the same rule of moral obligation, her evident duty to marry Mr Rushworth if she could

– though she had neither respect nor affection for him.[4] No doubt this is irony; and Maria's failure to understand moral obligation is spelt out with fearful precision in later chapters. 'Lady Bertram did not think deeply, but, guided by Sir Thomas, she thought justly on all important points; and she saw, therefore, in all its enormity, what had happened' – the elopement of Maria and her loss of reputation; and so she 'neither endeavoured herself, nor required Fanny to advise her, to think little of guilt and infamy'.[5] But we have seen that this reflects the morality of Sir Thomas, which is dour, and condemns Maria to something approaching life imprisonment with Mrs Norris. Can this really be the moral code of Miss Austen herself?

It is instructive to compare Lady Bertram's reception of the news that Maria has eloped with that of Fanny. In considerable measure Fanny, Edmund, Sir Thomas and Lady Bertram take a common view – although it is evident that in Edmund, the parson, and Fanny, his pupil, there is a religious, even theological element, in which the guilt and sin of adultery is uppermost, whereas to Sir Thomas moral principle and social disgrace are nearer the centre of his code. Sir Thomas's view is echoed in a sort of crude parody in Fanny's father's 'If she belonged to me, I'd give her the rope's

---

4 *MP* I, c. 4, pp. 38–9.
5 *MP* III, c. 16, p. 449.

end as long as I could stand over her.'⁶ In contrast, Mrs Norris, the parson's widow, is ready to take a much more liberal view. But Fanny has the sternest view of all – yet mingled almost from the start with quite other thoughts, of a much more cheerful complexion.

> The horror of a mind like Fanny's, as it received the conviction of such guilt, and began to take in some of the misery that must ensue, can hardly be described. At first it was a sort of stupefaction; but every moment was quickening her perception of the horrible evil . . .

and Miss Austen dwells at length on the 'too horrible confusion of guilt' whose contemplation gave Fanny deep misery through a sleepless night. But – 'What would be the consequence? Whom would it not injure? Whose views might it not affect? Whose peace would it not cut up for ever? Miss Crawford herself – Edmund; but it was dangerous, perhaps, to tread such ground . . .'⁷ Fanny tried conscientiously to set aside the more cheerful, selfishly cheerful, prospects which opened to her. But a letter from Edmund – breathing nothing but gloom, but announcing that he was coming next day to take her back to her beloved home at Mansfield – brought them forward at once.

> Never had Fanny more wanted a cordial. Never had she felt such a one as this letter contained. To-morrow! to leave Portsmouth tomorrow! She was, she felt she was, in the greatest danger of being exquisitely happy, while so many were miserable.⁸

The immediate cause of this change of heart is the return to Mansfield: but it is evident from the hint already given – and from much of what follows – that a deeper content had already made its way. The elopement of Maria and Henry Crawford would remove all pressure on her to marry Henry; would make such a union impossible in the eyes of Sir Thomas and Edmund, who had hitherto so strongly urged her to accept him. Beyond that, it must separate Edmund from Mary – that was dangerous ground indeed: Fanny had been trying to react in a thoroughly moral and religious way; but she was deeply in love with Edmund, and other thoughts must intrude. On the journey to Mansfield, Edmund and Fanny were accompanied by her sister Susan, and so there was little opportunity for confidential talk; but one brief moment at an inn – when Susan was a little way apart – enables Edmund to say 'You must feel it – you must suffer. How a man who had once loved, could desert you! But *your's* – your regard was new compared with – Fanny, think of *me*!'⁹ It becomes clear that Fanny

---

⁶ *MP* III, c. 15, p. 440.
⁷ *MP* III, c. 15, pp. 440–1.
⁸ *MP* III, c. 15, p. 443.
⁹ *MP* III, c. 15, p. 446. For what follows see c. 16, pp. 456–9.

takes it for granted that Edmund must break with the sister of a man who has seduced his own sister; but Fanny – and so the reader – are kept in some suspense as to whether Edmund is quite so sure himself. He had had one interview with her since the event, and been deeply shocked by her reaction: she had seen the wrong only in terms of public scandal, with no hint of sin and guilt; and this has opened his eyes – though most reluctantly – to the gulf which separated them.

Some readers have seen clear daylight here between Fanny's immediate perception that Edmund must renounce his love for Mary Crawford – and Edmund's slower realisation of it. Of this I am doubtful; but there seems no doubt that their responses are differently portrayed. In Edmund's mind, through most of the book, religious conviction and his feeling for Miss Crawford are in tension if not in conflict. Fanny shares his convictions – she learned them from him – and they are greatly strengthened by her love for Edmund. She is in love with him before Mary comes on the scene; she is soon jealous of Mary; she fights against both emotions – for till near the very end the possibility of marriage with him seems infinitely remote. But her love and her convictions are inextricably united: each serves to strengthen the other. Her love up to a point is unselfish, and helps her profoundly to accept his beliefs and principles; up to a point it is selfless, and makes her seek Edmund's true interests as she conceives them; yet it is also and equally the selfishness of love which makes her so virtuous, so prim, so determined in her convictions. There is a deliberate ambiguity.

This may seem a strange morality, hardly that of the parson's daughter; and we saw long ago that it will not do to read the morality of the Bertrams as a transcript of Jane Austen's.[10] She was an artist, portraying the springs of human action at a very deep imaginative level. Fanny's strong principles and her love for Edmund cannot be disentangled in the roots of her convictions.

In *Emma* the pattern is somewhat differently arranged. Her sound principles and fundamental good feeling – expressed above all in her patience, kindness and affection for her father – were already embedded before the book opens. Mr Knightley attributes them to Miss Taylor; Emma – once she is in love – allows something too to the early influence of Mr Knightley. 'I am sure you were of use to me . . . I was very often influenced rightly by you – oftener than I would own at the time.'[11] There was still much in the younger Emma which Mr Knightley had not cured – her vanity, her whimsies, her fantasies, her wilfulness; and they come to a head in her crushing discourtesy to Miss Bates at Box Hill.[12] This was a kind of catalyst: after it, conscience – and her growing awareness of her love for Mr

---

[10] See pp. 21–6.
[11] *E* III, c. 17, p. 462.
[12] See p. 107.

Knightley – started a cure of several of these faults. It is not enough to say that Miss Taylor gave her principles and her lover – soon to be her husband – gave her more; rather, the principles were a part of the attraction he found in her: not only principles, but a quick understanding, a lively mind – which might lead her often astray – but helped to bring her into subjection to him when he already knew that he was in subjection to her.

In *Persuasion* Captain Wentworth seeks a wife who is firm and capable, knows her mind and sticks to it. He recalls only too vividly the youthful attractions – the charm and intelligence and taste – of the young Anne Elliot; but has convinced himself that she lacks these other necessary qualities – and for that reason had deserted him. But at Lyme 'he had received lessons of more than one sort. The passing admiration of Mr Elliot had at least roused him, and the scenes on the Cobb, and at Captain Harville's' – her presence of mind, good sense, strength of purpose in a crisis – 'had fixed her superiority.'[13] The scene at Lyme is most carefully devised to bring out these qualities – those which revealed how much she had in common with an active, fearless naval commander. *Persuasion* is about more than the renewal of an old romantic attachment: it reveals and deepens the convictions which unite the lovers. The young Captain Wentworth had lacked the polish, the outward show of good breeding and gentlemanly conduct which would have appealed naturally to Lady Russell – and so she regards him as rash, unmannerly, imprudent and unworthy of Anne. Lady Russell plays the role in *Persuasion* of Miss Taylor in *Emma*: both inculcated sound principles of conduct in their pupils; both were admirable women, utterly devoted to Anne and Emma. Yet both were imperfect in their interpretation of their charge – Lady Russell in being less observant, less perceptive, less intelligent than Anne; Miss Taylor in being too indulgent. In *Persuasion*, as in *Emma*, the teaching of the mentor needs to be supplemented by union with the lover – though there the difference ends, since Anne has more to teach Captain Wentworth than vice versa.

Such is the pattern in the most mature novels of all. The deep underlying convictions unite husband and wife in the end in a bond of love and common principles. If it were possible for the reader to deduce, to rationalise the principles, then one might still say that Miss Austen was a didactic novelist. But that is clearly not the case, for two good reasons. In the most obviously moral of the novels, Fanny Price and Edmund concur in the end in a morality at once admirable in some of its fruits, but almost unbearably harsh in others. In all of them, and especially in *Emma*, any attempt which might be made to catalogue and analyse the virtues hero and heroine in the end admire and try to practise simplifies and crudifies an exceptionally subtle exposition.

But if it be the case that the deeper morality in the later novels is revealed

[13] *P* II, c. 11, p. 242.

in the long-formed union of conviction and affection between hero and heroine – how stands it with the earlier novels? In *Northanger Abbey* Catherine's and Henry's knowledge of one another is recent and superficial compared with the later novels. The theme of gratitude – in this case Henry's gratitude to Catherine for loving him, and hers to him for instructing and caring for her, and to his sister Eleanor for befriending her in friendless Bath – takes the place of long attachment; and gratitude is a favourite theme in the early novels. In *Sense and Sensibility* and *Pride and Prejudice* gratitude is a powerful and explicit element in the love of Marianne for Colonel Brandon and Elizabeth for Darcy; and Marianne and Elinor had plenty of time to study their lovers' characters – though nothing like that allotted to Emma and Fanny. But in these three earlier novels, it is only in *Pride and Prejudice* that particular care is taken to show how the heroine came to true knowledge of her lover's character. This is a very interesting case, for every effort is made in the first part of the novel to build up a false picture of Darcy in Elizabeth's mind: he has treated Wickham in the most disgraceful manner, and he has separated Bingley from Jane. Then he proposes to her, and she rejects him with horror and indignation. In her conversion there are many subtle stages – culminating in the overwhelming effect of finding what he has done for Lydia: gratitude is piled on the gratitude she had earlier felt for his loving her, and continuing to love her, in spite of her forceful repudiation of his first proposal. But crucial to all these stages is the discovery that she has been completely mistaken in her assessment of his character and actions, and this is achieved by two devices – very striking in themselves, yet (one might think) relatively crude compared with the means of self-revelation opened in the later novels. First of all, Darcy writes her a letter. After only a few readings of it, within a few hours, she realises at least the falsehood of her former opinion of him. He has staked all on convincing her that Wickham was the villain, not he – and she is convinced. To achieve this he has had even to expose his sister's attempted elopement, a revelation much mitigated by Georgiana's free confession to Darcy of the plot, yet it is hard for the reader to credit that Darcy should say so much. Nevertheless, it is said, and it alone is sufficient.[14] Next, she visits Pemberley, and hears the encomium of the old housekeeper on the young squire.

> 'I have always observed, that they who are good-natured when children, are good-natured when they grow up; and he was always the sweetest-tempered, most generous-hearted, boy in the world . . . He is the best landlord, and the best master . . . that ever lived. Not like the wild young men of now-a-days, who think of nothing but themselves. There is not one of his tenants or servants but what will

[14] See p. 80.

197

give him a good name. Some people call him proud; but I am sure I never saw any thing of it. To my fancy, it is only because he does not rattle away like other young men.' 'In what an amiable light does this place him!' thought Elizabeth.[15]

These devices are powerful, but less subtle than the weapons she uses in later novels. I have scouted any notion that Jane became an Evangelical between *Pride and Prejudice* and *Mansfield Park*;[16] but some conversion does seem to have taken place. In all the later novels she gives her heroes and heroines a better chance to know one another more naturally than Elizabeth and Darcy had had. Yet it is not a total conversion: Wentworth's conviction of the firmness of Anne's mature character is brought on by a catastrophe as dramatic as the devices in *Pride and Prejudice*. In both cases what is revealed is not only good principles working at a deep level – but an unexpected capacity to live up to them. In the end it is not only good principles which Jane Austen seeks in her more sympathetic characters – but the union of theory and practice which converts principles into true convictions.

In *Mansfield Park*, sexual indulgence – from flirting to adultery – plays a central part in the story. It is only a part of the moral world of Fanny and Edmund: of equal, perhaps of far greater importance, are the feelings of gratitude, loyalty, and devotion which Fanny has towards Aunt Bertram which win her aunt's devotion to her in return. Only once in the book does Lady Bertram move 'with no indolent step' – and that is to welcome Fanny back after her long sojourn in Portsmouth. Sir Thomas's repentance takes the form of a searching enquiry into his whole method of education and upbringing.

> He feared that principle, active principle, had been wanting [in his daughters], that they had never been properly taught to govern their inclinations and tempers, by that sense of duty which can alone suffice. They had been instructed theoretically in their religion, but never required to put it into daily practice . . . the necessity for self-denial and humility, he feared they had never heard from any lips that could profit them.[17]

It does not do to make sexual mores the only moral theme of *Mansfield Park*.

Yet it is a very striking feature of the book, and many modern readers naturally think how different are the mores of the late twentieth century. Yet this can easily be exaggerated. Even today, when it is very widely

[15] *PP* III, c. 1, p. 249.
[16] See pp. 21–2, 126.
[17] *MP* III, c. 15, p. 447; c. 17, p. 463.

accepted that a traditional pattern of Christian morality – or any other kind of morality which makes chastity a virtue – cannot be widely enforced or expected – there are many millions scattered about the world to whom chastity, and especially its sister, fidelity in marriage, are at the heart of family life and family values. In the Epistle to the Ephesians the secret of marriage is called 'a great truth' – thus the *New English Bible* and the *Revised English Bible*; 'a great mystery' in the Authorised Version. In the Latin Vulgate this was rendered 'sacramentum magnum', a great sacrament; and so, when the seven sacraments were defined in the mid and late Middle Ages, in a theological milieu receptive of the idea that marriage was a religious calling, marriage became a sacrament – and so it remains today for countless Christians, Catholic and non-Catholic alike.[18] But the early reformers, led by Luther, rejected its sacramental nature, while retaining their reverence for the married state. Thus Jane Austen would presumably not have used the word sacrament; but would have accepted that it was – in the words of the Prayer Book, devised by Thomas Cranmer, himself very much a marrying man – 'an honourable estate . . . signifying unto us the mystical union which is betwixt Christ and his Church': these words echo the same passage in Ephesians. It is doubtless the case that many who hold marriage to be a sacrament or at least an honourable estate today are equally wedded to a deep respect for other people's beliefs and practices; and that we might well expect Jane Austen to be a good deal less tolerant of different views than many of us are at the end of the twentieth century. But what is beyond question is that she lived in a world in which practice was fully as diverse as in the twentieth century – save only for the difference that modern methods of contraception make to the consequences – and so to the mores – of sex. She lived under the Regency, notorious in certain circles for its laxity. The laxity of many London families is emphasised in *Mansfield Park*; and many a contemporary reader must have been reminded, when Admiral Crawford openly lived with his mistress, of a greater admiral than he; and Jane's brother Frank had been quite close to Nelson. There is an amusing passage in one of her letters of 1813 in which she tries hard to like the Princess of Wales, wife of the Prince Regent, 'because she *is* a woman, and because I hate her husband' – a sentiment she doubtless forgot when she dedicated *Emma* to the Prince Regent in 1815. But she admits to doubts, including this: 'the intimacy said to subsist between her and Lady Oxford is bad'.[19] Jane Harley, wife of Edward Harley earl of Oxford, was a woman of exceptional charm alleged to have had frequent affairs, and her children were profanely labelled (after a respectable antiquarian series of books) the Harleian Miscellany. We could pursue the history of sex through every region of English social life in the age of Jane Austen; but the

---

[18] On marriage as a sacrament, see Brooke 1989a.
[19] *Letters*, L no. 82, p. 208; C no. 78.1, p. 504; M-F 244-7.

point is made: there was immense variety, in practice and theory and attitude.

But if we could cross-question Jane Austen herself, I imagine that she would have said that sexual fidelity was only part, though a significant part, of a much wider range of qualities comprised by fidelity in marriage – and that fidelity itself was only a part, though an important part, of the moral way of life which must grow from the common convictions of husband and wife. And that would seem to be the heart of the matter.

It will not have escaped observation that Jane herself was unmarried, and that study of moral growth among married couples sheds little light on the very private question of her moral code for bachelors and spinsters. Her letters show that she suffered the temptations of Emma to be vain of her accomplishments and to speak her mind, and unloose her wit, with abandon.[20] We are none of us so good as the characters we most admire; but letters and memoirs conspire to give the impression of a personality – ever prone to such temptations – yet constantly seeking to combine candour with modesty, penetrating frankness with sensitive tact; seeking on her own, or with the help of her family, above all of her sister, to conquer what she would have deemed unchristian and irreligious – or simply wrong – in her nature.

[20] See pp. 37, 168.

17

Epilogue: Reflections on the Feminism of Jane Austen

In 1913 the young Virginia Woolf – who greatly admired Jane Austen – sought the reason why she could not be wholly congenial to women of her generation.

> The chief reason why she does not appeal to us as some inferior writers do is that she has too little of the rebel in her composition, too little discontent, and of the vision which is the cause and the reward of discontent.[1]

It is true that Jane did not mount the barricades – there were not barricades available to her, anyway. It is true that in the structure of her novels she followed the conservative tradition: she did not preach political reform or sedition. Yet Virginia Woolf's comment seems to me amazingly unperceptive from so penetrating a critic. It may be that like her great-nephew Augustus Austen Leigh, Provost of King's College, Cambridge, she was at once conservative and revolutionary.

Recent students of Jane Austen – especially feminist critics – have mounted a fierce attack on 'the family record' as a portrait of the author of the novels. It is entirely true that the brilliant wit, the penetrating mind, the subtlety of perception, and the devastating portrayal of human folly and weakness hardly fit a picture of a pious, modestly spoken conformist daughter of the rectory such as might be deduced from a literal interpretation of many passages in the family memoirs – though this does much less than justice to them, especially to the latest version by Deirdre Le Faye.[2] It may also be the case that Jane sought to avoid the fate of Mary Wollstonecraft, whose stout defence of women's rights led to angry polemic.[3] But there is more to it than that: her novels were evidently meant to entertain,

---

[1] Virginia Woolf (1913), quoted in Southam 1968–87, II, 241.
[2] There is a vast feminist literature on Jane Austen. Of the best of what I have read, Kirkham 1983a is a sympathetic representative.
[3] See esp. Wollstonecraft 1792; and for the polemics to which her defence gave rise, Kirkham 1983a.

not to offend; they are not in any superficial sense didactic or moralising or polemical. They are, up to a point, models of decorum. They undermine many cosy social assumptions all the more devastatingly for that: mercenary marriages, gross and petty snobbery, the treatment of less privileged women – the treatment of women altogether. She had much to say; but like Lady Bertram, she said it without raising her voice.[4] There is no overt feminist doctrine in Jane's novels, as we understand the term; but she knew a woman's worth; and she put into the mouth of Fanny Price, a shy, nervous, retiring, little prig, her stoutest defence against male pretension.

> I think it ought not to be set down as certain that a man must be acceptable to every woman he may happen to like himself . . . We think very differently of the nature of women, if they can imagine a woman so very soon capable of returning an affection as this seems to imply.

Jane Austen was the unmarried daughter of a parson of modest means; she was poor all her life. The news that a rich uncle had left nothing to her mother or herself brought on a severe attack of the illness from which she died.[5] The world she portrays in her novels is mostly peopled by families better off than she was. From her visits to Godmersham Park, the home of her brother Edward, she knew what life was like in a great house at first hand: and many of the scenes in her novels are set in manor houses great and small – especially *Mansfield Park*. This has the effect, oddly enough, of sharpening the edge on the vision of women's disabilities which she portrays in all her novels.

In *Sense and Sensibility*, *Pride and Prejudice* and *Persuasion* the plot turns in part on the predicament of families of girls brought up in houses and on estates entailed to male heirs – in the first to a stepbrother, 'related . . . by half blood',[6] in both the others to cousins. The women are disinherited. In two cases most of the women escape the perils of disinheritance by marriage; but in *Sense and Sensibility* we are brought face to face with life after the elder Mr Dashwood's demise. The fate of Mrs Dashwood, a deeply distressed widow with three teenage daughters, is to be elbowed out of her comfortable home by a selfish step-daughter-in-law – and left with a

---

[4] *MP* II, c. 5, p. 218. For what follows, see *MP* III, c. 4, p. 353.
[5] *L*, L no. 157, p. 338; *C* no. 144, p. 491; M F-445. On 6 April 1817 she wrote to her brother Charles: 'A few days ago my complaint appeared removed, but I am ashamed to say that the shock of my Uncle's Will brought on a relapse, and I was so ill on Friday and thought myself so likely to be worse that I could not but press for Cassandra's returning . . .' Jane would have received £1000 if she had survived her aunt, but her mother – her uncle's sister – got nothing. Meanwhile Jane was very up and down with her illness: she had halted *Sanditon* on 18 March, ten days before her uncle's death (above, p. 45; *FR* p. 222).
[6] *SS* I, c. 2, p. 8.

tiny income and no home to move to, save a cottage in a remote village provided by another and more distant relation. In *Pride and Prejudice* and *Persuasion* the disastrous consequences which may come for the women are – save in occasional hysterical outbursts from Mrs Bennet – only implied; but the implications are only too clear. In all three they are set in relief by the characters of the heirs: John Dashwood, self-centred husband of an even more selfish wife, both of them obsessed with money and their own need of it; Mr Collins, the absurd clergyman – more amiable than Mr Dashwood, but it is a harsh fate indeed which leaves the female Bennets at his mercy; and Mr Elliot, one of the most repulsive of Jane Austen's villains. Of her heroines, only Emma is securely possessed of a large inheritance. In *Emma* it is Jane Fairfax who represents the unprivileged woman: in spite of her excellent upbringing and education and accomplishments, she is to be a governess, a member of one of the very few professions open to women – yet one which is likened to slavery.

When Mrs Elton importunately offers to find her an eligible situation as a governess, Jane Fairfax demurs. When the time is ripe,

> 'there are places in town, offices, where enquiry would soon produce something – Offices for the sale – not quite of human flesh – but of human intellect.'
>
> 'Oh! my dear, human flesh! You quite shock me; if you mean a fling at the slave-trade, I assure you Mr Suckling was always rather a friend to the abolition.'
>
> 'I did not mean, I was not thinking of the slave trade,' replied Jane; 'governess-trade, I assure you, was all that I had in view; widely different certainly as to the guilt of those who carry it on; but as to the greater misery of the victims, I do not know where it lies.'[7]

The novels as a whole suggest an obsession with the inferior rights and opportunities of women – softened for her readers by the happy and successful marriages with which she endows her heroines. In *Sense and Sensibility* Colonel Brandon's cousin had been forcibly married to his elder brother for the sake of her inheritance – then divorced and left with a 'legal allowance [which] was not adequate to her fortune' – and her daughter's fate is nearly as parlous owing to Willoughby's seduction and negligence.[8] In *Mansfield Park* the heroine is a poor relation, constantly reminded of her inferior status. In the eyes of Sir Thomas and Lady Bertram, she is morally bound to accept the first eligible suitor – in her case Henry Crawford. She has rich rewards – she comes to dote on her new homes and she marries in the end an admirable husband whom she adores. But her inferior status is constantly

---

[7] *E* II, c. 17, pp. 300–1.
[8] *SS* II, c. 9, pp. 205–11, esp. p. 207.

before us: her brother William is a naval officer, while Fanny remains the indigent niece, her aunts' slave.

Jane Austen occasionally draws a moral. After comparing the fates of Maria Bertram, briefly Mrs Rushworth, and Henry Crawford, she observes:

> that punishment, the public punishment of disgrace, should in a just measure attend *his* share of the offence, is, we know, not one of the barriers, which society gives to virtue. In this world, the penalty is less equal than could be wished; but without presuming to look forward to a juster appointment hereafter, we may fairly consider a man of sense like Henry Crawford, to be providing for himself no small portion of vexation and regret . . .[9]

This is powerful understatement – the folly of human justice is none the less eloquently portrayed.

It is perhaps the case that her male villains stick in the mind more than their female counterparts. Henry Crawford does more evil than his sister, corrupted though her mind is shown to be. Willoughby does far more evil than Lucy Steele, though both – in their different spheres – are equally necessary to the plot of *Sense and Sensibility*. Wickham is more consistently villainous than Lydia. Mrs Clay is a scheming woman and a hypocrite, and she may conquer Mr Elliot in the end – but her evil character is altogether more commonplace than his. Doubtless Jane Austen's wicked men owe something (as has often been observed) to the melodramatic villains of contemporary novels; but she persisted in portraying them, evidently, because they answered to her experience of life. Men, even those outwardly courteous and urbane, were often predatory, and society in a measure condoned a man's share in seduction. It was in the nature of things that in a world where men had far greater opportunities of every kind, they had greater responsibility too – and their wickedness could strike deeper. But in truth the novels offer a rich tapestry of male and female fools and knaves – and a remarkable gallery too of sympathetic portraits of men and women – including women both highly intelligent and well educated; nor do the women have it all their own way. There is no one in the mature novels more admirable than George Knightley.

In the final stages of the last of her novels to be completed, she embarked on a remarkable debate between Captain Harville and Anne Elliot on the difference between men and women. Anne develops the theme that women's feelings are longer-lasting. They are comparing the sailor at sea full of activity and hardship and the wife or lover at home, condemned to waiting for the sailor's return.

[9] *MP* III, c. 17, pp. 468–9.

Thus Anne:

'Your feelings may be the strongest . . ., but the same spirit of analogy will authorise me to assert that ours are the most tender. Man is more robust than woman, but he is not longer-lived; which exactly explains my view of the nature of their attachments. Nay, it would be too hard upon you, if it were otherwise. You have difficulties, and privations, and dangers enough to struggle with. You are always labouring and toiling, exposed to every risk and hardship. Your home, country, friends, all quitted. Neither time, nor health, nor life, to be called your own. It would be too hard indeed' (with a faltering voice [– for she is aware that Captain Wentworth is not far off]) 'if women's feelings were to be added to all this.'

Later on, Anne continues:

'I hope I do justice to all that is felt by you, and by those who resemble you. God forbid that I should undervalue the warm and faithful feelings of any of my fellow-creatures . . . No, I believe you capable of every thing great and good in your married lives. I believe you equal to every important exertion, and to every domestic for-bearance, so long as – if I may be allowed the expression, so long as you have an object. I mean, while the woman you love lives, and lives for you. All the privilege I claim for my own sex (it is not a very enviable one, you need not covet it) is that of loving longest, when existence or when hope is gone.'

Her words are overheard by Wentworth, who sets to work at once to scribble a proposal to her.[10] It is an argument very apropos its context, very characteristic of Anne Elliot, who has been yearning for an estranged sailor fiancé for eight-and-a-half years; but there is piquancy in it too – especially in the notion that a woman lives longer than a man, for it was written at the turn of July and August 1816, and in July 1817 its author died.

At the end of the day Jane Austen is one of the profoundest critics of male dominance – or of any notion of female inferiority in any intellectual or imaginative enterprise – simply by illustrating her apparently effortless superiority. Men humbled by her can – if they wish – take comfort from Chaucer and Shakespeare, who were as clever as she, if one can measure such things. But among the great creative writers of the last two hundred years, in sheer intelligence and penetration of mind, she makes rings round all her male rivals. One has only to contemplate how Dickens and Trollope, or even Henry James, handled the themes and problems of her

---

[10] *P* II, c. 11, pp. 232–5. This was part of the second ending to *Persuasion*: the first ending was finished on 18 July, the second on 6 August 1816 (*P*, p. 273; *MW*, facing p. 242) – she died in July 1817.

novels to see how unfair the competition is. I do not claim that she was more creative than they – that her reputation will outlive theirs; that is more than one can reasonably say. I am looking at only one aspect of her: sheer power of mind. The strongest competition comes perhaps from another woman, from George Eliot. But this is foolish talk such as would have aroused her impatience. She liked to be admired, but saw through flattery in the twinkling of an eye.

I do not for a moment mean that she never made mistakes or is above criticism. But it has been the assumption of this book that one learns more by trying to understand what she was at than by telling her not to. Marilyn Butler brilliantly demonstrated her debt to Tory novels, but failed in her attempt to tell Jane Austen how to copy them. I have tried to listen – as have many thousands of other devotees – to what she was saying. But the conclusion must be an admission of failure. No 'sensible man' would try to penetrate her mind. The rewards of trying are rich indeed: a small glimpse of one of the noblest works of creation. But as I bring the book to a close, I hear Mr Bennet again: 'For what do we live, but to make sport for our neighbours, and laugh at them in our turn?'[11]

---

[11] *PP* III, c. 15, p. 364. Cf. the echo in *MP* III, c. 17, p. 472, on 'such a contrast . . . as time is for ever producing between the plans and decisions of mortals, for their own instruction, and their neighbours' entertainment'.

Appendix of Dates

The purpose of this Appendix is to give an outline of dates for quick reference, and also to give a skeleton of the early evidence on which they are based. Much of the material can be found in *Letters* C, Index I, s.v. Austen, Jane; virtually all the dates in Deirdre Le Faye's *FR* pp. xv–xxiv – but the evidence has to be sought in the scattered pages of the book. My debt to both these authors is great.

STEVENTON, 1775–1801

1775, 16 Dec.	Birth	*Biographical Notice*, p. 3
?1795–7	Writes *Elinor and Marianne*	*FR* p. 83
1796–7	Writes *First Impressions*	See p. 44
1797	Starts *Sense and Sensibility*	See p. 45
?1798–9	?First draft of *Northanger Abbey*	See p. 45

BATH, 1801–1805 and 1805–1806

1801, May	Arrival	*Letters*, L and C no. 35
1803	Completion of *Northanger Abbey*	See p. 48
1805, 21 Jan.	Death of Jane Austen's father	*Letters*, L and C no. 41
Aug.	Godmersham, Goodnestone	*Letters*, L and C, nos. 45–7
Sept.–Nov.	Worthing	*FR* pp. 134, 267 n. 20
1806, July	Leaves Bath	*Letters*, L no. 55, p. 138; C no. 54, p. 208
July–Oct.	Clifton, Adlestrop, Stoneleigh	*FR* pp. 137–40, 267

SOUTHAMPTON 1806–1809

1806, July	Arrival in Southampton	*FR* pp. 140, 267
1809, May–June	Godmersham	*FR* pp.153–4, 268 partly based on Fanny Knight's diaries

CHAWTON 1809–1817

1809, 7 July	Arrival in Chawton	Caroline Austen 1986, p. 20; *FR* p. 154; cf. *Letters*, L. no. 69; C no. 68
1811, *c*. Feb.	*Mansfield Park* begun	See p. 45
Nov.	*Sense and Sensibility* published	*SS*, p. xiii
1812, Nov.	*Pride and Prejudice* sold to publisher	*Letters*, L no. 77; C no. 74.1 (p. 501)

1813, Jan.	*Pride and Prejudice* published	*Letters*, L no.79; C no.76
soon after June	*Mansfield Park* finished	See p. 45
1814, 21 January	*Emma* begun	See p. 45
May–June	*Mansfield Park* published	*MP*, p. xi
1815, 29 March	*Emma* finished	See p. 45
8 Aug.	*Persuasion* begun	See p. 45
Dec. or early 1816	*Emma* published	*E*, p. xi
1816, 6 Aug.	*Persuasion* finished	See p. 45
1817, 17 Jan.–18 March	*Sanditon* written	See p. 45

WINCHESTER May–July 1817

24 May	Journey to Winchester	*Letters*, L no. 160; C no. 146 (Saturday before 27 May)
18 July (Friday)	Death	*Biographical Notice*, p. 5; cf. *Letters*, L pp. 343–5; C pp. 513–14 (a Friday); Monumental Inscription in Winchester Cathedral

Bibliographical References

The Writings of Jane Austen

Quotations from the novels are from the first or second editions; reference is also made to the admirable editions of R.W. Chapman (1923) in their revised form, *The Oxford Illustrated Jane Austen* (based on Chapman's 3rd edn, 1932–4). Quotations from her other works are from ibid. VI, *Minor Works*, ed. R.W. Chapman, revised B.C. Southam (Oxford, 1969). Quotations from the Letters are from the originals as shown in Jo Modert, *Jane Austen's Manuscript Letters in Facsimile* (Carbondale and Edwardsville, Ill., 1990) or – for those not known to survive – from Lord Brabourne's edition (London, 1884, cited from the reprint of 1912) – checked by the immaculate editions of R.W. Chapman and D. Le Faye.

For bibliographical details see Chapman's Introductory Notes to the novels, and esp. Gilson 1982.

E   *Emma*, 1st edn, 3 vols, John Murray, London, 1816
Fragment of a Novel [ed. R.W. Chapman], Oxford, 1925 [*Sanditon*, also in *MW* pp. 363–427 and facsimile edn, ed. B.C. Southam, Oxford, 1975]
Letters, C   *Jane Austen's Letters*, ed. R.W. Chapman, 2nd edn, Oxford, 1951
Letters, L   *Jane Austen's Letters*, ed. Deirdre Le Faye, Oxford, 1995
Letters, M   *Jane Austen's Manuscript Letters in Facsimile*, ed. J. Modert, Carbondale and Edwardsville, Ill., 1990
See also below under Brabourne
MP   *Mansfield Park*, 2nd edn, John Murray, London, 1816; with occasional reference to the 1st edn, T. Egerton, London, 1814
MW *Minor Works* (see above)
NA   *Northanger Abbey*, 1st edn, *Northanger Abbey and Persuasion*, 4 vols, John Murray, London, 1818
P   *Persuasion* (see above)
PP   *Pride and Prejudice*, 1st edn, T. Egerton, London, 1813; with occasional reference to the 2nd and 3rd edn, 1813, 1817
SS   *Sense and Sensibility*, 2nd edn, T. Egerton, London, 1813; with occasional reference to the 1st edn, 1811

Other Books and Articles

Anstey, R., 1975, *The Atlantic Slave Trade and British Abolition, 1760–1810*, London

Austen, Caroline, 1952, *My Aunt Jane Austen: a Memoir*, London (repr. by Jane Austen Soc., 1991)

Austen, Caroline, 1986, *Reminiscences*, ed. D. Le Faye, Jane Austen Society

Austen-Leigh, M.A., 1920, *Personal Aspects of Jane Austen*, London; *and see FR, Life, Memoir*

Babb, H.S., 1962, *Jane Austen's Novels: the Fabric of Dialogue*, Columbia, Ohio

Bates, A., 1969, *Directory of Stage Coach Services 1836*, Newton Abbot

Bath 1806: Bath Illustrated by a Series of Views from the Drawings of John Claude Nattes, London

Bendall, S., C.N.L., Brooke and P. Collinson, 1999, *A History of Emmanuel College*, Woodbridge

Best, G.F.A., 1964, *Temporal Pillars: Queen Anne's Bounty, the Ecclesiastical Commissions and the Church of England*, Cambridge

Biographical Notice: Biographical Notice of the Author [by Henry Austen] in *NA* pp. 3–9

Blair, H., 1777–1801, *Sermons*, 5 vols, Edinburgh

Brabourne, Edward, Lord, 1884, *Letters of Jane Austen*, 2 vols, London; cited here from repr., 2 vols, in *The Novels of Jane Austen*, 11–12, Winchester edn of Edinburgh, 1912

Bradbrook, F.W., 1967, *Jane Austen and her Predecessors*, Cambridge

Branton, C.L., 1955, 'The ordinations in Jane Austen's novels', *Nineteenth-Century Fiction* 10, 156–9

Brooke, C.N.L., 1985, *A History of Gonville and Caius College*, Woodbridge

Brooke, C.N.L., 1989a, *The Medieval Idea of Marriage*, Oxford

Brooke, C.N.L., 1989b, 'The University Chancellor', in *Humanism, Reform and the Reformation: the Career of Bishop John Fisher*, ed. B. Bradshaw and E. Duffy, Cambridge, pp. 47–66

Brooke, C.N.L., 1993, *A History of the University of Cambridge*, IV, *1870–1990*, Cambridge

Brooke, C.N.L., J.M. Horn and N.L. Ramsay, 1988, 'A Canon's Residence in the Eighteenth Century: the case of Thomas Gooch', *Journal of Ecclesiastical History* 39, 545–56

Brooke, C.N.L., and G. Keir, 1975, *London 800–1216: the Shaping of a City*, London

Brooke, N.S., 1977, 'All's Well that Ends Well', *Shakespeare Survey*, 30, 73–84

Butler, M., 1987, *Jane Austen and the War of Ideas*, 2nd edn, London

Carpenter, E., 1936, *Thomas Sherlock, 1678–1761*, London

Chapman, R.W., 1926, *Two Chapters of Persuasion*, Oxford

Chapman, R.W., 1948, *Jane Austen, Facts and Problems*, Oxford

Cheney, C.R., *Handbook of Dates for Students of English History*, London

Collins, I., 1993, *Jane Austen and the Clergy*, London

Collinson, P., N. Ramsay and M. Sparks ed., 1995, *A History of Canterbury Cathedral*, Oxford

Complete Peerage, The, ed. V. Gibbs *et al.*, 9 vols, London, 1910–59

Constable, G., 1964, *Monastic Tithes from their Origins to the Twelfth Century*, Cambridge

Cowper: W. Cowper, *The Task and Selected Other Poems*, ed. J. Sambrook, London, 1994

Cripps, H.W., 1850, *A Practical Treatise on the Law Relating to the Church and the Clergy*, 2nd edn, London

Cripps 1914: *Memoirs of Father and Mother (Henry William and Julia Cripps)*, by three of their children, London

Davie, D., 1993, *The Eighteenth-Century Hymn in England*, Cambridge

DNB: Dictionary of National Biography

Duncan-Jones, E., 1957, 'Proposals of Marriage in *Pride and Prejudice* and *Pamela*', *Notes and Queries*, 202, 76

Fordyce, J., 1766, *Sermons to Young Women*, 3rd edn, 2 vols, London

Fordyce, J., 1776, *The Character and Conduct of the Female Sex*, London

Forster, E.M., 1936, *Abinger Harvest*, London

FR = W. Austen-Leigh, R.A. Austen-Leigh and D. Le Faye, *Jane Austen: a Family Record*, London, 1989

Gibson E., 1713, *Codex Iuris Ecclesiastici Anglicani*, London

Gilson, D., 1982, *A Bibliography of Jane Austen*, Oxford

Gombrich, E., 1960, *Art and Illusion*, London

Gregory, J., ed., 1995, *The Speculum of Archbishop Thomas Secker*, Church of England Records Society, 2

Hammond, G., 1982, *The Making of the English Bible*, Manchester

Hill, C., 1956, *The Economic Problems of the Church, from Archbishop Whitgift to the Long Parliament*, Oxford

Horn, J.M., 1974, 1992 = J. Le Neve, *Fasti Ecclesiae Anglicanae 1541–1857*, III, VII, compiled by J.M. Horn, London

Horn, J.M., and Sherwin Bailey, D., 1979 = J. Le Neve, *Fasti Ecclesiae Anglicanae 1541–1857*, V, London

Hubback, J.H. and E.C., 1906, *Jane Austen's Sailor Brothers*, London

Hudson, A., 1988, *The Premature Reformation: Wycliffite Texts and Lollard History*, Oxford

Humphreys, K.W., ed. 1990, *The Friars' Libraries*, Corpus of British Medieval Library Catalogues, London

Ireland, S., 1795, *Picturesque Views on the Upper or Warwickshire Avon*, London

Jane Austen 1983: Jane Austen: New Perspectives, Women and Literature, New Series 3, ed. J. Todd, New York

Jane Austen Society, *Collected Reports, 1949–65* (1967), *1966–75* (1977), *1976–85* (1989)

Killop, A.D.M., 1921, 'Jane Austen's Gothic titles', *Notes and Queries*, 12th Series, 9, 5 Nov., pp. 361–6

Kirkham, M., 1983a, *Jane Austen, Feminism and Fiction*, Brighton

Kirkham, M., 1983b, 'Feminist irony and the Priceless Heroine of *Mansfield Park*' in *Jane Austen 1983*, pp. 231–47

Lampe, G.W.H., ed., 1969, *The Cambridge History of the Bible*, II, Cambridge

Leavis, Q.D., 1983, *Collected Essays*, ed. G. Singh, I, Cambridge

Life: W. and R.A. Austen-Leigh, 1913, *Jane Austen, her Life and Letters: A Family Record*, London

Lobel, M.D., ed., 1989, *British Atlas of Historic Towns*, III, *The City of London from Prehistoric times to c. 1520*, Oxford

Lodge, D., 1962–3, 'A Question of Judgement: the theatricals at Mansfield Park', *Nineteenth-Century Fiction*, 17, 275–82

Lowther Clarke, W.K., 1944, *Eighteenth-Century Piety*, London

Malton, J., 1798, *An Essay on British Cottage Architecture*, London

Manning, B., 1941, *The Hymns of Wesley and Watts*, London

Martin, B., 1950, *John Newton*, London

Mather, F.C., 1992, *High Church Prophet. Bishop Samuel Horsley (1733–1806) and the Caroline Tradition in the late Georgian Church*, Oxford

Memoir: J.E. Austen-Leigh, *A Memoir of Jane Austen*, London, 1870, also cited from the 2nd edn, 1871

Moir, E., 1964, *The Discovery of Britain: the English Tourists 1540 to 1840*, London

Namier, L.B., 1957, *The Structure of Politics at the Accession of George III*, 2nd edn, London

Olney Hymns in Three Books [by J. Newton and W. Cowper], London, 1779

Parker, K.L., 1988, *The English Sabbath: a Study of Doctrine and Discipline from the Reformation to the Civil War*, Cambridge

Perkin, H., 1989, *The Rise of Professional Society: England since 1880*, London

Pevsner, N., 1968, 'The Architectural Setting of Jane Austen's Novels', *Journal of the Warburg and Courtauld Institutes*, 31, 404–22

Piggott, P., 1979, *The Innocent Diversion: a Study of Music in the Life and Writings of Jane Austen*, London

Pinion, F.B., 1973, *A Jane Austen Companion*, London

Pollock, J., 1981, *Amazing Grace: the Dramatic Life Story of John Newton*, London (repr. Oxford, 1996)

Pott, B., and J. Weinsheim, 1973, *An Annotated Bibliography of Jane Austen Studies, 1952–1972*, Charlottesville

Pott, B., 1985, *An Annotated Bibliography of Jane Austen Studies, 1973–1983*, Charlottesville

Rattenbury, J., 1941, *The Evangelical Doctrines of the Hymns of Charles Wesley*, London

Repton, H., 1803, *Observations on the Theory and Practice of Landscape Gardening*, London

Repton, H., 1806, *An Enquiry into the Changes of Taste in Landscape Gardening*, London

Roberts, W., 1979, *Jane Austen and the French Revolution*, London

Rosenfeld, S., 1962, 'Jane Austen and Private Theatricals', *Essays and Studies*, 15, 40–51

Rupp, G., 1986, *Religion in England 1688–1791*, Oxford

Sales, R., 1994, *Jane Austen and Representations of Regency England*, London

Searby, P., 1997, *A History of the University of Cambridge*, III, *1750–1870*, Cambridge

Sherlock, T., 1812, *Discourses Preached at the Temple Church and on Several Occasions*, 4 vols, edn of Oxford

Sherlock, W., 1702–13, *Sermons Preached upon Several Occasions*, 2 vols, 2nd edn, London

Southam, B.C., 1964, *Jane Austen's Literary Manuscripts*, Oxford

Southam, B.C., ed., 1968–87, *Jane Austen: The Critical Heritage*, 2 vols, London

Southam, B.C., ed., 1980, *Jane Austen's 'Sir Charles Grandison'*, Oxford

Stone, L., 1977, *The Family, Sex and Marriage in England 1500–1800*, London

Taylor, S., 1995, ' "Dr Codex" and the Whig "Pope": Edmund Gibson, Bishop of Lincoln and London, 1716–1748', in R.W. Davis, ed., *Lords of Parliament: Studies, 1714–1914*, Stamford, pp. 9–28, 183–91

Temperley, N., 1979, *The Music of the English Parish Church*, I, Cambridge

Thistlethwaite, N., 1990, *The Making of the Victorian Organ*, Cambridge

Thistlethwaite, N., 1994, 'Music and worship 1660–1980', in *A History of Lincoln Minster*, ed. D. Owen, Cambridge, pp. 77–111

Tucker, G.H., 1983, *A Goodly Heritage: a History of Jane Austen's Family*, Manchester (revised reprint as *A History of Jane Austen's Family*, Stroud, 1998)

Virgin, P., 1989, *The Church in an Age of Negligence: Ecclesiastical Structure and Problems of Church Reform, 1700–1840*, Cambridge

Walsh, J., 1966, 'Origins of the Evangelical Revival', in *Essays in Modern Church History in Memory of Norman Sykes*, ed. G.V. Bennett and J.D. Walsh, London, pp. 132–62

Walsh, J., S. Taylor and C. Hayden, 1993, *The Church of England c. 1689–c. 1833: from Toleration to Tractarianism*, Cambridge

Ward, W.R., ed., 1994, *Parson and Parish in Eighteenth-Century Surrey: Replies to Bishops' Visitations*, Surrey Record Society 34

Ward, W.R., ed., 1995, *Parson and Parish in Eighteenth-Century Hampshire: Replies to Bishops' Visitations*, Hampshire Record Series, 13

Warner, R., 1801, *Excursions from Bath*

Whitaker, K.B., 1940, *The Eighteenth-Century English Sunday*, London

Willis, A.J., 1964–65, *Winchester Ordinations 1660–1829*, 2 vols, privately printed

Wodehouse, P.G., 1938, *The Code of the Woosters*, London

Wollstonecraft, M., 1792, *A Vindication of the Rights of Women*, London

Wood, D., ed., 1994, *Studies in Church History 31: The Church and Childhood*, Oxford

Wrigley, E.A., and R.S. Schofield, 1989, *The Population History of England 1541–1871: A Reconstruction*, 2nd edn, Cambridge

Index

Counties (pre-1974) are usually noted for genuine place-names – not for those invented by Jane Austen.

215